God, Guns, and Guts of Firearm Defense

The Bible View

By Sig Swanstrom

A 36READY Preparedness Guide

Peer Reviewed for Bible Scholarship

2 Timothy 2:15 - Acts 17:11

Oxbridge Press

Oxbridge Press

www.OxbridgePress.com

First Print Edition

ISBN 13:978-0615863931

COVER: Photo of the author carrying both a Bible and a .45 ACP SIG pistol in a shoulder holster. In reality the author prefers a pancake holster worn on his belt, but a shoulder holster was used here to illustrate the concept of being equipped to use the Bible and a firearm.

CONTENTS

Contents Continued

Introduction

Does the Bible have anything to say about a topic such as this? Does Jesus actually talk about weapons and the use of deadly force for defense? The answer is a resounding, "Yes."

You're probably aware that guns were invented less than a thousand years ago,[1] long after the New Testament was written. However, deadly weapons have been in use since the beginning of human history, so it's no surprise that the Bible has a lot to say about this topic. Although guns may be a more modern invention, the core moral concepts regarding weapon use are firmly established in the Bible.

What's surprising is that you've probably never heard a pastor preach on this topic. Even so, it's important for us to understand what the Bible has to say about these issues. Subjects such as firearm ownership by civilians, concealed carry, the use of deadly force and our Right of self-defense, are pivotal issues for us today. Thankfully, all of these topics are addressed in the Bible—*if you know where to look.*

I've written this book for four different audiences: 1) Those who are interested in firearm self-defense from a biblical perspective; 2) For those who want to better understand gun rights from the perspective of the Founding Fathers of the United States; 3) For every follower of Jesus who strives to live according to the precepts of the Bible, including those who are not interested in firearms; and 4) For book clubs and Bible study groups who want to stimulate lively and useful discussion.

My motivation for writing is to expose common but dangerous misconceptions, and especially to promote what the Bible, and Jesus, has to say about this important and timely topic.

---

[1] During our four years living in Guatemala, our installation was attacked by Marxist guerillas three times. Additionally, during our travels around the region we encountered bombings and guerilla operations on numerous other occasions.

As to my background, I am a retired police officer and SWAT operator who served in the Los Angeles area. In the line of duty, I have personally encountered many deadly force situations. Day after day I faced violence and dealt with the aftermath of violent crime. And now, as the owner of a firearms self-defense training academy, I teach on these subjects. Our most popular class is *"God, Guns, and Handgun Self-Defense,"* so I have facilitated many discussions on this specific topic. Throughout these experiences I've learned that most people aren't adequately prepared for the real-world. I want to help.

This isn't a feel-good churchy pie-in-the-sky treatment of the subject. It's a needed exposé of the truth of what the Bible actually teaches.

You won't be subjected to gory details in this book, but you will be exposed to difficult choices. Importantly, you'll be given the tools needed for making hard life and death choices.

Today I teach operators and civilians on these subjects, so my personal experience has also been informed by the experiences of others. In the process, I've come to the realization that there is a lot of confusion regarding the use of deadly force and gun ownership. So it's the need for clarification that has prompted me to write this guide book. Muddled thinking leads to inaction or incorrect action. This can be deadly.

In the course of my teaching I've also discovered that even those who don't live according to the teachings of the Bible, still generally respect the moral precepts of the Book. This is especially true in regard to the teachings of Jesus. It's common for those who do not believe in Jesus as God, to still regard Him as a great moral teacher.

So even if you don't plan to ever carry a gun, I encourage you to better understand this issue from a biblical perspective. One thing is certain, we are living in a society that seems to be winding down, and violence abounds—and it's probably going to get a lot worse. If you think I'm exaggerating the gravity of our circumstances, jump to the chapter, *Summary of Relevant Crime Statistics.*

Why is it important to understand this subject from a biblical perspective?

It's because most of us are good at self-justification. Therefore we need a reliable moral compass outside of ourselves. The Bible aptly meets this need, and it has withstood the test of time.

In addition to this, its precepts are foundational to Western culture, and it was used to build the foundation on which the United States was built. The U.S. Constitution, the rule of law, and our concept of justice were all derived from the Bible.

In the modern world the Bible is still the gold standard for honest, ethical living, even by those who don't see it as the Word of God. There is a reason why more Bibles have been printed than any other book; it's a reliable guide for living. If everyone does whatever is right in their own eyes, the results are disastrous.[2]

The reason that it's important to understand the biblical perspective on this subject is also intensely practical. If you have not come to grips with this *God, guns, and defense* issue, you may hesitate at the wrong time. The result may be tragic. Whether we act, or fail to act, there are consequences either way.

If you use, or fail to use deadly force to respond to a violent situation, or if you find yourself consoling someone who was involved in a deadly encounter, your buried inner conflict may make matters worse. Now is the time to deal with this emotional topic. Even those who see the world in black and white realize that there can be a lot of gray with this topic, especially if we don't have an external standard to help us identify the right decision.

If you act or fail to act, and someone dies or gets hurt, you will need to live with that for the rest of your life. Speaking from personal experience, I encourage you to fully resolve these issues now, in advance of the need.

Whether I'm with secularists or religious people, the conversation often includes reflections such as, "I might be able to shoot someone if they were going to harm my family, but I couldn't use a gun to protect

---

2 Proverbs 6:12-19

myself." Or, "God has promised to protect me. That's what the Bible says, so I don't worry about it." Or yet another extreme, "If someone messes with me or my family, they'll have hell to pay, and I'll gladly give them a donation from Mr. Smith and Mrs. Wesson (as delivered by the popular handgun, the Smith & Wesson M&P pistol).

What do you think? Do you harbor any confusion on this topic? If not, are you sure your viewpoint is right? How do you know? Is it based on something other than your personal opinion?

As a firearms instructor, I've discovered that even police officers and those who have a license to carry a gun, are often plagued with contradictory thoughts on this subject. On the one hand they realize that self-defense is reasonable and right, but on the other they embrace the truth that life is sacred.

To one degree or another, many people are conflicted. They don't see how to bridge the two beliefs, so they simply block it from their mind. And this, too, is unhealthy. And can also be dangerous.

For me, becoming a police officer wasn't a job choice, it was a calling. So I was forced to deal with this issue because I personally felt conflicted on the use of deadly force. My father had served in the military during wartime, but he didn't talk much about his experiences. Conversely, my teachers in high school, university and even church, often talked about these issues, but their views didn't seem practical or realistic. I needed to discover what the Bible truly says.

I've written this short book to provide you with a real-world and healthy perspective on the use of deadly force. It's not *just* about our Right of self-defense or our Right to carry a gun. It's also not simply about what the law allows us to do. It's about personal responsibility and preparation, about moral choices and knowing what is right and wrong, and if called upon, having the guts to do the right thing, right now—this instant, when a split-second decision is required.

-- Sig Swanstrom

"The prudent person sees danger and takes precautions; the foolish person goes blindly on and suffers the consequences."

Proverbs 22:3, Holy Bible

"But now," he [Jesus] said, "take your money and a traveler's bag. And if you don't have a sword, sell your cloak and buy one!"

Luke 22:36, Holy Bible

The information contained in this book is not instruction in the law, nor is it legal advice. It is the responsibility of the reader to obtain counsel in legal matters from suitable sources.

Acknowledgements

Since this book has become controversial in some quarters, I will not name the thirty theologians, seminary professors and pastors who were asked to review my initial manuscript. By design, we sought manuscript review and criticism from Bible scholars who represent different orientations; conservative, liberal, and in-between viewpoints. This included Baptist, Assembly of God, Methodist and Free Methodist, Catholic and Anglican, Presbyterian, Lutheran, Church of God, Anabaptist, and Independent Bible. As a result of their input, this book has been vastly improved. They will remain unnamed, but my appreciation is heartfelt. Thank you.

My favorite criticism came from a liberal seminary professor who said, *"I can't fault the accuracy of your scholarship, but I am very uncomfortable with your viewpoint."* You may be similarly uncomfortable with what I've written. That's okay. But I do hope that you will read this with an open mind, and then do your own personal research.[3] The footnotes and endnotes contain many Bible verse references, so if you want to dig deeper into what the Bible actually teaches, this is a good place to start.

[3] Acts 17:11

About Bible Translations:

Since many dedicated, sincere and knowledgeable Christians and Bible scholars have different viewpoints on the issue of which Bible translation is best, in this book I have consistently used both the historic King James Version (1611 AD) alongside a highly-regarded modern-English Bible translation.

The King James Version (KJV) provides the reader with a consistent baseline for comparison, and the newer translation makes the Bible verse(s) easier to understand. In each case, the modern translation was selected based on its ability to faithfully communicate the intent of the original language manuscript. By using this side-by-side approach, the reader can quickly confirm the author's premise, and at the same time gain greater insight into the meaning of the text. In the process, the traditions and preferences of different readers are honored.

As you probably know, the Bible was originally written in the Hebrew and Greek languages, and the Geneva Bible (first mass-produced study Bible) and the King James Version (KJV) were the first English-language translations widely used by both ordinary people and scholars. However, since the Geneva Bible was published in 1560 and the KJV in 1611, both more than four hundred years ago and in the same era as Shakespeare, today it is hard for many non-scholars to understand the archaic English. Consequently, a modern translation is always included side-by-side with the historic.

The Geneva Bible was popular among reformers such as John Calvin and John Knox, and heavily used by the Puritans and early American leaders, partially due to its extensive helps, cross-referenced verses, maps, and other study aides. However, today there are many English-language study Bibles and the Geneva Bible is no longer popular, so it was not included.

On the other hand, the King James Version remains popular today despite its old-world English vocabulary, primarily because it is seen as an authoritative translation of the text, presented unencumbered by the study notes of scholars. With this in mind, in this book we are enriched by using both the historic KJV translation alongside a carefully selected modern-English translation. This makes it a simple task for the reader to confirm that the author has accurately handled the Bible text.

No controversial translations of Bible verses were used in this book. The KJV, and the various modern-English translations which accompany it, are all highly respected and broadly accepted by pastors and Bible scholars. Each of the modern translations used in this book are in common use by churches that are committed to accurately handling the Word of God.

If you have an Internet connection and would like to access a different translation as you read, visit: www.BlueLetterBible.org. *'Blue Letter Bible'* is not a Bible translation, but rather a free online resource which includes more than a dozen English translations of the Bible, plus Hebrew and Greek manuscripts.

Chapter 1

A Shocking New (Old) Concept: Personal Responsibility

Guns in church? Missionaries with guns? For some, these are shocking new concepts, but they really aren't new. And they aren't unbiblical, either; they are actually biblical concepts that aren't usually taught by milquetoast preachers who engage in Bible-light teaching, or confused theologians who refuse to separate their political views from biblical truth. As a result, most of us haven't been taught biblical truth in regard to *God, Guns, and Guts of Firearm Defense.*

If you read the introduction, you already know that I am a retired police officer. But let me tell you a little bit about my experiences *after* I retired from law enforcement...

Having just moved with my family to worn-torn Guatemala, we were anxious to get involved in a local church. For many years I'd served as a board member and part of the welcoming committee at our church back home, so I was also looking forward to experiencing the role reversal of being a first-time visitor.

As with many Christian churches in the U.S., we were intentional about making our church a welcoming place. By design, we staffed each entry door with greeters who had outgoing personalities and a friendly demeanor. Our whole congregation went to great lengths to provide a friendly welcome, especially to first-time visitors.

So I was surprised by what we experienced as we walked up to the main entrance of this Christian church in Central America. There were two people standing in front of the massive, closed front door of the church. But they weren't smiling greeters. Both were uniformed police officers, and they were armed with submachine guns and stern faces.

As we approached they looked me over like a potentially toxic organism, then they scrutinized my wife and children before stepping aside so that I could pull open the formidable wood door. Once inside, we found another all-business police officer similarly armed–and then we walked into a courtyard with lush tropical flowers, and smiling ushers who extended to us a very warm welcome. It was surreal in contrast.

As a former police officer I have continued to be alert and observant. Old habits die hard, so I am still in the practice of looking for curious things such as concealed handguns. As I approached the first usher who had his hand outstretched to shake mine, I noticed the telltale bulge of a gun under his finely tailored suit coat. The next usher was wearing a colorful, casual un-tucked shirt, and he also had a similar telltale bulge. As I looked around, I noted that all the ushers were carrying concealed handguns.

This was certainly unexpected. Yet, under the circumstances, it was actually quite comforting.

At that time Guatemala was plagued by a protracted and bloody civil war. Just that week our embassy had warned me that there were a dozen kidnappings a day in Guatemala City alone, so we needed to be vigilant. These were threats of violence unlike anything we had experienced in the Los Angeles area where I'd been a police officer. (But perhaps not as different as I'd like to think!)

Over the next few months as we became increasingly involved in this church, we learned that it wasn't just the police officers and ushers who were armed. Many of the regular church members carried concealed handguns, too, including a number of the seasoned missionaries who worshiped with us.

I remember thinking, "Missionaries with guns? This is a lot different from California where only the cops and criminals carry weapons."

We attended this church for three years, and during that time no one attacked the church. Not surprising, as it was common knowledge that our parishioners were armed. (Several attacks had occurred at this church previously, before the church leaders became intentional about armed defense. That's why the church members had undertaken these protective measures.)

You might be surprised, but even after this experience, and even though I had carried a gun 24-hours a day, 7-days a week for years when I was a police officer, it took another year before I started carrying a gun in Guatemala. I am law abiding, and I didn't have a license to carry a gun in Guatemala, so I didn't.

A year later things changed. I had changed, too. I had become increasingly aware that it isn't reasonable to rely solely on the police and military for protection. As this old adage reminds us, *"When seconds count, the police are only minutes away."* And even when the police do arrive, sometimes they need help.

Why had I changed?

Guerrilla insurgents[1] had attacked the little community where we lived. Though the military fought valiantly, my family and I, and our neighbors, were left to fend for ourselves. Within minutes, our peaceful, gated community became a casualty of war and anarchy.

I realized that American society had programmed me to think that it is the job of law enforcement, military and other government professionals, to protect the public. We see them as the experts. And, since they are the specialists, I thought that after leaving my law enforcement career, I didn't have any personal responsibility in this regard. I was wrong.

This wasn't just wrong-thinking for life in Guatemala. It is wrong-thinking for anywhere.

Is "public safety" something that is solely the job of government *specialists?* Or, is public safety the responsibility of the good people within a society? If it is our job, too, what are we to do? How did we arrive at this point?

Chapter 2

Firearm Self-Defense: The Effect of the 1960s and the "Peace Movement" on Church Teaching

In the 1960s the secular peace movement, and those espousing socialist or progressive political agendas, started manipulating Christians by using Bible verses to advance their cause. In essence, we let people who didn't know Jesus, and didn't know the Bible, teach us about both. No wonder our understanding has become confused.

Using Bible verses out of context, the peace activists were able to secure the aid of many well-meaning Christians and Jews who were either sympathetic to their cause, or had only elementary Bible knowledge. It was only later that we realized the scope of the confusion that this caused.

For example, when we use terms such as "social justice," these words mean different things to different people. Christians generally intend a meaning such as justice-for-all, but in the secular world "social justice" typically indicates a *progressive* or *socialist* political agenda. The same words, but they communicate a completely different meaning.[2]

Similarly, a popular verse used out of context during this period was Isaiah 2:4 which reads, *"And they will hammer their swords into plowshares and their spears into pruning hooks. Nation will not lift up sword against nation, and never again will they learn war."*[3] Peace activists even erected a statue at the United Nations which artistically represents this lofty-sounding biblical concept, but few read this verse in context to learn about it from a biblical perspective. If they had, they would have learned that this is an unattainable human quest. The Bible says that this isn't going to happen until Christ rules the earth after His second coming. It makes it very clear that this cannot be achieved by humanity.

On the surface, the slogans and rhetoric of the 60-70s peace movement sounded Jesus-like, but the actual motivations of the proponents were rarely altruistic, and they certainly weren't biblical. For example, this U.N. statue was paid for by the Union of Soviet Socialist Republics (USSR), an oppressive communist country which ferociously crushed dissent and expanded its socialist agenda by bribery, assassination and military conquest. Their idea of peace through totalitarian control is far from the biblical concept of peace.

We need to understand that when Jesus taught about loving others and being advocates for peace and justice, the heart of His message was very different from that of those who are proponents of a radical secular agenda. Jesus, and the Bible teach us to pursue peace, but it is a peace which includes personal liberty, uniform justice for all, and independence from overbearing government control.

Over time this Peace Movement misuse of the Bible has been somewhat corrected, but often not by greater knowledge of the Scriptures. More often it's attributed to the personal experiences of those involved, and their observations of the results. Because of this, most sincere Christians withdrew from the *peace movement* because it wasn't really about peace. Yet, since that time, many remain confused about the subjects of peace, love, justice, the role of government, the justified use of force, and the role of Christians as peacemakers.

Thousands of the Christian social activists of the 1960-70s are today's senior pastors, seminary professors, church leaders and parents, so the ongoing confusion, or at best a lack of clarity on the subject, has served to propagate confusion and inaction. Unfortunately, a dangerous lack of understanding of a biblical worldview persists and this aggravates the problem.[4]

Well-meaning leaders and parents have unwittingly transferred these lingering misunderstandings to the next generation. Today, many young adults and emerging leaders are similarly confused about love, justice and the use of force. The legacy of the 1960-70s is confusion, mixed messages and viewpoints which are thought to be "Christian" but don't have their basis in the Bible.

As a child of the 1960-70s and a peace activist in college myself, I eventually had to come to grips with this issue from a biblical viewpoint. Not because I was so astute, but because I felt called to become a police officer. So I was forced to deal with it.

Initially, I thought that being a 'Peace Officer' and carrying the requisite firearm was incompatible with my Christian beliefs (as I understood them at the time). This circumstance, and being exposed to violent atrocities in Haiti during this same period,[5] forced me into a deeper study of the Bible. I needed to discover what God actually has to say about these issues, rather than listen to the platitudes of my progressive friends.

In the process, I learned basic truths such as the fact that Commandment #6 of the Ten Commandments is not *"Thou shalt not kill,"* as translated in the King James Version of the Bible. It is *"You shall not murder,"* which is a more accurate translation of text of Exodus 20:13.[6]

Unlike the rhetoric of the 1960-70s, we now clearly understand that this Commandment does not prohibit the use of deadly force, but rather homicide (murder). It sounds almost foolish now, but this was my first discovery as I started down the path of understanding.

Next, I realized that otherwise reliable pastors and church leaders sometimes misused Bible verses. Occasionally this was due to a desire to advance their political agenda, but more often it was inattention to principles of sound scholarship, or the result of a personal philosophy deeply buried in their cultural upbringing.

In my own process of discovery, I learned that anything important needs to be understood in the context of the whole Bible, not just by reading a handful of cherry-picked verses. Further, that God expects even His ordinary followers, like me, to engage in a systematic study of the Bible: Actual, diligent Bible study, not just absorbing what "experts" say about the Bible.

Eventually I came to understand that as the title 'Peace Officer' implies, the use of deadly force to resist evil is not just permissible, it is required of us. Those who strive to obey God and follow Jesus must literally be peace*makers* (Matthew 5:9). And peace-*making* involves more than just being kind, forgiving, and working to heal relationships; it can also involve forging peace.

Thankfully, when the day came for me to take my oath-of-office as a police officer, I was able to take it enthusiastically and without reservation. I understood that the use of force is essential to combat evil. Interestingly, the preamble of that oath also has relevance for anyone who desires to be a responsible citizen. Here is how the standard oath-of-office for U.S. police officers and sheriff's deputies begins:

"As a law enforcement officer, my fundamental duty is to serve mankind; to safeguard lives and property; to protect the innocent against deception, the weak against oppression or intimidation, and the peaceful against violence or disorder; and to respect the Constitutional rights of all to life, liberty, equality and justice." [7]

Today, as a citizen who is no longer a police officer, my responsibility toward others nevertheless remains much the same. As a Bible-obedient citizen, a similar oath is still valid and might read something like this:

"My fundamental duty is to love God, and serve mankind; to safeguard life, to protect the innocent against deception, the weak against oppression or intimidation, and the peaceful against violence or disorder; to insure equality and impartial justice, and to protect the God-given and Constitutional Rights of all to life and liberty."

What is the Code that you live by? How would you summarize your own guiding principles?

– – – – – – –

The remainder of this book is a summary of what I have learned about the use of deadly force and responsible citizenship from a biblical perspective. It includes my conclusions, offered in the real-world context of someone who has repeatedly confronted evil and violence.

Using the Bible itself, I found that God has a lot to say on this subject. More to the point, it was easy for me to reach my conclusions once I undertook a serious study of the Bible.

It was the Bible itself that I used to identify the proper course of action. Frankly, it was a bit laborious, but my efforts were rewarded with clarity. Hopefully, this book will provide you with the framework for your own study, and help you jump-start your own process of discovery.

For me, it was tempting to just ask my pastor, or simply tap into my cultural upbringing to find answers. But the easy approaches aren't necessarily reliable. For me, this was too important of a subject to unquestioningly trust these other sources. I wanted answers which I could count on to be right, so the Bible was my only completely trustworthy resource.

What I found was answers to my questions which are straightforward and Bible based, and I will share these with you in this book. Yet, the prospect of using deadly force against another human is still difficult to embrace. And, it should be difficult. If we have a cavalier attitude toward this subject, something is wrong.

My hope is that my investigation into the topic, combined with my real-world experiences as a police officer, might be helpful to you as you think through these same issues and seek answers.

Why bother? It's because, if you haven't already been a victim of violent crime, you probably will be at some point in your life. (See the chapter, *Summary of Relevant Crime Statistics*.) With this reality in mind, every person needs to consider this issue and form their own conclusions. It's simply too important an issue to ignore.

We live in a dangerous world—and it's getting more dangerous. It's no longer just random criminal violence that we face. Added to the mix, we now live with terrorism, street gangs, political violence, porous borders, murderous drug violence, and post-event anarchy.

The New Orleans area, after hurricane Katrina, is a poignant reminder of how quickly social order can dissolve. And it also serves as a reminder that when the time comes, and you need help, the police may not be there to solve your problem. You might be alone.

\- - - - - - - -

A book such as this is only an introduction to this topic. If you have lingering questions after reading this book, I encourage you to prayerfully re-read the verses referenced, ideally in the context of the other verses around them. Look up the verses cited in the endnotes, and then identify and read cross-references. Prayerfully reflect on what you have read in the light of the whole Bible. Since one of the main purposes of the Bible is to teach us how to live, we can expect God to bring us clarity, especially with a vital issue such as this.

Further, the New Testament cannot be properly understood without a parallel study of the Old Testament (Tanakh). We need to look at the *whole* Bible, and identify principals for living that are consistent with the Bible in its entirety. Jesus came to fulfill what was started in the Old Testament, not to replace it as if it had become irrelevant.[8]

Jesus and the Apostles regularly quoted from the Old Testament, so I have followed their example and included Old Testament references as well as verses drawn from the New Testament. If we are going to follow Jesus' example on how to live life, it's clear that we need to study the Old and New Testaments together.

Additionally, we need to keep in mind that the absence of criticism or reproof on an important topic is also significant. Likewise, the Bible is a cohesive book that does not contradict itself. If there seems to be a contradiction on a topic we have not dug deep enough. God does not contradict Himself. Clear answers are available to us if we are willing to take the time to prayerfully investigate.

Chapter 3

Jesus' Viewpoint: What Did Jesus Teach About the Use of Weapons?

Jesus did teach on this subject, but few pastors ever preach on this aspect of Jesus' life. It's a surprise to many people, but Jesus was very pro-weapon. If He was living on earth today He would be pro-concealed carry. How do I know? It's actually clear, if you take the time to look.

At least one member of Jesus inner circle, his disciple Peter,[9] carried a deadly weapon. And Peter was obviously a civilian, so being armed isn't just a police-only or military-only way of life.

A sword, usually carried in a sheath hung from the belt, was the handgun of Jesus' day. Jesus disciple Peter, a civilian, routinely carried this type of deadly weapon. So it's not a fantasy-leap to conclude that if Peter was living today, he would carry a gun.

It is important to note that Peter was more than just one of the masses who followed Jesus. Peter is an Apostle, and is considered to be the founder of the Christian Church. Further, this commission came from Jesus himself.[10] Peter was with Jesus every day for several years, and Peter carried a sword. So what does this tell us about Jesus' viewpoint on this subject?

Additionally, carrying a sword could not have been something that Peter did without the knowledge of Jesus and the other disciples. They traveled together, and they lived together. So it's unreasonable to think, as some suggest, that this was a secret.

Peter's sword may not have been huge, but it was a sword nevertheless. The Greek word which is used in the original text is *machairan*,[11] which was a military term for a personal-use sword. So there can be no confusion between the word "sword" and "knife" as some claim. Just as in English, the difference between the two is obvious.

Further, it is ridiculous to suggest that Jesus didn't know that Peter carried a sword. A máchairan was a deadly weapon, and it was 2-feet or longer in length. Frankly, it's absurd to suggest that Jesus didn't know about it. The fact is this: Peter routinely carried a reasonably large and very menacing, deadly weapon.

In Jesus' day as today, it was prudent to be able to protect yourself and others from those who use violence to rob or otherwise harm the innocent. Jesus recognized this fact. It's true that Jesus probably didn't carry a weapon as His role was unique. Yet, He did recognize the need for His followers, like Peter, to be armed. Let's face it, Jesus wouldn't have allowed a deadly weapon to be carried by a key member of His inner-circle if He felt otherwise.

Also, the Bible tells us that Peter used his sword to defend Jesus in the Garden of Gethsemane, when Jesus was about to be illegally arrested (John 18:1-11).

> *"Simon Peter then, having a sword, drew it and struck the high priest's slave, and cut off his right ear; and the slave's name was Malchus. So Jesus said to Peter, 'Put the sword into the sheath; the cup which the Father has given Me, shall I not drink it?'"*
>
> John 18:10-11 NASB

King James Version:

10 Then Simon Peter having a sword drew it, and smote the high priest's servant, and cut off his right ear. The servant's name was Malchus.

11 Then said Jesus unto Peter, Put up thy sword into the sheath: the cup which my Father hath given me, shall I not drink it?

John 18:10-11 KJV

When we study the above Bible passage, it is clear that Peter was not rebuked for using the sword as some suggest. No, that didn't happen. That's not what this passage tells us. Rather, Jesus simply stopped Peter from using his sword because it wasn't appropriate in light of the prophetic events which were unfolding.[12]

The core message contained in these Bible verses is that we need to exercise sound judgment. We should only use a deadly weapon when it is appropriate to the circumstance.

In the days when Jesus walked the roads of Israel with His disciples, Peter carried a sword. Why? It was prudent for civilians to carry a weapon due to robberies and other crimes of violence. It is similarly sensible for us today if we are, like Peter, emotionally balanced law-abiding citizens.

Likewise, there is another condition which is essential to this responsibility. We need to be properly trained.

These verses remind us that we need to be adequately trained. (Notice that in this high stress circumstance, Peter missed.) Moreover we need to be emotionally balanced, and not prone to violence or emotional outbursts. Further, we must be able to properly evaluate the circumstances we face, and we need to understand applicable laws—and obey them unless they are superseded by one of God's laws. Plus, we need to be prudent in our actions.

Sound judgment, training and common sense are essential prerequisites for using a weapon.

Chapter 4

Jesus' Teaching: We are to be peace-*makers,* not pacifists

We are to establish peace and advance the cause of justice. Jesus, and the Bible, makes it clear that we are not to be uninvolved bystanders. Nor are individual citizens to act as judge and jury; we are specifically prohibited from engaging in acts of revenge or personal retaliation. Nevertheless, God does expect us to be peace-*makers,* not pacificists.

What does this "peace-maker" role look like?

We are to actively work for peace, but *not* the peace-at-any-cost form of peace. Compromise with evil is not the kind of peace that God wants. Nor does He want us to secure peace by accepting enslavement or subjugation. (Spiritual peace is the ultimate quest, of course, but that subject is outside the scope of this book.) God expects our focus to be on righteousness; not just honesty, but rather living life as God's agent of peace and reconciliation in a violent world.

> ***"Blessed are the makers and maintainers of peace, for they shall be called the sons of God!"***
>
> [Jesus] Matthew 5:9 AMP

> ***"Blessed are the peacemakers: for they shall be called the children of God."***
>
> [Jesus] Matthew 5:9 KJV

The 'Jesus lifestyle' is one which advances national and community peace, and this can only occur when righteousness and justice prevail. We are to be His agents of peace, truth and virtue. For some these are out-of-vogue concepts, but in Jesus' world they are always relevant.

They never go out of style.

Just as a 'real estate agent' represents a 'real estate company,' followers of Jesus are to be God's agents and represent Him in our fallen world. If we read the Ten Commandments in context, we see that Commandment #3 (Exodus 20:7) seems to add emphasis to this point. It's unlikely that God was only concerned about swearing.

Throughout Scripture as well as with Commandment #3, God makes it clear that His people have a duty to properly represent Him to the world. Not taking God's name in vain[13] involves far more than just not swearing. It means that His people are to take-up His name properly and publically, serving as His ambassadors and agents, representing Him and His agenda rightly. This expectation is integral to using the Bible as our guide-book for living life, as well as for understanding this topic.

Some people are fortunate and live in a time and location that is peaceful. Others may enjoy the benefits of living in a community which is protected by professional law enforcement officers and a peerless military. Nevertheless, even those who are blessed with peace are not without 'peace-maker' responsibilities.

Our circumstance does not annul, or even subordinate our personal responsibility to be maintainers of peace. Abuse of power becomes inevitable if we abdicate our responsibilities in this arena.

Though some people want to ignore or even bury this truth, the foundation of the United States was intentionally built on biblical principles. There was a good reason for doing this, and there are good reasons for maintaining this today. The nation's Founders made it clear why this was, and is, important. Here are a few quotes which explain their motivations:

George Washington, Founding Father, 1st U.S. President [14]

> "Believing as I do, that [Christian] Religion and Morality are the 'essential pillars' of civil society,"

John Quincy Adams, Founding Father, 2nd US President [15]

> "Our Constitution was made only for a moral and religious [Christian] people. It is wholly inadequate to the government of any other."

Oliver Ellsworth, Founding Father, Chief Justice of the Supreme Court [16]

> "[T]he primary objects of government are the peace, order, and prosperity of society. . . . To the promotion of these objects, particularly in a republican [constitutional] government, good morals are essential. Institutions for the promotion of good morals are therefore objects of legislative provision and support: and among these . . . religious institutions are eminently useful and important. . . . [T]he legislature, charged with the great interests of the community, may, and ought to countenance, aid and protect religious institutions—institutions wisely calculated to direct men to the performance of all the duties arising from their connection with each other, and to prevent or repress those evils which flow from unrestrained passion."

James Madison, Founding Father, 4th U.S. President [17]

> "I have lived, sir, a long time, and the longer I live, the more convincing proofs I see of this truth, that God governs in the affairs of men. And if a sparrow cannot fall to the ground without His notice, is it probable that an empire can rise without his aid? We have been assured, sir, in the Sacred Writings [Bible], that 'except the Lord build the House, they labor in vain that build it.'[18]
>
> I firmly believe this; and I also believe that without His concurring aid we shall succeed in this political building no better, than the Builders of Babel: We shall be divided by our partial local interests; our projects will be

confounded, and we ourselves shall become a reproach and bye word down to future ages. And what is worse, mankind may hereafter from this unfortunate instance, despair of establishing governments by human wisdom and leave it to chance, war and conquest.

I therefore beg leave to move that henceforth prayers imploring the assistance of Heaven, and its blessings on our deliberations be held in this Assembly every morning before we proceed to business, and that one or more of the clergy of this city be requested to officiate in that service." [This practice of opening Congress with prayer continues to this day.]

Noah Webster, Father of American Scholarship and American Education

"The most perfect maxims and examples for regulating your social conduct and domestic economy, as well as the best rules of morality and religion, are to be found in the Bible. . . . The moral principles and precepts found in the Scriptures ought to form the basis of all our civil constitutions and laws. These principles and precepts have truth, immutable truth, for their foundation. . . . All the evils which men suffer from vice, crime, ambition, injustice, oppression, slavery and war, proceed from their despising or neglecting the precepts contained in the Bible. . . . For instruction then in social, religious and civil duties, resort to the scriptures for the best precepts."[19]

Daniel Webster, Early American Jurist, Voted Top-5 Senator of All Time

"[I]f we and our posterity reject religious instruction and authority, violate the rules of [God's] eternal justice, trifle with the injunctions of morality, and recklessly destroy the political constitution which holds

> us together, no man can tell how sudden a catastrophe may overwhelm us that shall bury all our glory in profound obscurity." [20]

Just as our nation's Founders believed, today we can't expect our government to be just, and the enforcement of laws to be just, if these biblical foundations are allowed to languish. This happens as a result of anti-Bible influences, but they also crumple, or become confused, when we fail to embrace our personal responsibility to be our Creator's representative in society. Personal compliance to biblical principles isn't enough. We are to be ambassadors.

Power corrupts, but the best way to avoid corruption is when a discerning, Bible-following and Jesus-representing citizenry is actively holding their leaders accountable. It is true that Christians see themselves as citizens of the Kingdom of Heaven, but they are also His ambassadors where they live. As my history-professor dad often reminded me, if Christians are only heavenly minded, they won't be of any earthly good—to God or anyone else.

> *"You are the salt of the earth; but if the salt has become tasteless, how can it be made salty again? It is no longer good for anything, except to be thrown out and trampled underfoot by men.'*
>
> *"You are the light of the world. A city set on a hill cannot be hidden; nor does anyone light a lamp and put it under a basket, but on the lampstand, and it gives light to all who are in the house.'*
>
> *"Let your light shine before men in such a way that they may see your good works, and glorify your Father who is in heaven."*
>
> [Jesus] Matthew 5:13-16 NASB

King James Version

> *Ye are the salt of the earth: but if the salt have lost his savour, wherewith shall it be salted? it is thenceforth good for nothing, but*

> *to be cast out, and to be trodden under foot of men.*
>
> *Ye are the light of the world. A city that is set on an hill cannot be hid.*
>
> *Neither do men light a candle, and put it under a bushel, but on a candlestick; and it giveth light unto all that are in the house.*
>
> *Let your light so shine before men, that they may see your good works, and glorify your Father which is in heaven.*
>
> [Jesus] Matthew 5:13-16 KJV

Jesus tells us that we are the salt of the earth. What does He mean?

If we dig deeper in the use of the word "salt" as it was understood in Bible times, we can gain additional insight for today. When Jesus said, *"You are the salt of the earth. But what good is salt if it has lost its flavor? … It will be thrown out and trampled underfoot as worthless,"* his audience would have immediately considered the three primary characteristics of salt.

In Bible times, salt was recognized as having three important attributes. First, it was used as a preservative to keep food from spoiling. Second, it was recognized as a substance which created thirst. Third, salt was used as a spice to add flavor to food, making it taste better.

When Jesus used this example of us as salt, He was telling us:

First, our reputation should be as an asset to the community. Our personality should not be seen as combative, officious, or self-righteous. Yet we should be unabashedly effective in improving the health and safety of our community, society, and culture. In other words, we are to stand resolutely against corruption, and against the advocates and effects of evil. We are to be God's agents of righteousness, healthy transformation, and justice.

Second, our lifestyle should help people develop a thirst for God. Therefore, we need to be winsome and positive; we need to live in such a way that God's Spirit can work through us to bring about a thirst for a relationship with our Creator.

Think about it—ordinary people asked Jesus to attend their parties[21] and He enjoyed going. (In the New Testament, these individuals were often referred to as *sinners and publicans.* The lowest-of-the-low social outcasts were often denoted by the term *tax gatherers.*) So it's reasonable to conclude that Jesus has a personality which would be described as gracious and upbeat—perhaps even fun, but at the very least He demonstrated that He was very sociable and caring toward people at all levels of society.

Jesus was interested in spending time with children[22] and ordinary people. Why else would they routinely invite Him to their social gatherings? It wasn't as if these were scholarly or ecclesiastical gatherings. They were parties where the guests were feasting and drinking quantities of wine.[23] Jesus wasn't carousing with them in wild living, but He did know how to be a good friend. He honestly cared about the welfare of ordinary people.

Third, our life should bring positive transformation. It's not enough to simply live as a good, honest, moral person. As a result of our life and activities, our community should be transformed into a better place to live—a place where people want to live. Just as salt can be used to make food taste better, we need to make community life better.

Are we living up to all three aspects of Jesus' expectation? And, are we keeping this subject of 'defense' in balance with the big picture of living a God-honoring, God-representing life?

Peace-making is critically important but it is only one aspect of community involvement. However, since peace-making is a role that has been largely abolished by individuals in modern times, it deserves a new level of attention and higher priority.

Chapter 5

Jesus' Strategy: Overwhelming Violence of Action

There is no evidence to suggest that Jesus personally carried a deadly weapon. That would have been counter to His unique role in human history. Nevertheless, He did personally engage in overwhelming violence of action.

For us today, the issue isn't "What would Jesus Do?" It's, "What is Jesus teaching *us* to do?"

In all of history, no one has come close to the way Jesus lived a life of love and kindness. But He was no milquetoast. There was nothing wimpy about Jesus. When He preached, *"Blessed are the meek"*[24] He wasn't extolling weakness, He was urging us to not assert our own rights, but rather to focus on advancing the Kingdom of God.[25] Jesus understood the big picture, and He understood sound strategy and tactics to accomplish an important objective.

One of the best examples of Jesus being strategic was when He used violence to force the vendors out of the Temple in Jerusalem. On that occasion, He used *overwhelming violence of action* as part of a strategy to make a profound point with community and church leaders, and the general public. Everyone who was there that day would have remembered this incident for the rest of their life. Doubtless they told the story again and again, for years, to their children and friends. It was that dramatic.

In the process, Jesus teaches us an important lesson regarding the occasional need for strategic, overwhelming violence of action. Even if you're well acquainted with this famous story, there are a couple of important details that you may have missed.

Here's what happened: Merchants were selling animals on the Temple grounds, and bankers had booths to exchange foreign currencies right there on the sacred Temple square. Together, these business people had a lively trade serving the pilgrims who were visiting the Temple. But in the process, they turned the Temple into a marketplace, desecrating this holy site. It was a serious insult to God our Heavenly Father and Creator, and Jesus wasn't about to tolerate their insolence.

The priests who were responsible for the Temple building and grounds, and the ultra-strict and straight-laced Pharisees, apparently allowed this desecration, so the authorities were of no help in correcting the violation. In fact, many of them were businessmen and may have profited from this illicit trade.

Since this was a very serious issue; literally an affront to God, Jesus couldn't allow it to continue. Obviously He didn't relish the idea of violence, but the unusual circumstance required it. This was a crime in progress as far as Jesus was concerned, and violence of action was necessary to rectify the outrage.

This same event is mentioned in three of the New Testament gospel accounts,[26] but only the Apostle John gives us much in the way of detail. Here is what John had to say about what he witnessed that day:

> *"It was nearly time for the Jewish Passover celebration, so Jesus went to Jerusalem. In the Temple area He saw merchants selling cattle, sheep, and doves for sacrifices; He also saw dealers at tables exchanging foreign money. Jesus made a whip from some ropes and chased them all out of the Temple. He drove out the sheep and cattle, scattered the money changers' coins over the floor, and turned over their tables. Then, going over to the people who sold doves, He told them, 'Get these things out of here. Stop turning my Father's house into a marketplace!'*
>
> *Then his disciples remembered this prophecy from the Scriptures: 'Passion for God's house will consume me.'"*
>
> John 2:13-17 NLT

King James Version

13 And the Jews' Passover was at hand, and Jesus went up to Jerusalem,

14 And found in the temple those that sold oxen and sheep and doves, and the changers of money sitting:

15 And when he had made a scourge of small cords, he drove them all out of the temple, and the sheep, and the oxen; and poured out the changers' money, and overthrew the tables;

16 And said unto them that sold doves, Take these things hence; make not my Father's house an house of merchandise.

17 And his disciples remembered that it was written, The zeal of thine house hath eaten me up.

John 2:13-17 KJV

As we read about this incident, in John 2:16 we see that it includes a very important detail. In Israel, bird vendors used large cages to display their birds, but these were actually stacks of small cages attached to each other. This made it possible for the merchant to easily transport the entire collection of cages, but when onsite he could open the door of just one small cage to remove one or two birds. This also made it possible for each customer to select the birds they wanted to purchase, and when the merchant removed the birds, there was no risk of others flying out. This same method is still used today throughout the Middle East.

So why is this important? In verse 16 of this Bible passage, Jesus is teaching us something of pivotal importance about the proper use of 'overwhelming violence of action.' The text gives us a vital clue; "*going over to the people who sold doves, He told them, 'Get these things out of here.'*"

In other words, Jesus was not in an angry, uncontrolled rage. His actions were not an out-of-control response to the situation. Rather, He was completely in control of His emotions, and was very strategic in the use of overwhelming violence of action. This is an example of "tactical Jesus," and we need to learn from Him the importance of shrewd, strategic thinking and measured force.[27]

Jesus was passionate, but He was 100% in control of His emotions. We need to follow His example of enthusiasm guided by shrewd tactics and self control.

Jesus turned over the banker's tables to scatter their coins. He made a whip and used it to drive out the cattle. However, He simply instructed the bird vendors to leave. Why? Because turning over the bird cages might have caused injury to some of the doves, and He didn't want to harm the birds. The problem wasn't the birds. It was the vendors who were desecrating the Temple by selling the birds inside the Temple grounds.

This is an essential detail. We can learn something important here.

Control: Jesus used violence when there was no other option for correcting an egregious trespass against God's righteousness. Yet, He was fully in control of His emotions. He wasn't out-of-control, nor was He having a temper tantrum. He was tactical. He used violence of action as a last resort, and delivered it using measured but overwhelming violence. It was strategic violence which was appropriate to the circumstance, designed to accomplish a legitimate and critically important purpose.

Measured: It is important that we learn from Jesus about the use of *measured* violence, as well. Like Jesus, we should only use violence-of-action as a last resort and as a strategic form of battle. Plus, it needs to be controlled and regulated so that it provides the desired effect, but without unnecessary injury—especially unnecessary collateral damage.

Those who have engaged in the use of "overwhelming violence of action," readily acknowledge that in the heat of the moment, it is easy for violence to escalate to an unacceptable level. Therefore, we need to be particularly careful to *only* deliver the measure of violence which is necessary and appropriate to the situation. This is how we should live.

It is also our responsibility to hold others accountable to this same standard.

Explosive Action: Jesus' action was decisive. On this occasion His strategy was to use explosive action. It was a strategic decision. Jesus didn't start small, or by arguing or pushing vendors around. He made a whip, and then He exploded into action. This was extremely shrewd. He strategically used the element of surprise. He was alone in His action; one man, but a whirlwind of action. Because of His shrewd plan, He was able to single-handedly drive out the entire crowd of merchants.

Shrewd Planning: Jesus didn't just respond to the circumstance. He formulated a shrewd plan, made a whip from cords prior to initiating action, and then He implemented His plan decisively. In other words, He applied the principles of sound tactics, preparation/readiness, and decisive action.

Think about what Jesus accomplished. He took on a large group of men using the element of surprise, and rapidly engaged in overwhelming-violence-of-action to accomplish a specific objective. Because of this tactic, He was victorious. Jesus won, in spite of the fact that He was up against what we would consider to be insurmountable odds.

Personal Responsibility: In this situation Jesus didn't just kneel in prayer and ask God to solve the problem. He didn't ask God to send angels to fight, nor did He beg the Holy Spirit to convict the miscreants. He accepted personal responsibility to act. He had the guts to do the right thing, the right way, at the right time.

Jesus was the Son of God, but He didn't use His divine power, either. Jesus routinely performed miracles but not on this occasion. He could have, but He didn't perform a supernatural miracle that day. He took action; in this situation, violent action. Why?

This incident was undertaken to teach us several important lessons about violence of action. With this event, Jesus is teaching us to act shrewdly in our planning, and strategically in our actions. Furthermore, that it may sometimes be necessary to use extreme measures, such as overwhelming violence of action. (This is the only recorded incident in Jesus life where He used violence, so we can assume that this type of strategy is reserved for rare or unusual circumstances.)

What is your gut-level reaction to this incident in Jesus' life?

Does it make you extremely uncomfortable? If so, you may need to make some changes in how you think, and how you live your life. You may need to dig deep and find the guts to stand a little straighter. You may need to be more deliberate about putting on the full armor of God (Ephesians 6:16-18), fortifying yourself with deeper resolve and passion.

We all need to look into our own heart and see if we need to become more assertive when it comes to taking a stand for Jesus, and for righteousness and justice. Many of us need to step-up and accept a higher level of personal responsibility. What about you? Ultimately, it's about being personally righteous, being equipped and prepared, using sound strategy, keeping our eyes focused on what's truly important, and having the guts to do the right thing at the right time.

Conversely, if you read this and say, "Yes! Finally someone is saying what I've felt all along." Well, maybe you need to cool down and be more circumspect in your actions. Maybe you need to put more emphasis into diplomacy and shrewdness.

We shouldn't look to the Bible to find ways to justify our natural tendencies. We should look to the Bible, and seek the help of God's Holy Spirit, to curb our natural-self and live according to Jesus' teaching. Early Christians referred to this as *The Way* because it was the only path compatible with a God-honoring life.

Jesus made it clear that our body is to be regarded as the Temple of God;[28] so we first need to take decisive action to clean up our own life. We need to let the Holy Spirit work in us so that we can follow Jesus teaching. His will, His way. We need to seek His Kingdom first and His righteousness,[29] not overly fixating on temporal issues and concerns.

Action Appropriate to the Circumstance: This Temple incident was not typical for Jesus. As far as we know, this was the only time in His life that Jesus used overwhelming violence of action—but He was prepared to use it when it was needed.

At the Temple in Jerusalem, Jesus made a very public stand. He used overwhelming violence of action because it was necessary for the circumstance, but violence of action wasn't part of His daily routine. "Yes," Jesus was ready to use it, but violence was only one of the many tools in His strategy-toolbox. He only pulled it out when it was the best tool to fix the problem.

Ready for Action: When violence of action was needed, Jesus was ready. When appropriate and necessary, He responded with measured, overwhelming force of action. In this Temple incident, it wasn't an uncontrolled emotional response. It was a shrewd tactic.

Discernment in Action: For those who strive to live according to the Bible, *discernment* and *balance* are integral to this lifestyle.

We need to routinely exercise sound judgment. We need to know when to act soft and kind; and when to act tough as nails with powerful intensity. We need to understand when violence is truly necessary, and when it can make matters worse.

Sometimes circumstances require immediate action. Other times we should call the police, observe, and wait for law enforcement to act. But when the circumstances are desperate and the government is failing to act, or if the dire circumstance is chronic and the government is unable or fails to adequately help, then it is appropriate to develop a personal or community strategy.

For us, even personal action should generally include getting the counsel of others in advance. In situations where immediate action isn't necessary, if possible, we need to seek wise counsel before taking action. We need to be strategic not just righteous.[30]

In these situations, and with the help of others, we need to evaluate and consider practical details, including public opinion, adversarial courts, and how opponents will try to skew the facts and manipulate the outcome. We need to understand that nonviolent alternatives are more desirable. When violence of action is actually required, we need to respond with *measured* violence which is appropriate to the situation. We need to avoid collateral damage as well as unintended consequences. It's not enough to act righteously; we also need to act shrewdly.

When violence is necessary we need to discharge it wisely and strategically; oftentimes rapidly and with surprise. It must always be undertaken without vengeance or malice, and without other inappropriate motivations. We need to discern the degree and type of violence that is appropriate to the circumstance, and plan for it to achieve the desired outcome, recognizing both the short-term and long-term effects of our actions.

Jesus used this Temple incident to teach us several important lessons about strategic violence of action. With this event, Jesus provides instruction on being creative and shrewd in our planning; tactical in our operations, self-controlled, and that we should only use the violence which is actually necessary to accomplish a legitimate, godly purpose.

This particular incident was an unparalleled action in the life of Jesus. Throughout His whole life on earth with His disciples, He didn't do anything else even remotely like it. Yet in this single event, He showed His disciples, and us, that we need to recognize events and circumstances which effectively draw a line in the sand. We need to be willing to engage in decisive, overwhelming violence of action when the line has been crossed and action has become necessary.

Further, though His actions make it clear that we need to be willing to use extreme measures such as overwhelming violence of action, this is rarely necessary. Yet, it is a tool in our toolbox. We should not rush to use it; but just because it is infrequently used, we should not forget that it's there, and that it is an option.

It is also important to remember that in spite of this incident, Jesus has the reputation of being the most loving and kind person who ever lived. Importantly, this 'clearing of the Temple' is the only recorded incident in Jesus life where He used violence to accomplish an objective.

Therefore, we can reasonably assume that this type of behavior is reserved for unusual circumstances. Zeal for the Lord is commendable,[31] but earning a reputation as a person of violence needs to be avoided, if possible.

Historically, though Jesus employed violence on this occasion, His reputation is not as that kind of person. He is remembered as a man of peace and kindness. We need to take pains to garner this same reputation.

Though Jesus used acts of violence in the Temple that day, He is still recognized as the epitome of brotherly love. Why? It's because throughout His life, most of His actions were peaceful, selfless, loving, and oriented toward healing and restoration.

Further, those who witnessed this Temple incident also understood that Jesus' actions were appropriate. They weren't confused by His actions. They grasped the biblical truth that love requires us to take a stand for righteousness and godly justice. Today, it's important for us to also grasp that without public understanding, this Temple strategy would have failed.

The week following Jesus' violent act of clearing out the Temple, the merchants were likely back at it again; continuing to desecrate this sacred parcel of land. So why did Jesus do it? Does this mean that Jesus failed with His strategy? Absolutely not.

His objective was not simply to correct that serious problem of His day, but to provide us with a teaching event which is relevant to us today. He is teaching His followers about the tactical advantage of surprise, and the righteous and judicious use of overwhelming violence of action as a legitimate option.

Chapter 6

Jesus' Final Instructions: Be Prepared—and Carry a Sword

Jesus directed His able bodied followers to carry a sword. He taught that we have a responsibility to be armed.[32] These are literally Jesus' instructions, not my interpretation.

Jesus didn't just say that if you feel like it, it's okay to carry a weapon. What He said is much more shocking than that.

Recorded in the New Testament are four longer speeches made by Jesus.[33] In the last one, often referred to as Jesus' Farewell Discourse (or Last Supper Discourse), Jesus actually issued an injunction about being armed. He told His followers that if they were not already carrying a deadly weapon (sword),[34] that they should start carrying one. He made it clear that they needed to have quick access to a weapon.

This powerful injunction was delivered in the context of telling His followers what to expect in the future. He warned them that they would face periods of adversity and violence, and they needed to be ready.

It is extremely significant that this injunction was part of Jesus' final instructions, delivered to his followers at the end of His final dinner with them, just prior to His arrest. (He was crucified the next day.) If you would like to read this discourse in the context of the whole biblical account of Jesus teaching that night, it is included in the appendix of this book.

The Last Supper was obviously a critically important time so we can expect Jesus' final instructions to be momentously important to us, too. Jesus was about to leave this world, so He utilized this last opportunity to provide an explicit warning with specific instructions for His followers. His parting words included a clear injunction. Jesus told His followers to arm themselves:

> ***"And He said to them, 'When I sent you out with no purse [money pouch] or [provision] bag or sandals, did you lack anything?' They answered, 'Nothing!'***
>
> ***"Then He said to them, 'But now let him who has a purse [money pouch] take it, and also [his provision] bag; and let him who has no sword sell his mantle [coat] and buy a sword."***
>
> Luke 22:35-36 AMP

Since this teaching is so important yet so controversial, I will repeat these same verses using other highly regarded English translations of the original Greek text. I want to make sure that it is crystal clear that there isn't any ambiguity here, and that I haven't "cherry picked" these paragraphs from some obscure or unusual Bible translation.

New American Standard Bible:

> *And He said to them, "When I sent you out without money belt and bag and sandals, you did not lack anything, did you?" They said, "No, nothing." And He said to them, "But now, whoever has a money belt is to take it along, likewise also a bag, and whoever has no sword is to sell his coat and buy one."*
>
> Luke 22:35-36 NASB

New Living Translation:

> *Then Jesus asked them, "When I sent you out to preach the Good News and you did not have money, a traveler's bag, or extra clothing, did you need anything?"*
>
> *"No," they replied.*
>
> *"But now," he said, "take your money and a traveler's bag. And if you don't have a sword, sell your cloak and buy one!'*
>
> Luke 22:35-37 NLT

New International Version:

'Then Jesus asked them, "When I sent you without purse, bag or sandals, did you lack anything?"

"Nothing," they answered.

He said to them, "But now if you have a purse, take it, and also a bag; and if you don't have a sword, sell your cloak and buy one.'

Luke 22:35-37 NIV

***New* King James Version**

'And He said to them, "When I sent you without money bag, knapsack, and sandals, did you lack anything?"

So they said, "Nothing."

Then He said to them, "But now, he who has a money bag, let him take it, and likewise a knapsack; and he who has no sword, let him sell his garment and buy one.'

Luke 22:35-37 NKJV

King James Version

'And he said unto them, 'When I sent you without purse, and scrip, and shoes, lacked ye any thing?' And they said, 'Nothing.'

Then said he unto them, 'But now, he that hath a purse, let him take it, and likewise his scrip: and he that hath no sword, let him sell his garment, and buy one.'

Luke 22:35-36 KJV

The central theme of this injunction is that Jesus wants His followers to be prepared for any contingency. As part of this preparation, He specifically directed them to get a sword. It was now time for His followers to start carrying a weapon. It was the dawn of a new era.

In the middle of His ministry, Jesus sent his disciples out as His ambassadors (Luke 10:9, 10). On that occasion, He told them that they should not bother to prepare, but just go. Unfortunately, today these verses are often taken out of context and misused as if they are instructions for us today.

Many well-meaning teachers fail to take note of Jesus' final instructions (Luke 22) which supersede the circumstances which surrounded the earlier event. They ignore that the Luke 10 episode was part of a singular teaching event, conceived by Jesus to teach His disciples about having faith in God. It was a one-time specific teaching episode, not instructions for all-followers for all-time. Yes, we need to have faith and trust God, but Jesus was not telling us to go out as His disciples did on that occasion.

By the end of Jesus' ministry, circumstances had changed radically. It was a new era (John 16:4). Jesus' injunction of Luke 22:36 was for those who would live as His followers in the days after His death and resurrection. We are living in that era; this instruction is for us.

Faith and trust in God is still a bedrock principal. But Jesus explained that His followers need to do their part, too. According to their ability, they need to get ready for the times ahead.

Jesus' final instructions included that they should expect uncertain and violent days ahead. He wanted them to be more than prepared. He wanted them to be ready, and He didn't want them to be surprised when the circumstances of life changed.

With these instructions Jesus was very intentional and specific. He wants us to be unencumbered by unnecessary debt, and to have ready access to finances (according to our ability). He doesn't want us to focus on our 'wants,' but rather on what we really need to travel down the road of life.

In addition, Jesus specifically mentioned that we need to have a provisions bag ready, as this is the most basic level of preparation. (In Jesus' day, a "provisions bag" contained essential items for life on the road. Today this is often referred to as a knapsack GO-Bag.[35])

And, Jesus wants us to have a weapon for defense. He wants us to be equipped and ready to defend ourselves and others.

Does this sound radical?

It is.

Jesus doesn't want us to be overly attached to the 'things' of this world. He wants us to be ready for any contingency, and for the opportunities He will give us to minister to others. Life shouldn't be about seeking pleasure or our own agenda. Jesus wants us to seek first the Kingdom of God, and His righteousness (Matthew 6:25-34).

That Last Supper night Jesus told His followers that if they didn't already own a sword they should sell something—even their coat if necessary, to get the money they needed to buy one. Jesus was that serious about their need to have a weapon. Jesus made it clear that it is important for us to be armed and prepared for defense.

Are Jesus' instructions actually relevant for us today? Yes.

Not only are they relevant, they're important, too. Jesus is telling us that we must prepare ourselves for any eventuality. We need to be ready to face uncertain times, adversity, and also violence. That is why He told His followers to carry a sword; they would need it. We do, too.

If we are sincere about being a follower of Jesus today, we can't ignore these instructions. They were for those He was speaking to face-to-face that night, and they are also for us. The context makes this clear. So we need to take these instructions seriously.

In my view, these instructions from Jesus couldn't be clearer. It's a real stretch to try and apply a different meaning to this passage. Thankfully, there are many theologians and pastors who get it right, but most don't talk about it. It's not politically correct.

Regrettably, the most vocal theologians and seminary professors seem to have a predisposition to pacifism or Progressive philosophy, so they try to assign some abstract meaning to this portion of Scripture. There are yet other theologians who are uncomfortable with this facet of Jesus' character, so they smile and bypass these verses, claiming that Jesus was just telling his disciples a joke.

What do you think?

Personally, I think Jesus' point is obvious. Further, that His message is of exceptional importance for us today. We can't continue to ignore it. We've got to step up and embrace all of Jesus' teaching, not just the parts we find comfortable.

At the Last Supper, Jesus' knew that it was His last opportunity to provide definitive instructions to His followers. It wasn't a time for jokes or vague allusion to an obscure meaning as some commentators inanely suggest (John 12:27-30). If we are willing to shed our predispositions and listen, the meaning is obvious.

Yet for many Christians and others who carry the cultural baggage of our day, being told to carry a sword sounds totally radical. Especially for those who grew up under the strong influence of the 'peace movement' or 'Progressive' thinking. But this is Jesus talking here.

We need to intentionally shed our cultural baggage. We need to look at what Jesus and the Bible actually teach about uncomfortable subjects such as living as a peace-*maker;* standing against evil, the use of measured force and overwhelming violence of action, and the application of coercive force and deadly force.

If your 'cultural baggage' is so great that you can't yet countenance the idea of carrying a gun, then perhaps you should become highly proficient in martial arts. If not martial arts, then you need some other effective way to defend yourself and protect others.

To becoming proficient in martial arts, carrying pepper spray[36] or a stun-gun, or having a baseball bat, are all better than having nothing. But these solutions have limited effectiveness. In any case, if you are not prepared both physically and mentally to use a weapon, then don't carry one. You will only get yourself into trouble.

We don't know how many of Jesus' other disciples carried a sword routinely, but in addition to Peter, at least one other disciple did carry a sword (Luke 22:38). So we can properly conclude that Jesus endorsed carrying a weapon. He recognized that His followers needed to be armed and ready to thwart violence.

This was true even *before* He gave His final instructions. His final instructions were something new, and different. He was requiring something more; something beyond their current practices.

What made His final instructions different is that He expanded this into an injunction for *every* able-bodied follower of Jesus. Even so, as important as this injunction is, let me be clear that an *injunction* is not the same as a *Commandment.*

Unlike a *Commandment* which is something required of every person, an *injunction* is a command for those who are able. For example, both adults and children are to not steal (*Commandment*), but this injunction about carrying a weapon only applies to adults. Similarly, a physically infirm person must obey the *Commandment* to not commit adultery, but they only need to obey this injunction on weapons if they are physically able to do so. Those with a mental handicap are to worship only God (*Commandment*), but a person who has mental problems, or even struggles with anger issues, should not have a weapon.

An injunction is situational. But it is not based on feelings or desires; obedience to a biblical injunction is based in our capacity to obey.

To be concise, Jesus subscribed to personal responsibility and self-defense as a lifestyle. His final instructions made it clear that each of us is to be suitably prepared. Not simply prepared to the degree we find it convenient or according to our personal priorities or comfort with the subject, but measured by our capacity and actual ability.

Fortunately, Jesus' core teaching of peace and love is abundantly clear and unmistakable. Yet, for some, this Luke 22:36 injunction creates a dichotomy, so they opt for the message of "love" and ignore that our Lord is also the God of justice and peace-*making*.

Without a doubt, Jesus expects us to be kind, peaceable and loving.[37] However, when we try to take on these admirable characteristics without also embracing God's nature as the God of justice, who is devoted to righteousness and the sacredness of life, then we become fenced-in and divided by a false understanding of Jesus' teaching on love.

Holiness is far more important than establishing peace corrupted by a compromise with evil.[38] Living with an attitude of forgiveness is essential,[39] and we must quickly acknowledge that no one is perfect,[40] but this does not absolve us from being people of action. Our peacemaking efforts must be realistic in regard to expectations,[41] but this is different than compromising with evil in order to obtain peace.

The first mention of the word "love" in the Bible is when God told Abraham to sacrifice his son, Isaac.[42] God orchestrated this incident to give us a raw understanding of God's sacrifice of His Son, Jesus. So love is not just an emotion, it also involves sacrifice, and we can't forget this as we contemplate taking a stand against evil.

This "love" issue is the source of a lot of our confusion about God, and these misunderstandings are not unique to our era. Woven throughout the history of the Church are zigzagging eras of God's people shuttling from one side of this subject to the other.

What makes this a more serious problem today is that this pendulum-swing which favors an unbiblical understanding of love, is hitting us at a very inopportune time. In our current era, the effect of this misunderstanding is also physical danger.

There is reason to expect darker days ahead. (Read the editorial "Signs of the Times" in the appendix of this book.)

If we fail to realign ourselves with God's nature of justice and accept our duty to be peace-makers, we won't be able to effectively stand against evil. And yet that's our job.

It is likely that we will suffer dire consequences if we fail to accept personal responsibility, including our personal responsibility to be physically prepared (Luke 22:36). These preparations, along with developing the guts [43] to make hard choices and the readiness to do the right thing, is necessary.

We are now entering an age of social upheaval with new forms of violence. So the failure to properly understand and embrace God's teaching on these topics will mean that we are ill-equipped for what we will face in the future. Unfortunately, just as with Jesus' disciples at the time of the Last Supper, many of us still don't seem to get it. Or, we aren't willing to obey and follow Jesus.

We need to get serious about being prepared and ready.[44] It's time to keep a weapon at hand, and to be trained and ready to use it.

Chapter 7

Nehemiah: An example of the Bible's teaching on being armed, vigilant and ready for action

In Nehemiah's time it became the duty of every citizen to help build a security wall to defend their hometown, and each of them carried a weapon with them wherever they went.[45] This Old Testament account of God's people, who were living in Jerusalem, includes the same weapon-carrying principle as that which Jesus taught in Luke 22:36.

Today, even secular teachers use examples drawn from the Bible's book of Nehemiah to illustrate valuable leadership techniques. Without a doubt, the man this book was named after is a great model of effective, as well as godly leadership. Yet, there is more to the story than just leadership techniques. This historical account also provides us with yet another type of model, that of an entire community embracing their personal responsibility for community safety and security.

Once inspired by Nehemiah, it's important to note that the people of Jerusalem didn't evade their duty. They listened to Nehemiah and prayed to God, and they embraced their personal responsibility for family and community security. They owned it.

After Nehemiah presented his plan for community security, there is no record of anyone trying to avoid participation. No one tried to sidestep their personal responsibilities. No one said that the physical labor of building a security wall was better suited to the skills of stonemasons and construction workers. Nor did they try to avoid security duties by saying it was the job of the police or military. No one tried to get out of carrying a weapon because they lacked that kind of experience. They all recognized and accepted these tasks as duties of personal responsibility.

The people in Nehemiah's time were experiencing rampant crime, and they were discouraged about it and felt helpless. And, they were also facing another security problem, one which is oddly contemporary with us, Arab terrorism.[46] Yet under Nehemiah's leadership, they were reminded that God was with them, and that they needn't succumb to fear or despair.

They took action; they didn't make excuses. Even the priesthood didn't claim an exemption because they were clergy. Each person was part of the security force and kept a weapon with them night and day.[47]

The people didn't hesitate. Together, they worked to build the security wall and gates, and they all worked together on security and armed defense. The "specialists" no doubt directed the efforts, but each person recognized that security is a fundamental responsibility of each member of the community.

If you're inclined to read the Bible, I encourage you to read through the book of Nehemiah, looking for other details which relate to this topic. There are many. For example, it was a group of civilians who stood guard with spears and bows while others were involved in the various construction efforts. (Today, the weapons which are equivalent to *spears* and *bows* are *tactical shotguns* and *assault rifles*).

Importantly, even those who were doing the heavy-lifting jobs of construction as well as the other laborious duties all kept a weapon with them constantly. As a minimum, all the workers carried a sword—which was the handgun of the day. Picture trying to build a stone wall with a sword strapped to your side. It doubtless got in the way, and it was almost certainly inconvenient. (It's worth noting that carrying a sword would have been far more inconvenient than carrying a handgun, but they did it anyway.)

This is a reminder for us. It is inconvenient to carry a gun, but we can't let *convenience* get in the way of *prudence*. Nor can we let convenience override our *duty* toward public safety, and our need to be obedient to Jesus (Luke 22:36).

If we want to reclaim our communities which have become hotbeds of crime, we will need to reassert our personal responsibility toward public safety and security. Wrong thinking on this topic has produced disastrous consequences.

Public safety is not just the responsibility of government; it is *first* and foremost our responsibility. Government is simply our employee and there to help. Gun ownership by responsible people is important as it is a great equalizer, but it is only one component.

We need to embrace that this is an important key for unlocking restoration and community health, particularly in crime-ridden inner cities and lawless regions. Our government officials and agencies, and our courts, need to be restored to their intended purpose, too. Their role should be to support individual and cooperative public safety efforts, and to provide a framework for impartial justice. It's a private/public partnership. It's not the exclusive role of government.

Rather than supplant our duty, government needs to support our efforts. We've now proven that more police, more laws, and more government does not work. We need to get back to God's plan, building safe communities His way, on a foundation of biblical principles which include morality, justice, liberty, and personal responsibility.

The people in Nehemiah's time didn't wait for the government to rebuild Jerusalem's security wall and defensive gates; they got busy and did it themselves. Nehemiah was a volunteer, and he provided the crucial leadership, but it was the people who willingly accepted the responsibility for their own defense.

In Nehemiah's day, the people prayed and looked to God for protection, but they also did their part. They kept their swords handy when they worked during the day. At night they posted sentries, and everyone else kept their swords close at hand while they slept. They were always ready and prepared for an emergency. If needed, at a moment's notice, they were ready to fight.

This model worked then. It still works today.

When my family and I lived in Guatemala, General Rios Montt [48] invited me to have lunch with him at his house. This controversial former president of Guatemala, who at this time was retired, was credited with breaking the back of the guerilla insurgency in that country. Because of this reputation, I was additionally interested in this one-on-one time as I wanted to ask him about his strategies which eventually brought an end to the protracted civil war (1960-1996).

After a few minutes of talk on a broad range of subjects, I was able to probe more deeply with my questions. Asking him about his successes in the war when so many other leaders had failed, I expected to hear an answer designed to impress me with his military might and the skill of the soldiers under his command. What he answered was nothing even remotely close to my expectation.

The General told me that he spent time on his knees in prayer, and he thanked God in advance for His intervention. He knew that God wanted to bring peace to his troubled country, and he knew that it was God who had given him the opportunity to serve as peace-maker to the nation. Then he proceeded to tell me about what God inspired him to do.

General Montt said that they were able to create a tipping-point. They were able to reverse the downward spiral of violence in Guatemala by doing two simple things:

First, he armed the civilians in remote communities. This made it possible for these citizens to take an active role in protecting their community from the guerillas. And second, they built roads. Simple dirt roads made it possible for villagers to establish relationships with each other, and to work together cooperatively. As a result, they could also come to each other's aid for community defense.

The military did its part too, of course. But the key that unlocked success where others had failed, was that Rios Montt equipped the ordinary citizens to do the people's work. He made public safety the job of the citizenry, not just the professionals.

This was similar to what Nehemiah did in his day. Nehemiah made sure that each individual citizen was armed, he established communication, and he developed a shrewd plan for defense. He made it possible for public safety to be everyone's job.

In Nehemiah's day, the people worked together to build a security wall. They put aside their regular work and made it their full-time volunteer job for nearly two months. As they worked, they were also ready to defend themselves and their neighbors. This was only possible because day and night, during work and after work, they had ready access to their weapons.

> *"At last the wall was completed to half its height around the entire city, for the people had worked with enthusiasm. But when Sanballat and Tobiah and the Arabs, Ammonites, and Ashdodites heard that the work was going ahead and that the gaps in the wall of Jerusalem were being repaired, they were furious. They all made plans to come and fight against Jerusalem and throw us into confusion. But we prayed to our God and guarded the city day and night to protect ourselves.*
>
> *Then the people of Judah began to complain, "The workers are getting tired, and there is so much rubble to be moved. We will never be able to build the wall by ourselves."*
>
> *Meanwhile, our enemies were saying, "Before they know what's happening, we will swoop down on them and kill them and end their work."*
>
> *The Jews who lived near the enemy came and told us again and again, "They will come from all directions and attack us!" So I placed armed guards behind the lowest parts of the wall in the exposed areas. I stationed the people to stand guard by families, armed with swords, spears, and bows.*
>
> *Then as I looked over the situation, I called together the nobles and the rest of the people and said to them, "Don't be afraid of the enemy! Remember the Lord, who is great and glorious, and fight for your brothers, your sons, your daughters, your wives, and your homes!"*
>
> *When our enemies heard that we knew of their plans and that God had frustrated them, we all returned to our work on the wall. But from then on, only half my men worked while the other*

half stood guard with spears, shields, bows, and coats of mail.

The leaders stationed themselves behind the people of Judah who were building the wall. The laborers carried on their work with one hand supporting their load and one hand holding a weapon. All the builders had a sword belted to their side. The trumpeter stayed with me to sound the alarm."

Nehemiah 4:6-18 NLT

King James Version

6 So built we the wall; and all the wall was joined together unto the half thereof: for the people had a mind to work.

7 But it came to pass, that when Sanballat, and Tobiah, and the Arabians, and the Ammonites, and the Ashdodites, heard that the walls of Jerusalem were made up, and that the breaches began to be stopped, then they were very wroth,

8 And conspired all of them together to come and to fight against Jerusalem, and to hinder it.

9 Nevertheless we made our prayer unto our God, and set a watch against them day and night, because of them.

10 And Judah said, The strength of the bearers of burdens is decayed, and there is much rubbish; so that we are not able to build the wall.

11 And our adversaries said, They shall not know, neither see, till we come in the midst among them, and slay them, and cause the work to cease.

12 And it came to pass, that when the Jews which dwelt by them came, they said unto us ten times, From all places whence ye shall return unto us they will be upon you.

13 Therefore set I in the lower places behind the wall, and on the higher places, I even set the people after their families with their swords, their spears, and their bows.

14 And I looked, and rose up, and said unto the nobles, and to

> *the rulers, and to the rest of the people, Be not ye afraid of them: remember the Lord, which is great and terrible, and fight for your brethren, your sons, and your daughters, your wives, and your houses.*
>
> *15 And it came to pass, when our enemies heard that it was known unto us, and God had brought their counsel to nought, that we returned all of us to the wall, every one unto his work.*
>
> *16 And it came to pass from that time forth, that the half of my servants wrought in the work, and the other half of them held both the spears, the shields, and the bows, and the habergeons; and the rulers were behind all the house of Judah.*
>
> *17 They which builded on the wall, and they that bare burdens, with those that laded, every one with one of his hands wrought in the work, and with the other hand held a weapon.*
>
> *18 For the builders, every one had his sword girded by his side, and so builded. And he that sounded the trumpet was by me.*
>
> Nehemiah 4:6-18 KJV

Today, in addition to other family and work responsibilities, God expects His *able* followers to be suitably armed and prepared. He expects us to take family, neighborhood and community defense and safety seriously. If the police aren't at hand *and we are sufficiently trained and able,* we are to take appropriate action to stop those who perpetrate grievous criminal violence. This is how 'Public Safety' has historically worked.

We are not to operate as vigilantes, but rather actively support and augment the lawful work of the police and sheriff in our community. Neighborhood Watch and other similar programs which assist law enforcement are important. Participation is everyone's responsibility, but since everyone won't embrace it, these tasks generally become the responsibility of a few community-minded citizens. This is less than ideal, but it can still work.

If a motivational leader like Nehemiah hasn't surfaced yet, that's okay. We don't need to let that stymie our efforts. However, it may be prudent to be more low-key until God blesses us with the people and resources we need. In the mean time, we need to pray and ask God to bless our efforts, and for His protection; remembering that while we wait, we can still do our part.

Once a cadre of responsible people develops, if circumstances change and the neighborhood becomes more dangerous, these individuals are positioned to become the nucleus for an expanded neighborhood or community effort.[49] Cooperation and unity within a leadership team can often become a capable substitute for an individual leader like Nehemiah.

Nehemiah's people didn't make excuses and we shouldn't either. Our failure to individually embrace these community responsibilities is why many neighborhoods have become unsafe. We can change this.

In peaceful neighborhoods, it may not be essential to coordinate this effort through a formal Neighborhood Watch-type program. An informal, but intentional alliance of responsible neighbors may be sufficient. However it does need to be deliberate, and yet some measure of organization is necessary. (Phone trees for emergency contact of neighbors, knowing who has CPR and medical training, which neighbors can be called upon for firearm defense, etc.)

Even those in wheelchairs or house-bound elderly people can have a role in these efforts. This isn't just a task for physically powerful men. It just needs to be a group of people who are reliable, even-tempered and discerning, who care about their neighbors and are willing to be vigilant.

Ideally, a few of these will be physically fit and armed. At least a small team of men and women need to be suitably armed, trained, and ready to step into the gap if the police are not available to quell deadly violence. As desirable as it would be, today we cannot expect every neighbor to arm themselves and obtain firearm self-defense training. At least not until something serious happens.

"Do not stand idly by when your neighbor's life is threatened. I am the Lord."

Leviticus 19:16b NLT

King James Version

"...neither shalt thou stand against the blood of thy neighbour: I am the Lord."

Leviticus 19:16b KJV

In all situations we need to understand and evaluate the risks associated with both action and inaction. We need to face the fact that we might get injured or killed (Mathew 26:52b). However, this potential for personal risk does not mean that it's not our duty to get involved.

In Judges 20 we read a sobering story in which the people of Israel took a stand against evil in their nation. It became a civil war. They prayed, and God confirmed the rightness of their cause. Nevertheless, 40,000 of the good guys died. They paid a terrible price. Yet, it was necessary to put an end to the egregious evil that was becoming a cancer to their society. Even though God was in it, and despite the fact that God had approved their actions, a lot of good people died.[50]

We need to keep in mind that God does not promise us a painless life, but rather a purpose-filled life. Routinely this involves spiritual battles (Ephesians 6:12), and occasionally this purpose is fulfilled in physical battle (1 Corinthians 15:54-58).

"Do not be afraid of sudden fear, nor of the onslaught of the wicked when it comes; for the Lord will be your confidence..."

Proverbs 3:25-26 NASB

"To do righteousness and justice is desired by the Lord more than sacrifice."

Proverbs 21:3

"Like a trampled spring and a polluted well Is a righteous man who gives way before the wicked."

Proverbs 25:26

Jesus said, *"Do not fear those who kill the body but are unable to kill the soul; …"*

"Do not think that I came to bring peace on the earth; I did not come to bring peace, but a sword."

Matthew 10:28a, 34

"The righteous are bold as a lion."

Proverbs 28:1b

"For God has not given us a spirit of timidity, but of power and love and discipline."

2 Timothy 1:7

King James Version

"Be not afraid of sudden fear, neither of the desolation of the wicked, when it cometh. For the Lord shall be thy confidence, and shall keep thy foot from being taken."

Proverbs 3:25-26 KJV

"To do justice and judgment is more acceptable to the Lord than sacrifice."

Proverbs 21:3

"A righteous man falling down before the wicked is as a troubled fountain, and a corrupt spring."

Proverbs 25:26

"And fear not them which kill the body, but are not able to kill the soul"

Matthew 10:28a

"Think not that I am come to send peace on earth: I came not to send peace, but a sword."

Matthew 10:34

"the righteous are bold as a lion."

Proverbs 28:1b

"For God hath not given us the spirit of fear; but of power, and of love, and of a sound mind."

2 Timothy 1:7

God expects us to be prepared and ready to act when circumstances dictate action. When it is time to act, we need to boldly and fearlessly take a stand. *It's our duty*. Doing our duty often requires guts, and we need to embrace the fact that it may be costly. Occasionally it may result in injury or even death, but it's still our duty.

Doing our duty may also be lonely, or even painful. We certainly need to avoid being unnecessarily contentious, and we need to strive to build unity; nevertheless, being active almost always comes with criticism or worse. We need to understand that it's always costly to care for others. Nevertheless, we have a moral and spiritual obligation to stand for righteousness and justice.

It is our duty. And, it takes guts to do our duty.

Chapter 8

Church History & Secular History: What Can We Learn From It?

It's worth noting that throughout Jewish history and the history of the Christian church, people have faced changing and challenging times, so we shouldn't expect anything different. When times are good, we need to be thankful. When times are hard, we need to dig deep for the tenacity that our Creator planted in our soul.

Church history is filled with stories of adversity, persecution and martyrdom. What most people don't realize is that more Christians have been martyred for their faith in Jesus during the past century than in all prior history.

Most of us are aware that Bible and Church history is full of instances of martyrdom and incredible sacrifice made by people who were willing to stand-up for their Faith. Many of these men and women were not church leaders; they were ordinary people like you and me. They were just doing their duty. They made the decision to persevere. These men and women fulfilled their personal responsibility to be ambassadors for justice and righteousness.

Today, most people don't realize that these same sacrifices are still happening. In fact, more Christians are suffering persecution and martyrdom today than at any other time in the history of the Church. On average, there are 100 Christians who are martyred for their Faith in Jesus every month.[51]

While most Americans are caught-up with the quest to make more money, buy a new car, or make plans for a fun vacation, many of our brothers and sisters in Christ are making the ultimate sacrifice. They are fighting the good fight.[52]

Similarly, while Hollywood élites lecture us about feeding the world's poor, we forget that most starving people suffer, not because their land isn't fertile but because they are the victims of injustice. It's not that we lack the will or the ability to feed the world's poor; we lack the will to stop the warlords and tyrants who steal the food.

To a lesser but nevertheless real degree, something similar is happening in the inner cities of the United States. This is happening because we have allowed the government to criminalized gun ownership and concealed carry of a firearm, and because we have allowed government agencies and courts to maliciously prosecute good people.

As a result of poverty (lack of guns and training) and unconstitutional laws, these people are not equipped to defend themselves. All across the United States, in affluent and poverty-prone areas alike, all across the "land of the free and home of the brave",[53] people are unable to protect themselves due to a lack of access to firearms, ammunition and training, or due to anti-gun laws and a wayward government.

Unfortunately, this situation is enabled by unbiblical Church teaching. In congregations across America, the UK, Europe and the rest of the Western world, a perception exists that there is a dichotomy between love and the use of force, particularly deadly force. This isn't new. It's important for us to understand that this is not just a contemporary problem, but one that our early Church Fathers also encountered.

Confusion about what the Bible says isn't new. Nor is it insurmountable. Thankfully, the teaching of some of these early Church leaders has been so insightful that it has stood the test of time. Unlike today, many of these highly-visible leaders had a firm grasp on the balance between love and the occasional need for deadly force to maintain public safety.

Therefore, what I am advocating in this book isn't something new, but rather a return to balance. Historically, Christian theologians have had a much clearer understanding of the balance between loving kindness, justice and the use of deadly force, than most seminaries teach today. What we see today is an aberration that needs to be corrected.

To document this historic sense of balance, I've included quotes from two leaders of the early Christian Church. The words of these *Church Fathers* demonstrate that I am not advocating a strange new interpretation of Jesus' injunction (Luke 22:36), and that confusion on these matters isn't new.

As these early Church leaders acknowledged, Jesus' words in Luke 22 are intended to be understood as straightforward teaching. Jesus told His followers to carry a sword, and that is literally what He meant.

St. Cyril of Alexandria (c. 376-444 AD) said this about Luke 22:36:

"The saying in appearance had reference to the apostles but in reality applied to every Jew [every believer in Jesus Christ]. Christ addressed them. He did not say that the holy apostles must get a purse and bag. He said that whosoever has a purse [money], let him take it. This means that whoever had property in the Jewish territories should collect all that he had and [be ready to] flee, so that he could save himself, he might do so. Some did not have the means of equipping themselves for travel [escape and/or self-defense], and from extreme poverty must continue in the land (area of conflict / location of danger]. 'Let such a person,' Jesus says, 'sell his cloak and buy a sword.' From now on, the question with all those who continue in the land will not be whether they possess anything or not, but whether they can exist [without a sword] and preserve their lives." [54]

St. Ambrose of Milan (c. 340-397 AD), said this about the supposed dichotomy of Jesus' teaching on this subject:

"Why do you [Jesus] who forbid me to wield a sword now command me to buy one? Why do you command me to have what you [previously] forbid me to draw? Perhaps He may command this so that a defense may be prepared, not as a necessary revenge, but that you may be seen to have been able to be avenged but to be unwilling to take revenge. [In regard to self-defense], the law does not forbid me to strike back [when being attacked]... This seems wicked to many, but the Lord is not wicked, He [Jesus] who when he could take revenge chose to be sacrificed." [55]

As we note in this teaching from these early Church leaders, there is a big difference between allowing oneself to be martyred for our Faith, and quite another to foolishly and unnecessarily die at the hands of a violent adversary. To accept violence by failing to act in our own defense, or to fail to defend another, are not examples of martyrdom or godliness. Occasionally, this inaction is the result of confusion on what the Bible teaches, but more often it is simply the result of cowardice.

In Luke 22, when Jesus was teaching about being prepared and carrying a sword, just like today, His disciples didn't understand the magnitude of His directive. Two of Jesus' disciples already carried swords (Luke 22:38), and they mistakenly thought that was sufficient. Just like most people today, Jesus' disciples didn't recognize the signs of the times—and yet circumstances were changing. They just didn't see it.

Jesus' disciples seemed to think that the future was going to be life as usual. That wasn't the case. Jesus was talking about something new. They were facing a new era unlike anything they had previously experienced. There is a good chance that we are too.

What about you? What do you see as the signs-of-the-times today?

Jesus' disciples didn't get it, and today most people still don't get it. Jesus became exasperated with His disciples. He must be sick and tired of how dull we are, too.

When Jesus said, "It is enough" (Luke 22:38), He wasn't saying that two swords were sufficient for the group, but rather that He had given sufficient instruction (John 16:12-13). He didn't need to talk at greater length—His followers needed to start listening.[56] Jesus knew that the Holy Spirit would help them recall His instructions, so he didn't need to say more on that occasion.[57]

Today, psychologists use the term '*normalcy bias*' to describe this social phenomenon. For those generations alive today, particularly those who have lived their life inside the United States, Canada, the UK or Western Europe, it's hard to avoid this mental condition. As a result, most of us are infected with a false sense of security. Sure, there have been economic ups and downs, gas shortages and strikes, major storms and earthquakes, acts of terrorism, and we have watched a downward spiral of social and moral decay; but most of us can't envision *life-changing* major upheaval.

Jesus' disciples suffered under this same misconception. That's why Jesus cautioned His followers to look for the "signs of the times" (Matthew 16:1-3). We need to live with an attitude of heightened awareness if we are to obey Jesus' injunction and prepare for the future.

Simply put, Jesus' followers should be prepared for any contingency. This preparation isn't simply to help us survive, but rather to prepare us for ministry in the midst of difficult days. It's not about surviving; it's about thriving. It's about seizing opportunities to serve.

Protecting people from violent miscreants is simply one of the many practical aspects of our ministry to others. The Bible's message is clear, and it's relevant for us today. This isn't a new religious philosophy; it's a return to historic time-tested Bible teaching.

We need to abandon the false-Jesus of today's political correctness, and pay attention to what the unchanging historical-Jesus of the Bible is teaching us. In addition, we need to respond to the "signs of the times" with discernment and sensible preparations. Like our brothers and sisters-in-Christ who have traveled this path of faithful intercession before, we need to become spiritually, emotionally, and physically ready for service in the days ahead.

Even though the purpose of this book is to discuss the moral and spiritual aspects of firearm defense from a biblical perspective, it's worth noting that the duty of good people to be armed is not just a concept of those who want to live according to the precepts of the Bible. These same conclusions are found in the writings of other cultures and times, including many historical figures that are universally respected.

The Right to Keep and Bear Arms is a biblical concept. True.

And, it is also a perspective held by those who don't care about the Bible, but they do care about lessons learned from the study of mankind and human history.

As we deal with those who don't think that ordinary citizens need to be armed, we need to remember that their viewpoint isn't new. Similarly, the view that an armed citizenry is necessary isn't new either.

Importantly, it is the pro armed-citizen viewpoint that has historically been the view of informed freedom-loving people throughout history. This is irrefutable.

The concept of an armed citizenry isn't historically unusual, either. It is the obvious conclusion of anyone who is willing to honestly embrace the lessons taught by personal experience and human history. Today as we deal with anti-gun opponents, it is Important to recognize that the Right to be armed isn't a concept that is limited to people of Bible-honoring faith.

Thoughtful people and philosophers from other perspectives have come to these same conclusions. These same moral principles of promoting an armed citizenry have broad historic acceptance even outside Bible-oriented and religious cultures. Therefore, even if an individual doesn't respect the time-tested precepts of the Bible, or Jesus, or the Christian Church, they need to understand this fact:

There is an abundance of other thoughtful and secular sources which promote these same values and conclusions. For them it is a rational conclusion reached by observing human nature and history.

For example, Plato in his book *The Republic* argues that individuals have a right to be armed,[58] but warns that this would eventually result in an egalitarian democracy.

Most westerners would see this as a good thing, whereas Socrates wasn't in favor of a democratic form of government so he argued that this was a negative, yet inevitable outcome of having an armed population.[59]

Aristotle reminds us that the Athenians were disarmed under tyranny, and when armed, there was a natural progression toward democracy and a government which provides justice and equality for everyone.[60]

These men were not religious, but they were realists. So whether the conclusion is based on the Bible or secular history, the result is the same. A disarmed citizenry is doomed to suffer victimization as a result of either crime or government tyranny, or both.

Both Aristotle and Plato made it clear that an armed populous leads inevitably to democracy. Whereas a disarmed population can only lead to rule by elitists who will eventually become tyrants.

At the peak of the Roman Empire when Rome ruled the world, their law not only endorsed the ordinary citizen's right to keep and bear arms, but codified that citizens had a responsibility to be armed. According to their law, this was for both personal protection, and to be ready to assemble a civilian militia to thwart government tyranny.[61]

Cicero said that the people should have *"the courage to strike down a dangerous Roman citizen (fellow citizen) more fiercely even than they struck down the bitterest foreign foes."*[62] In Cicero's view, carrying a personal weapon wasn't just acceptable; it was a personal responsibility to be armed and to act.

What many of us would call God's Law, Cicero called the *Law of Nature*. He said that the Law of Nature was ample justification for being armed, irregardless of the laws instituted by government. In his view, this alone was justification for the citizen's right to be armed with a weapon for personal protection, irrespective of the laws of a government which might condone or prohibit it.

Cicero said, *"And indeed, gentlemen, there exists a law, not written down anywhere but inborn in our hearts; a law which comes to us not by training or custom or reading but by derivation and absorption and adoption from nature itself; a law which has come to us not by theory but from practice, not by instruction but by natural intuition. I refer to the law which lays it down that, if our lives are endangered by plots [government] or violence or armed robbers or enemies [personal or public], any and every method of protecting ourselves is morally right."*[63]

(If you're looking for a more detailed summary of the expansive history of the Right to Bear Arms from a historic and secular viewpoint, read attorney Stephen P. Halbrook's book, "That Every Man Be Armed." Even though it's a scholarly tome it's very readable. The author is truly an expert, and is even cited in Supreme Court cases when an authoritative source is needed to explain the history of the Right to bear arms.)

Just as Caesar regarded the right to bear arms an obstacle to conquest,[64] so too do today's manipulators who have a political agenda which they know will eventually become unpopular with the public. These are the puppeteers who are pulling the strings of the gun control movement. (For more on this topic, see the editorial in the appendix of this book, "Gun Control, Politics of Deception.")

As we consider the Bible and church history, as well as world history generally, it is important to understand that the Right to self defense, and the Right to bear arms, has been recognized to be something that is not just acceptable, but rather a personal responsibility. Throughout history, being armed has been seen as essential for insuring public and personal safety, and as a bulwark against government tyranny.

Whether we look to the Old Testament and Jewish leaders in Bible days, to Jesus and the Apostles in the New Testament era, or to leaders of the early Christian Church, the Founding Fathers of the United States, or secular philosophers throughout history, there is agreement that an armed population is necessary for self defense and freedom. And, that *dis*arming the people will eventually lead to government tyranny and the loss of freedom.

Historically, the Right to own and carry a weapon has been recognized as a prerequisite to establishing, and maintaining, freedom and liberty. It's not a new idea. It's not just a biblical concept. For anyone who has studied human nature and history, it's common sense.

Good people need to be armed.
If they aren't, bad people will prevail.
It's that simple.

Chapter 9

Revenge: Is it ever justified?

Revenge is *not* an act of godliness; it is *not* an activity of justice. By definition, it is motivated by uncontrolled anger, spite, or a desire to retaliate or punish. Individuals motivated by these desires are not following Jesus.

Circumstances sometimes require violence of action, but to pursue revenge is the antithesis of being a peace-maker. There is no such thing as godly revenge, or biblically justified revenge or retaliation.

The Bible not only fails to condone revenge; it clearly condemns it. The Bible makes it very clear that only God has the Right to engage in acts of revenge, and He does not tell individuals that they are to be His instrument of revenge.[65]

> *"Never pay back evil for evil to anyone. Respect what is right in the sight of all men. If possible, so far as it depends on you, be at peace with all men. Never take your own revenge, beloved, but leave room for the wrath of God, for it is written, 'Vengeance is Mine, I will repay,' says the Lord… Do not be overcome by evil, but overcome evil with good."*
>
> Romans 12:17-21 NAS

> *"For God called you to do good, even if it means suffering, just as Christ suffered for you. He is your example, and you must follow in His steps. He never sinned, nor ever deceived anyone. He did not retaliate when He was insulted, nor threaten revenge when He suffered. He left His case in the hands of God, who always judges fairly."*
>
> 1 Peter 2:21-23 NLT

"Do not seek revenge or bear a grudge against anyone among your people, but love your neighbor as yourself. I am the LORD."

Leviticus 19:18 NIV

"Do not envy a man of violence and do not choose any of his ways. For the devious are an abomination to the LORD; but He is intimate with the upright. The curse of the LORD is on the house of the wicked, but He blesses the dwelling of the righteous."

Proverbs 3:31-33 NASB

"Don't say, 'I will get even for this wrong.' Wait for the LORD to handle the matter."

Proverbs 20:22 NLT

King James Version

17 Recompense to no man evil for evil. Provide things honest in the sight of all men.

18 If it be possible, as much as lieth in you, live peaceably with all men.

19 Dearly beloved, avenge not yourselves, but rather give place unto wrath: for it is written, Vengeance is mine; I will repay, saith the Lord.

20 Therefore if thine enemy hunger, feed him; if he thirst, give him drink: for in so doing thou shalt heap coals of fire on his head.

21 Be not overcome of evil, but overcome evil with good.

Romans 12:17-21 KJV

"21 For even hereunto were ye called: because Christ also suffered for us, leaving us an example, that ye should follow his steps:

22 Who did no sin, neither was guile found in his mouth:

23 Who, when he was reviled, reviled not again; when he suffered, he threatened not; but committed [himself] to him that judgeth righteously:"

1 Peter 2:1-23 KJV

"18 Thou shalt not avenge, nor bear any grudge against the children of thy people, but thou shalt

love thy neighbour as thyself: I [am] the LORD."

Leviticus 19:18 KJV

31 Envy thou not the oppressor, and choose none of his ways.

32 For the froward is abomination to the Lord: but his secret is with the righteous.

33 The curse of the Lord is in the house of the wicked: but he blesseth the habitation of the just.

Proverbs 3:31-33 KJV

"22 Say not thou, I will recompense evil; [but] wait on the LORD, and he shall save thee."

Proverbs 20:22 KJV

Attitude, intent, and purpose are key elements for differentiating revenge from the legitimate use of violence. For example, Jesus intentionally used an act of measured violence to make a point when the Temple was being desecrated (John 2:13-17), but He was clearly not engaging in an act of revenge. The prophet Elijah killed 450 men (1 Kings 18:22-40) one afternoon, but his purpose was not revenge.

Throughout Jesus' life on earth He never engaged in 'payback' even though He had numerous occasions when it might have seemed warranted (ex. Luke 9:51-56). Even when Jesus was about to be murdered He forgave His tormentors (Luke 23:34). Yet, violent acts are appropriate when the motivation is self-defense or the protection of others, but the same act is not justified when the purpose is revenge.

Retribution[66] is slightly different from revenge or retaliation. For example, if you found that one of the vendors serving your business was dishonest and charging you for goods not delivered, it would be foolish to let this fraud continue. Some form of just *retribution* would be required of us as part of our stewardship of the business. In a situation such as this we have the choice to confront and counsel, and forgive the debt or seek reimbursement, or we can call the police. Or, we can provide our own sanctions such as ceasing to do business with that supplier. We have the duty to forgive but we don't have a duty to forget. Retribution can therefore be a just act, but if it gets into punishment which is beyond moral consequences or a judicious lesson of redemption, then it becomes retaliation or revenge.

According to the Bible an act of 'retribution' can be just or unjust. Conversely, acts which involve retaliation, pay-back, or personal revenge, are always ungodly acts.

Retribution is appropriate when it provides justly deserved compensation, such as requiring repayment for the value of goods stolen. However, if our personal response moves beyond reasonable compensation and becomes punishment, at that point it becomes an unbiblical response.

Jesus' benchmark is a higher standard than what was allowed in the Old Testament. The old way of "eye for an eye, tooth for a tooth" (Exodus 21:24; Leviticus 24:20) might be legal, but it is not helpful because it goes beyond useful compensation and becomes penalty.

A court of law can assess a penalty which goes beyond compensation, and intentionally punishes, but this isn't acceptable behavior for individuals. There is a higher standard of behavior advocated by Jesus, and it applies to all situations, not just those where violence might be considered.

A 'preemptive strike' is a response that is more difficult to evaluate. These might be reasonable or unreasonable, based on the details of the situation.

For example, if you are in a wilderness campground and an outlaw motorcycle gang encamps nearby, and you overhear them organizing for a rampage of rape and plunder through the campground, a preemptive strike is reasonable. It might even be your duty.

David, before he became King of Israel, had several occasions when he engaged in preemptive strikes and pursuit-strikes as a civilian.[67] God blessed him when he responded according to the biblical principles which justified the action. As we read the Bible, a standard rule for engagement by civilians emerges. We need to be able to answer "Yes" to each of the following questions:

1) Would a reasonable and prudent person consider the threat to be real?

2) Do you have reliable information and facts on which to base your decision? (We cannot allow previous negative experiences with others, prejudice, dress and physical appearance, or other generalities to compromise our decision making.)

3) Is the threat of sufficient severity that action is appropriate?

4) Does the group (or individual) have the *present* ability to carry out the plan?

5) Is the danger imminent? Or, are government authorities unavailable, unwilling, or incapable of taking decisive action in a timely fashion?

Note: We are talking here about biblical standards for action, not national or local laws which might establish different standards.

It's worth noting that many of Jesus' disciples suffered all sorts of abuses. All of the Apostles had their rights violated. Many of them were murdered, yet their associates refrained from acts and even attitudes of revenge. Many of the heroes of the Faith suffered great abuse and injustice, yet they did not engage in revenge (Hebrews 11:36-12:1). Revenge is a radically different motivation than an aggressive but appropriate response to a situation.

Revenge or retaliation oftentimes comes to mind when fairness or justice has been thwarted. Yet, followers of Jesus are mandated to be peace-makers and justice-seekers, and they don't lose sight of the fact that we live in a fallen world. The Bible teaches us that people are ***not*** basically good. We have some residual good in us, but we are corrupted beings.[68]

Revenge often bubbles to the surface when our temper boils. This usually occurs when we have false ideals or unreasonable expectations.

Most people do strive to accomplish some good things, but we all fall short.[69] No matter how hard we try, we aren't perfect. Because of this reality, our expectation cannot be to expect godly behavior from fallen people. As much as we'd like it to be routine, godly conduct simply isn't 'normal' behavior.

The ugly head of retribution surfaces when we combine healthy indignation with a false expectation that the world is a place of fairness and integrity. Or, it can happen when indignation overshadows our awareness of our own shortcomings, and we allow ourselves to become puffed-up with a false sense of personal virtue; or, when we observe that justice has been thwarted or corrupted. Either way, our own unhealthy personal pride and false expectations is the root of revenge.

If we are willing to be honest, we recognize that a desire for revenge is a far more natural response than forgiveness. Thankfully, in Western culture most people still have an underlying sense of Bible-based morality, even if they decry religion. Those who don't revere the Bible still recognize that revenge is unacceptable, so they usually suppress this desire.

Oddly, most secular people will embarrassingly acknowledge that a desire for revenge is a normal human response, but they still find it unacceptable. Unfortunately, this is changing. We have legislated God and morality out of our schools and public life, so the anchor rope has now been cut and the cultural ship has been set adrift.

Many of our popular television dramas and action-oriented movies and video games now present revenge as not just acceptable, but commendable. This is often justified by a storyline which reminds us that our government, our legal system, or society has failed to deliver justice. Justifications aside, these influences have now displaced biblical morality and our society is suffering the consequences. Even people who participate in a church community are not immune to these beguiling influences.

We can debate what factors have caused this social decline, but even the most ardent secularists will agree that a negative social shift is occurring. Anyone who reads the newspaper or watches television can see that revenge is becoming increasingly acceptable.

As a result, the veneer of civilization is becoming thinner, and revenge and viciousness is becoming more commonplace as our society shifts away from the Bible as the standard for living. Notwithstanding, the Bible hasn't changed. Jesus still forbids personal revenge and expects us to be forgiving. There's no serious debate on these tenets of the faith.

When, and to the degree necessary, physical force and deadly force is needed to apprehend or stop a violent offender, or to stop a threat of dire criminal violence; it's still not okay to add revenge or retaliation into the response. Revenge cannot be used to justify any act, nor can we allow it to 'sweeten' a justified act.

An act or attitude of revenge or retaliation, to any degree, is not part of a righteousness response. We are human, so we may feel it, but we must suppress it. We cannot allow these feelings to play any part in our response to any circumstance.

Feeling a desire to retaliate is an unhealthy emotion but it is understandable. Acting on that urge by using unnecessary or excessive force, or, being motivated to act due to a desire for revenge, is the offense. These are unacceptable and anti-biblical behaviors. To be clear, the problem isn't necessarily the act itself, it is the motivation.

Revenge and retaliation are the exclusive jurisdiction of God. Thankfully, He rarely doles it out even when it is deserved. If we are willing to reflect on God's unmerited favor toward us, and pray for God's help, our urge for revenge can be defused.

God expects us to be gracious, kind and forgiving, but we also need to be ready to respond with dispassionate deadly force when it is required. The use of violence cannot be justified when it is used to obtain revenge, but it is justified when it is used appropriately to protect and serve.

To find this balance between forgiveness and violence of action, we need to constantly keep God's mercy in the forefront of our mind. Without God's unmerited favor we would all stand condemned due to our moral failures. So whenever we are tempted to harbor an attitude of revenge, we need to quickly consider our own lack of perfection.

We need to remember the unmerited favor Jesus offers each of us. He sacrificed His own life for us, and offers to pay the price for our failures. We just need to acknowledge that we have a problem we can't fix, and ask Him to take care of it. Because of Him, like a branch that is grafted back onto a healthy plant, we can experience the gift of new life. We didn't earn it; it's a gift. Since Jesus was willing to do this for us when we didn't deserve it, who are we to not forgive those who harm us? Even though a desire for revenge may be a normal human response, from our Creator's perspective it is not reasonable, nor is it healthy.

There isn't a contradiction here. God expects us to constantly maintain an attitude of forgiveness. At the same time, we are to be prepared and ready to engage in violence of action.

When we experience an inner urge to seek revenge it can be displaced by applying God's forgiveness. Ideally, we need to get beyond this urge for revenge before we engage in action, but this isn't always possible. If timing doesn't afford us this opportunity to get our head right, we need to be meticulous in separating our actions from our base urges. We cannot allow our response to be influenced by our emotions.

When times are tough, we must remember that the use of violence is never acceptable, nor is it ever godly, when we use unnecessary or excessive force. Our motivation cannot be to punish or retaliate; 'pay-back' and revenge are crimes against God's nature.[70]

As individuals, if we ever engage in revenge or retaliation we immediately move from lawful to lawless in God's eyes; from justified to guilty. It's that simple.

Chapter 10

Deadly Force: Literally a grave subject

We need to keep in mind that whether we act or not, we will live with our decision for the rest of our life. We may be able to sidestep decisions about the use of deadly force now, but we may not have that luxury in the future. So we need to consider these matters now; when our mind is clear and we have the opportunity to think things through. Today we can pray, think calmly, learn about the law and what the Bible has to say about these moral issues; tomorrow might be too late.

Throughout our consideration of this topic we need to always remember that the use of deadly force is one of the most serious subjects we are likely to ever face. Once you've pulled the trigger there's no going back. You can't change your mind. Whether your decision was right or wrong, there will be consequences.

If you shoot, you will live with the results. And if you fail to shoot but should have, you will live with the consequences of your failure. And if you didn't have a gun with you so you weren't able to act, that is yet another form of failure which will probably haunt you for the rest of your life.

For most people the tendency is to fail to act. Some are frozen by fear; some are confused or clueless; while others are cowards, or selfish and only care about themselves. While still others are surprised by the circumstance and don't know what to do.

If you are willing to deal with this now, you can probably avoid these failures.

Despite the abundance of news reports and television crime stories, when it comes to an emergency situation, most people haven't prepared themselves physically, mentally and spiritually. So when they face a sudden emergency they do nothing; they freeze with indecision.

When faced with a general crime problem most people ignore it, whine about it, or wring their hands and bemoan the circumstance in emails and conversations. Some may be glued to their television or news radio to learn more about an incident. Whereas others attend community meetings and then vote, deluding themselves that they have fulfilled their obligations of responsible citizenship. Yet, none of these activities are effective. In essence, these actions are all indicators of being frozen in a mode of ineffectual activity.

Jesus expects more of us. He expects us to be people of action. Wise and prudent action, of course; but He expects us to be people of judicious, timely and effective action. Being a follower of Jesus is a resolute lifestyle of meaningful action, not a philosophy.

In today's world, being armed and ready indicates that you want to be proactive. You are willing to be part of the solution, not an extension of the problem.

Yet, to contemplate using a firearm against another human being is a serious step. Justified or not, to use a gun to shoot someone is quite literally an act which may dispatch that person to hell. This is a grave subject, and most people find the topic so odious that they refuse to prepare.

The reality is this: *If you are not prepared and something does happen, at that point it's too late. At that point you won't have the time to think it through. If you aren't already armed, and physically, mentally, and spiritually ready to face the situation, you will probably fail. You will have chosen victimhood over victory.*

To delay might also be a deadly choice. If you procrastinate, you or a loved one might pay the ultimate price.

Notwithstanding, this is a serious issue and being armed and ready is not something to jump into casually. For a Christian, the prospect of using deadly force is even more sobering. Redemption is no longer possible for someone who is dead. Still, the Bible makes it clear that the use of deadly force *can be* justified. Sometimes it is even required.

When is shooting justified? What does the Bible have to say about this dilemma; the sanctity of life vs. the need to use deadly force?

The Bible teaches us that we are to do what we can to stop an act of violence that is likely to cause serious bodily injury or death. From the biblical perspective, we have a responsibility to do what we can to protect ourselves and others from armed aggressors. It is actually an act of love and compassion to prevent or stop acts such as murder, rape, kidnapping, robbery, etc. According to the Bible, we also have a responsibility to bring liberty, and to restore or enforce peace in a situation of serious or impending violence, lawlessness or anarchy.

Yet, there is a price to peace. It can be costly to be a peace-maker.

To acknowledge that people are not basically good isn't enough; we need to personally embrace this fact because it is foundational to deadly-force decision making.[71]

It's contrary to conventional fluffy thinking, but people are not basically good. Even young children are demanding and self-centered. Most people have some good in them, but goodness is not the norm when no one is watching.

We need to accept the fact that the natural tendency of humanity is not goodness. Our character is hopelessly flawed to one degree or another. That's why Jesus offers us the opportunity to be 'born again' with a new heart.[72] If this wasn't important, He wouldn't have come to earth and allowed himself to be hung on a cross. If there was another way to get to heaven He would have taken it. (Luke 22:39-24:46)[73]

Once we come to grips with the fact that we are dealing with fallen humanity,[74] and we can't expect godly behavior from godless people, we can get beyond the 'surprise' which often debilitates and stymies effective action. Being armed isn't enough; we need to be physically, mentally, and spiritually ready to act.

Evil should not surprise us. Further, in our corrupted world we will not experience peace without the use of force or the threat of force. We don't live in fantasyland. No matter how nice and loving we are, there will always be some evil person who is willing to use force to perpetrate their vicious deeds. The only way for us to curb this depravity is by applying the force necessary to empower justice.

Attempted murder, rape, kidnapping, aggravated robbery, violent carjackings, home invasions, gang attacks and acts of terrorism, violent anarchy, and the organized subversion of justice by those in power, are all examples of situations which may require the use of deadly force. Still, even in situations such as these, it is never something to be entered into lightly. Legal complications are the least of the problem. The more serious factor is sending even the most heinous criminal to hell for eternity (1 John 3:36; 5:11-12).

This acknowledged, the welfare of the criminal does not supersede the God-given Rights of the victim. Whether the victim is a nice person or not, once a violent aggressor threatens them with grievous bodily injury and has the present ability to carry it out, the aggressor becomes a legitimate target for our action. Decisive, deadly force is appropriate if we are protecting our own life or the life of another, from dire criminal violence or liberty-threatening aggression (kidnapping, etc). It doesn't matter if you are the intended victim, or if the victim is a family member, friend—or a stranger. It's not the relationship with you that is important, but rather the act itself and the risk to the victim.

When we talk about protecting the innocent, we're not making a judgement call about the victim's Jesus-like purity. An innocent victim is not necessarily a good person, it's simply that they are innocent in the circumstance. For example, when there is a gunfight between waring gang members there is no innocent victim. However, when a prostitute is about to be shot by her pimp, she may be engaged in illegal activity but she is still an innocent victim when it comes to attempted murder.

In all situations, our primary responsibility is to protect the weak or innocent victim. It is not to punish the criminal or avenge the victim; our mission is simply protection. We are not judge and jury, and it is not our job as individuals to *deliver* justice (Deuteronomy 32:35, 36a).

Today as in Bible times, it is our duty to courageously protect others; not just our own interests. This is quite literally another application of God's love. It is righteousness, justice and love in action.

It is our duty to protect life; our life, and the life of our family, friends and neighbors, but that is not where our responsibility ends. It's not just about "us" and "ours," it's about others, too. It's about *good* standing tall against *evil.* But it should never be about revenge, retaliation, or getting even.[75]

A more difficult subject is whether or not we should use deadly force to stop an illegal arrest (such as Jesus'). Or to stop theft, vandalism, or some other property-only related crime. In these situations, even if the law justifies a shooting, God's law may not concur. We must be particularly circumspect when it comes to the use of deadly force to protect property. The Bible is clear that it is reasonable to use deadly force to protect your home or your neighbors house (Nehemiah 4:14), but it's not as black and white when it comes to stopping someone who is trying to flee with your big screen television.

Each Christian or Bible-follower must consider all of these circumstances *before* they are actually encountered. What does the Bible have to say about property crimes and other related issues? The answer is not as straightforward as it is for situations where we are acting to protect a life; either our own, or protecting the life of another.

You've probably heard the term, *"having integrity at the time of decision."* But there is a related truism that few outside of the Boy Scouts talk about, and that is being *"fully prepared at the time of need."* We need to work through these issues now. We need to study the Bible, learn the law, and we need to seek wise counsel. And, we need to prepare to act. We need to be people of judicious action.

It's important for us to consider the various situations we might face, in advance—particularly those which might involve a deadly-force solution. We need to consider these things now when we have the opportunity to study the Bible, learn about the law, pray, think, reflect, and seek wise counsel. If we don't do it now when we have the advantage of time, and without the negative effects of stress and emotion, we probably won't make a sound decision later.

It's an easy decision to use a gun against a vicious murderer who is trying to kill a member of your family. The use of deadly force is a straightforward decision in that situation, but what about a circumstance which is less obvious?

We can identify these potential situations by projecting ourselves into news stories and the plots of television programs, by listening to the experiences of others, and by using our own creativity to construct various possible and likely scenarios. This is often referred to as *'running scenarios,'* and these mental exercises can help us hone our decision-making skills.

Shoot, Don't Shoot; Act, Don't Act –

Real-World Scenarios:

I've slightly changed the details of the below scenarios, but these are all real-world situations which were faced by individuals which I had the opportunity to interview.

If you were in each of the below situations, and you had access to a firearm, *"How would you respond?"*

Scenario #1: You are at the gas station putting gas into your car. While you wait for the tank to fill, you decide to go into the station's convenience store to buy a beverage. As you enter through the glass doors you find that you are facing the back of a gunman. He is holding a crying 8-year old child as hostage, and he is robbing the store. Not satisfied with the money from the cash register, he is using the child to motivate the cashier to open the safe. Suddenly, he moves the barrel of the gun away from the child's head, and begins to swing his gun toward the store employee while yelling, "You're a dead man." All the customers dive for the ground. The robber is only 10-feet in front of you. What do you do? Do you hit the ground with the others, or do you shoot?

Scenario #2: In the old cowboy days of the Wild West, it was a capital crime to steal a man's horse. This was because that horse was often necessary for survival. Many horse thieves were killed during that era. How would you respond to a modern version of a similar crime? What if you were in a remote wilderness area, having taken your infirm, elderly neighbor for a picnic to the lake where he used to camp with his family. You look up because you hear the noise of someone starting-up your Jeep. You had parked nearby because your friend can hardly walk, but you are too far away to physically stop the thief from driving away. They are stealing it. Would you shoot them to stop them from getting away with your vehicle? Your friend can't possibly survive a night in the wilderness. There is no cell phone coverage, and no way to summon help, but you do have a gun in your pocket. What would you do?

Scenario #3: What if, after a disaster, you didn't have enough food to feed your family (or yourself, or your friends)? It's been two days since they've had anything to eat. Would you use your gun to get food, so that you could feed your starving kids? What if the person who owns the food catches you and tells you to leave, and refuses to let you have any of it? He's a big, strong, physically fit guy armed with a baseball bat. Even though he has lots of food, he just sneers at you when you offer him $100 for a small bag of food. He laughs at you when you beg for his help. You're desperate. Would you shoot him to secure the food that your family desperately needs?

On what authority did you base your decision? Did you justify your action based on an emotional response, or was it based on an external moral standard such as the Bible?

Scenario #4: What if a team of law enforcement officers was going house to house in your neighborhood, demanding that the residents surrender their guns, even threatening to use force to disarm them. These officers say that martial law has been declared, and the mayor and police chief have ordered them to confiscate all guns from residents. They say that the government has suspended the 2nd Amendment of the

Constitution due to the current state of emergency and the public good. Would you surrender your guns? Would you fight? What would you do?

Note: This was the situation faced by thousands of good people after hurricane Katrina. Heavily armed police officers searched homes without permission, and took the homeowner's guns while holding them at gunpoint. At the time when this happened, most of the people who surrendered their guns assumed that the police would be there to protect them if they needed help in the aftermath of the disaster. Unfortunately, that didn't happen. As a result of surrendering their guns these people were unable to protect themselves. In the days that followed these seizures, roving gangs of violent criminals attacked many of these neighborhoods. The full scope of this disaster was not reported by the mainstream media.

Scenario #5: What if you find that Presidential Executive Order, "National Defense Resources Preparedness Act" (NDRPA)[76] has been invoked due to a collapse of the power grid and Internet. Computer hackers are to blame. As a result, there is no electrical power nationwide. The authorities have no idea how long it will take to restore electricity. Financial institutions and banks can't operate without power, and stores don't open because their computerized cash registers don't work and their buildings are dark and without ventilation. But this really doesn't matter, anyway, because during the week immediately after the incident, rioters broke into all the grocery stores and stole everything. Trucks can't get fuel, and those which do operate are often hijacked, so there are rarely any deliveries of food and other supplies to your community. Credit cards don't work without power, and prices have skyrocketed even for those who are lucky enough to have cash.

At this point, armed Department of Homeland Security agents come to your door and demand that you surrender your food, gas, and other provisions. The terms of NDRPA give them this authority. The DHS agents are only going to leave you a 3-day supply of food, which they say should be plenty as they expect the power to be restored very soon. Prior to the disaster you had the foresight to stockpile food and other supplies for you and your family, but they are going to take it.

They need your supplies, they say, to redistribute your provisions to others who are in need. What would you do?

It's easy to ignore bad laws, unlawful government agency policies, and these unconstitutional Executive Orders now in a time of peace, but what if they are implemented? How will you respond?

Scenario #6: Your neighbor, who is also your best friend, has developed mental problems. He has been getting psychiatric help, but his condition seems to be getting worse. You, and his family, are very worried about him.

You return home one day and your friend's wife runs up to you, telling you that your friend has just taken the neighbor woman and her daughter hostage. You can see them through the window of the neighbor's house, and you see that your friend has a gun, and you can hear him ranting.

You call the sheriff, and when the deputy arrives, the situation seems to deteriorate further. Your friend places his gun against the head of the neighbor woman. Both the neighbor woman and her young daughter are screaming in panic, and your demented friend is becoming increasingly agitated. The sheriff's deputy has called for back-up, and he has asked for the SWAT team and a hostage negotiator, but they won't arrive for at least 30-minutes.

You approach your friend to try and talk with him, but he acts like he doesn't even recognize you. You back-off because he placed the barrel of his revolver to the woman's head, and your friend cocked the hammer of the gun, and told you that he would kill the woman if you didn't leave. You believed him and cautiously left the house. You heard him lock the door as you left.

You and the deputy agree that the woman and her daughter are in immediate danger. The irrational wildness of your friend is becoming more pronounced, and it seems increasingly likely that your friend is going to shoot them both. The deputy says that he is only a mediocre shot, and doesn't think that He can get close enough to use his handgun.

His tactical shotgun is useless due to the proximity of his hostages. You both agree that the death of the woman and child is probably imminent. Your scoped hunting rifle is a few steps away in your gun safe, and you are a good shot. What would you do?

Scenario #7: You are in a shopping mall when a man suddenly runs past you. He is being chased by a man who has a gun in his hand. You are armed with a concealed handgun. The first man is screaming for help. What would you do?

If you have read these scenarios without answering the "What would you do?" question, I encourage you to go back now, and re-read each scenario. Then make a decision on each situation before proceeding to the next section of this chapter.

All seven of these scenarios actually happened. I have interviewed the people who actually faced these circumstances.

At this point I'll add some additional details regarding Scenario #7; information which was not available when the incident happened: It was later determined that the man with the gun in the shopping mall was an undercover police officer. This police detective who was in plain clothes, had failed to continuously identify himself as a police officer because he had become winded by the chase. The man he was chasing was a purse snatcher who had robbed a woman at knifepoint. During the foot pursuit, the criminal dumped the purse, but he still had the knife. This particular witness didn't see that weapon, but various other witnesses said that they saw it in the thief's hand during the chase. The robber was apprehended outside the mall by another police officer. Important to this scenario is that the witness failed to accurately comprehend the circumstance. Thankfully, he also failed to take any action. However this failure to act was not the result of good judgment. It was because he was surprised by the incident and frozen by indecision.

This explained, for our purpose here, with these scenarios it is generally irrelevant how the person actually handled the incident. What is important, is for you to think about how *you* would respond. What would you have done? If you had a gun and found yourself in each of these situations, how would you handle yourself?

We need to think about how we will personally respond to a potentially violent crime in progress, as well as unusual, and even nightmarish circumstances. All three types happen. Not only do we need to be armed with a gun; we need to also be armed with good judgment. By considering various possible scenarios you can prepare yourself for making appropriate "shoot" and "don't shoot" decisions.

For us to be level headed, and make good decision when the time comes, we need to take the time now to reflect on various potential difficult-choice circumstances. We need to think about shoot, don't-shoot situations today, when we can be level headed and objective.

You probably won't face a situation which is identical to any that I have included in this book, nor any other scenario which you will have previously considered. However, the task of thinking-through various possibilities is nevertheless constructive. These practical exercises can help you make a better decision when you face a crisis situation. Using this "what if" method, you can greatly improve your thinking processes for emergency situations, especially when you are under pressure or need to make a split-second decision.

Working through scenarios like these, and coming to informed decisions, can help you build mental *muscle memory*. This type of muscle memory is an important asset. It can help you make better decisions, especially if you ever find that you need to instantly come up with an action plan in the heat of the moment.

It is also important to periodically *'run scenarios'* based on your daily life. This will help you become more aware of your surroundings as you learn what is typical, and what is unusual. If you do this regularly, it can help you gain the mental conditioning which is needed. By practicing this technique you can learn to quickly identify threats and solutions, particularly those which might surface in your home community and work environment.

The military does something similar, and we refer to those training exercises as "war games." Homeland Security and FEMA do it too, but they simply refer to it as 'contingency planning.' Here in this book I call it, *running scenarios*. But whatever you call it, the concept is simple. You consider possibilities, and then come up with a reasoned, and realistic, plan of action. I'm not suggesting that you do something as elaborate as the government's exercises, but you can at least make it a habit to periodically *'run scenarios'* of what-if planning in your mind.

The following scenarios are based on activities drawn from my life today. You'll note that they are very simple situations, but they are nevertheless real-world practical. It's important to keep your scenarios straightforward and not too elaborate, at least in the beginning. The most beneficial scenarios are those which help you plan for circumstances which you are likely to actually encounter in your daily life.

Note: "Running Scenarios" is a mental exercise, only. It does not involve taking action in any form. Practical exercises accomplished with the help of friends can also be valuable training, but that is not the focus of this chapter.

Scenario #8: I stopped my car for a red light. What would I do if the panhandler walking between the cars pulled a gun, and tried to force his way into the car which is stopped in front of me? [77] What would I do?

Scenario #9: While sitting in a café having breakfast, what would I do if a pickup truck crashed through the front windows of the restaurant? At first I would think it's simply a traffic accident. But what if the driver got out and started shooting people. What would I do? (Does this sound farfetched? This really happened a few years ago, not to far from where I live.[78])

Scenario #10: I'm at home working on my computer when I hear the doorbell ring. I'm in the middle of something complex and I don't want to lose my train of thought, so I decide to not answer the door. I keep working. A minute or two passes, and the bell starts ringing again, so I go to the window to see who is being so persistent. What I see is someone I don't know, so I assume it's a salesman and I continue to ignore the bell. Everything is quiet for a couple of minutes, but then I hear glass breaking in the vicinity of my backdoor. I quickly grab my phone and dial 9-1-1, and they tell me that a police officer should arrive within 10-15 minutes. I realize that my pistol is in the safe in my bedroom, and that's at the other end of my house. I don't have 10-15 minutes to wait for the police. What am I going to do?

\- - - - - - -

These last three scenarios illustrate the value of using everyday places, and your ordinary activities of life, to develop your mental-training exercises. You can also use the experiences of friends and neighbors, as well as news stories, televisions shows, movies and other events to help you develop practical scenarios.

When you formulate various practical situations in your mind, you have the opportunity to use them to hone your crisis decision-making skills. But be sure to keep most of your scenarios real-world. These scenarios don't need to be elaborate; just use your everyday activities and news stories to engage in these "what if" contingency planning exercises.

Be sure to concentrate on more than just formulating the incident itself. You need to also devise your step-by step response to the situation. "What if the bad guy responded by doing so-and-so, and then I did …" When you apply this "if-then" process, you can use the same scenario to devise variations of the problem. As you consider the various potential developments, you will have the opportunity to sort through your options, and then identify your best tactical solution.

Remember, this isn't about picturing yourself as a hero or recklessly brave; it's about determining how to respond both morally and tactically. These go hand in hand. It's about threat assessment, biblical (moral) due-diligence, and formulating the appropriate response.

Ask yourself questions such as: "How would I move? When will I draw my gun? Can I get my gun out while still seated, and without being seen by the criminal? Can I safely run (or drive) to a place of safety? Can I wait for the police to come, or do I need to act? If I need to engage, can I do it from a place of cover? (Not just concealment, but cover which will protect me from gunfire.) How can I best utilize the element of surprise? Should I stay where I am and fight, or move to a new position? Where can I position myself to protect innocent by-standers if bullets do start to fly? What can I do to give myself a greater chance of success?"

Don't forget to also ask yourself questions such as: "Are there other criminals involved who are out of sight, or perhaps hiding so that they can provide cover fire along the escape route? Is there a getaway car? What is the motive of the criminal? Is this a planned-out or spontaneous crime, an act or terror, or the actions of a crazy person?" Details such these can help you respond with greater insight and safety. You need to consider options so that you can identify a moral and tactical response which provides the highest possible success coefficient.

There is far more to this practice than just identifying tactics. Considering tactical options and questions such as those mentioned are integral to the task of 'running scenarios.' However, don't neglect to regularly include moral issues in addition to tactical considerations.

Running scenarios in your mind can help you think-through options and actions. True. But not only are these scenarios practical from the standpoint of what kind of tactics should be employed, but also the identification and clarification of various moral issues. Tactics are only one part of planning an appropriate response. Be sure to also formulate scenarios which include moral questions or dilemmas. The real-world of firearm defense is tangled with difficult moral choices.

In the first seven scenarios which were presented earlier in this chapter, you'll note that all of them also include a significant moral decision. When I'm teaching my firearm self-defense classes, I often use these real cases as examples for this reason.

When I present the details of Scenario #1 (convenience store robbery with child hostage) to my students, invariably there are a few who can't countenance the idea of shooting the criminal in the back. They want to wait until he turns toward them to shoot. In their minds it somehow isn't "fair" to shoot the criminal in the back. It's as if morality requires us to adhere to some form of Marquess of Queensberry Rules for pistol dueling, rather than using deadly force to stop a violent criminal act.

What do you think? With this specific scenario, most people experience at least a check in their spirit, or a moment of confusion, when they consider the need to shoot. In the real-world, anything that causes confusion, or even a thought process which brings a split-second delay, can be deadly.

In this scenario, why is there uncertainty in regard to shooting the criminal in the back? Why are some people conflicted and sometimes distracted, or confused over a moral issue such as 'fairness'?

It's because many of us suffer the effects of conflicting worldviews, as well as the absence of a firm, reliable foundation on which to base righteous and just decisions. Plus, most people lack personal experience of this nature; they've never been in a situation in which they had to take this kind of action. This is why it is important to consider the intent of the Creator as taught in the Bible, and to see what we can learn from biblical accounts which have some relationship to these kinds of decisions. Too often we read these historical narratives as if they are just stories, rather than looking for the lessons which can be learned from the events. God has included these accounts in the Bible not just because they are interesting, but to teach us.[79] There's no fluff in the Bible; everything serves an instructional purpose.

Yet another incapacitating bit of urban folklore is the Progressive philosophy's backlash against the Castle Doctrine and Stand-Your-Ground laws, which assumes that we have a moral obligation to retreat. We've even had a U.S. Attorney General succumb to this baseless argument. This naïve and romanticized philosophy claims that an individual who is under attack has the moral obligation to retreat before resorting to the use of deadly force. The concept is that we are somehow morally obligated to demonstrate our non-aggression before we utilize our God-given Right of self-defense. This is foolishness.

This 'retreat' concept is an example of the illogical moral froth that develops when moral scruples are based on the mind games of academics, rather than on the Bible which has stood the test of time. If our objective is to stop an act of violence, perpetrated with intent to cause grievous bodily harm, it makes no difference if we retreat sheepishly or we advance aggressively. To put unreasonable conditions on our Right of self-defense clouds decision-making, and it increases indecision and promotes inaction. It can also cause needless injury and death.

Of course, disarming good people is the underlying motivation, not morality. Adding burdensome requirements such as the need to retreat on top of the thousands of other firearm laws already on the books, and the result is more public *confusion*, *inaction*, and *intimidation*. This discourages people from even trying to defend themselves.

When these 'Progressives' suggest that their approach is based in 'morality,' they are attempting to claim the high ground of the argument. Some weak-minded people without an understanding of history might actually believe this, particularly those who don't have a basis for morality outside of their own mind. However, for the 'Progressive' social engineers who sponsor such laws, they do it for another reason. They sponsor these efforts because they don't want good people to be able to engage in self-defense; they want us to turn to the government for protection.

When crime prevention and public safety become the exclusive purview of government, then the people naturally turn to government for protection. They insist on more government when they feel the need for more safety and security. Advocates for big government don't like independent and self-reliant people, they want the people to be dependent on their largess, and to demand more government and eagerly pay more taxes to get the protection they desire.

This is like a king who is able to progressively increase taxes to feed his opulent lifestyle, who is able to crush opposition and subjugate his people, through an insidious process of creating fear, and then coming to the rescue. The goal of the king isn't really protection of his people, it is power, control, and to have others feed his ego and lifestyle.

As we consider moral issues, it can be difficult to identify what is truly biblical and what is false morality. Knowing what the Bible really teaches is the only solution, of course, but we can also look to various warning signs. False morality is either instilled in us through a false application of fairness and loving kindness (such as the Marquess of Queensberry Rule example), or it is presented to us as a part of an anti-biblical agenda.

When the agenda is in opposition to the Bible, the proponents pompously act as if they own the high-ground of the argument. In the process they make statements such as, "everybody knows that this is the only right and moral viewpoint." There is no sound basis for their argument so they resort to snobby bravado. (This is the approach typically used by those who oppose reasonable laws which codify biblical principles, such as the Stand-Your-Ground and Castle Doctrine laws.)

If you would like to look into this further, study the life of the heroes of the Bible. One such example is David, a man who is described in the Bible as deeply appreciated by God; a man after God's own heart.[80] Though he made some very serious mistakes in his life, his desire was to be a man of God, and this is how he lived for most of his life. Therefore, it's fitting for us to look at his days of righteousness as a role model for us, all the more since he had a number of deadly-force encounters.

In regard to the use of deadly force, it is especially relevant to look at David's life during the days when he was a civilian,[81] before he became king of Israel. To the point, we see that when David faced violent aggression, he sometimes retreated, other times he stood his ground, and in yet other instances he courageously and aggressively moved forward. [82] On numerous occasions he ran after his opponent, aggressively pursuing a violent adversary and killing them after they had harmed innocent people. (For us, if it is practical to turn the pursuit of dangerous people over to the police, that is usually the prudent choice. The point here is that according to God's law, pursuit can be reasonable.)

We need to also note that when it was appropriate, David fled to avoid a violent confrontation.[83] The determining factor between fight and flight was based on sound judgment. He determined what was appropriate, and actually needed, in light of the big-picture circumstances. The important lesson here is that David didn't fight to protect his ego. He fought to protect life, land and liberty.

Further, David consistently failed to retaliate even when it seemed justified.[84] When possible, he sought to find a remedy through the use of non-violent dispute resolution,[85] and he even went out of his way to respect the authority of his oppressive government—even when he was unfairly treated. [86]

Notwithstanding, during a period of lawlessness when the government failed to do its duty in regard to protecting the people, David didn't just whine about it or protest. When the government continued in its failure to provide protection, David assembled an armed group of men to protect a nearby community.[87]

David recognized that it was essential to be vigilant, armed and ready to act. He was a man of action, and he did intervene when it became necessary to protect innocent people. [88]

Morality also requires knowledge of the law and obedience to the law of the land. Knowing the law is a facet of morality, but we need to remember that God's laws trump the laws of man. We obey laws in priority order—God's laws first.

Since knowing the laws of our nation and community is a subject of critical importance, this book has several chapters dedicated to this topic. The point I'm making is that even if you are a legal expert, this knowledge isn't enough. Knowledge of the law isn't an adequate basis on which to make informed moral choices. Similarly, having self-defense skills, and knowing effective tactics isn't enough, either. We need to understand and resolve moral issues before we contemplate our legal options and strategic tactics.

In regard to real-world moral decisions, I have been involved in a number of incidents where unresolved moral dilemmas produced very negative results. On one of these occasions I was almost killed because our SWAT sniper failed to shoot the guy who was trying to kill my partner and me. Apparently due to an internal moral conflict, he froze in indecision for just a moment, but it was long enough that he lost the window of opportunity to take the shot. Fortunately, two other team members were able to intervene, and they took the guy down. (Thank you again, Jack Calnon and Bob Cornuke.)

In the 'it-really-happened' Scenario #1 which I related earlier in this chapter, the person entering the convenience store was an off-duty police officer. When he opened the door and saw what was going on inside, he silently drew his gun but didn't immediately shoot. His concern was heightened because the criminal had his gun pointed at the head of the child he was holding hostage. As the robber twisted around, the officer had observed that the gunman's finger was on the trigger. Therefore the officer was afraid to shoot because he thought his bullet might cause a reflex action, resulting in the gunman firing his pistol. So, he waited for a safer opportunity. He got it a few seconds later when the screaming felon swung his pistol toward the store employee. The officer was ready; he took the shot. Problem solved.

This off-duty officer was able to take the shot because he was physically and morally ready. In that short 1-second of prime opportunity, when the assailant's gun came away from the head of the child, but before it was aimed at the store employee, the officer was able to take a safe shot. He had already kneeled so that his shot would be directed upward to avoid hitting any customers behind the criminal. Also, he had already selected his ideal point-of-impact. Even though the criminal was only 6-feet away, he carefully aimed using his gun's sights. At the moment of optimal opportunity, he shot the perpetrator in the head rather than the usual torso shot. He did this because he didn't want to there to be any chance of his bullet hitting the child who was being held tight to the robber's chest.

Assailant neutralized. Peace restored. Safety maintained; the hostage was uninjured. No one else was harmed. The entire incident took less than 10-seconds from the time the off-duty police officer opened the door and discovered the crime in progress, to the time when he fired the shot which ended the dangerous situation.

Beginning to end, less than 10-seconds: If he had not been in the practice of training and routinely running scenarios in his mind, this incident would have probably ended very differently.

The criminal died instantaneously, but his death was not the officer's goal. The goal was to decisively stop a dangerous situation, and the police officer did just that. Importantly, if the officer had missed or only injured the assailant, the perpetrator would have probably shot numerous innocent people. Moreover, if the officer had waited until the robber was facing him, rather than shooting him in the back, the incident would likely have ended in a bloodbath with many innocent people dead or injured.

I've used these two actual police cases to illustrate how important it is to consciously resolve moral dilemmas in advance; before we face a deadly-force situation, and before we plan our tactical response.

Scenario Development: As you practice developing your scenario exercises; first consider the most likely occurrences, and the most straight-forward potential encounters with violent criminals. These will naturally involve a number of different scenario situations, but they should primarily revolve around everyday crimes such as: home invasions, carjackings, attacks of all sorts in parking lots, man-with-a gun or knife situations in stores and restaurants, armed robbery, attempted rape, etc.

Violent encounters with people armed with guns, knives, axes, baseball bats, vehicles, and other deadly weapons can develop in many different forms, and they can occur in all the locations we routinely frequent. So as you go about your daily life, periodically 'run scenarios' in your mind. Don't make this an obsession, but do remember to occasionally engage in these mental exercises.

Next, after you are comfortable with the scenario development process, start adding unusual incidents to your planning. Someday you may face an emergency situation such as an active shooter in a theater or school. Or, it might be a criminal gang operating with impunity after a natural disaster, riot, or during some other out of the ordinary circumstance. Whatever the state of affairs, I encourage you to think about these uncommon occurrences, as well. These often require very different tactics, and they often include unusual moral dilemmas.

Unresolved moral dilemmas tend to make people freeze with inaction, so be sure to work through difficult moral decisions as you develop these mental exercises. For example, it's far easier to cope with killing a vicious criminal than to cope with killing a 12-year old neighbor child who was pointing a gun at someone. Yet, the risk to an innocent person may be identical. The decision to shoot the heinous criminal, and the child, both involve taking the life of a human being. Both situations involve saving an innocent life. These are both moral decisions, but one is still more difficult than the other. Why?

What is the process you use for making your moral judgments? What are the moderating factors which might legitimately, or illegitimately, affect your decision? Are you being driven by an emotional response, or a strictly legal response, or is there a biblical basis which supports your decision?

In the actual situation described earlier in Scenario #6, the man did decide to use his hunting rifle. He did use it to stop his best friend from killing the woman. Decisive action was necessary.

As often happens with the use of decisive force to neutralize a deadly situation, his action brought about the death of the perpetrator. In this case the perpetrator was his best friend. However, in the process he saved the life of the innocent neighbor woman and little girl. It was absolutely the right thing to do under the circumstances. (Micah 6:8; Isaiah 1:17; Psalm 82:3-4; 94:16) However, this does not mean that the decision was easy to make at the time, nor is it easy for him to live with today.

Life isn't fair. In this situation there wasn't a winning option. If he had failed to act he would have grieved over his failure to protect two innocent people, and that family would have been robbed of its mother and child. He did act, and his friend died. It was a huge personal sacrifice to pull the trigger, but sacrifice is sometimes required of us.

As this individual told me his story, he was in tears. It was several years prior but he still lives with the pain of his sacrifice. Yet, consider how much more difficult it would be if, in hindsight, he felt that he had made the wrong decision. What if he had let the woman and her daughter die?

We can't know the future and what might have been. We can only do our best. When called upon by circumstance, we need to have the guts to do our best. We need to take the full situation into account, and selflessly act on the best choice we know how to make.

My challenge to you is to be *fully prepared at the time of need.* What do you need to do to physically, mentally and spiritually prepare yourself?

Running scenarios is obviously important. Moreover, it is of *critical* importance to consider the moral implications of actions in advance.

Since these scenarios involve unpleasant events and a gritty thought process, some choose to ignore all of this. They choose to respond by making a decision that is easier, at least easier today. They choose to avoid this unpleasantness today, when everything is fine and everyone is safe. But of course this decision, which is to avoid making a decision, is foolish and shortsighted.

When we choose to not own or carry a gun when we have a legal right to do so, is similarly foolish. It's like failing to buy car insurance because you don't want to contemplate ever having a serious traffic accident.

We need to face these potential occurrences, honestly. We need to also recognize that there are individuals, such as pacifists, who are honestly motivated by a different understanding of the Bible. There are also other wonderfully kind people who make moral decisions based on the Hindu moral code which forbids killing, or by the moral code of some other established belief system. In those cases it's a thoughtful response. I disagree with these viewpoints, but I nevertheless respect these people. Further, I need to honor them and respect their viewpoint even if I think it is misguided.[89]

However more often than not, those people we encounter who

have a different viewpoint can't point to an external code of conduct which vindicates their viewpoint. These people are often motivated by underlying fear and cowardice. They profess a decision based on moral scruples, but it is really a false-morality which does not respect human life as something sacred, unique, and worthy of protection. We have a duty to treat all people with respect, but we don't need to honor arguments which are based on self-centeredness and vacuous arguments. These callous people need to be called out.

In my experience, when a kind person is naturally nonaggressive, or they consider themselves to be a pacifist, for them to live in the aftermath of failure-to-act moral negligence is additionally difficult. It seems to always bring deep regret and protracted anguish. We do need to remember that whether we act in error, or we fail to act but should have, God is always willing to forgive us for our failure. Even so, sometimes it's not easy to forgive ourselves.

University professor, pastor and theologian Dietrich Bonhoeffer[90] learned this first hand in Germany during World War II. He had studied nonviolent resistance under Gandhi, and ardently taught these tenants to others in Germany and the U.S. Yet, all this changed when he was forced to personally face evil. When Bonhoeffer encountered the real world in Nazi controlled Germany, his scholarly idealism gave way to biblical truth. He was forced to study the subject using a whole-Bible approach rather than rely on the wishful thinking of his progressive ideology.

After coming to grips with this difficult issue, Bonhoeffer became a member of the German Resistance (Widerstand). Later in the war he even participated in the *Wolf's Lair* assassination attempt which targeted Adolph Hitler. Yet, he was never beguiled by violence, nor did he compromise his integrity when it came to living according to his understanding of biblical truth.

Just before the end of the war Bonhoeffer was arrested and executed. He accepted his unfair verdict without a fight. He accepted his fate. (Matthew 26:52b; Revelation 13:10) Bonhoeffer was a hero, and he died a martyr.

Like Bonhoeffer, those who think of themselves as nonaggressive or pacifists, as well as those who are undecided or might hesitate, need to revisit the foundation of their beliefs. If their convictions are based in the Bible, or even the heritage of America or Western culture, we are in a position to help each other. We can listen to each other's concerns and arguments, and then study Scripture and history together.

If they are willing to listen, we need to explain to them the value of an external compass such as the Bible, and our understanding of what the Bible teaches. Conversely, if their worldview is based on something else, there is little hope of resolving this conflict. In this situation it's the worldview issue that needs to be addressed first.

The Bible is a reliable, external moral compass which has stood the test of time. Engaging in conversations about God, guns, and guts of firearm defense is a responsibility of being a loving person, and of loving justice. If we care, it's important to speak the truth into the life of those around us.

If we are parents, or leaders, it is our duty to know the truth—and to teach the truth. It's literally an obligation.[91]

Why bother? Because the way the world is going it is very likely that many of us will face a deadly-force situation in the future.[92] We need to help our family, friends, and those we are able to influence, come to grips with what the Bible really teaches. A progressive philosophy of wishful thinking will not defend our families. More laws, and more government programs, will not bring us public safety.

We need to help each other. Personal readiness, as well as family and community readiness includes far more than gun ownership and tactical training. It also involves spiritual (moral/biblical) and emotional (mental) development, as well as a *signs-of-the-times* and a big-picture (Bible view) focus on the future. We need to be prepared (equipped) and physically, mentally, and spiritually ready.

Statistically, there is a good chance that each of us will face a difficult deadly-force decision at some point in our life.[93] Armed or unarmed, good decision or bad, ready or not, we will live with the results for the rest of our life. This is a grave subject and it will be to our own peril if we fail to fully deal with it.

Are you personally prepared and ready? Are you helping others? Are you an advocate for justice?

Chapter 11

Shooting: Should We Shoot to Kill? Shoot to Wound? Or, What?

We should *not* shoot to kill. Likewise, we should *not* shoot to wound, either. So what should we do? We should shoot to *STOP*.

This may seem like splitting hairs because shooting to stop often results in the death of the perpetrator, but this isn't just nuanced word-play. From a biblical viewpoint, it is an important distinction. When a situation requires the use of deadly force we should shoot to *stop* the criminal act and protect innocent life.[94]

It's about taking what action is necessary to immediately, and decisively, stop the actions of the violent perpetrator. We shoot because we don't see any other viable way to stop the act of grievous violence or dangerous crime. Or, we don't see any other way to rescue someone who is about to become a victim of a violent crime such as kidnapping.

The practical reality is that we must be ready to respond very rapidly using focused, overwhelming force. Surprise is our ally. In many situations where deadly force is needed, it should not be threatened, but taken.

If the situation is handled decisively from the onset, rarely does a member of the public get into a protracted gun battle. When handled properly, these incidents are *usually* resolved very quickly. From start to finish, a well-handled critical incident often takes less than 10-seconds. It may be the longest 10-seconds of your life, but from the first act of engagement to the end of the incident, it is usually over quickly—*if you act decisively*. This is why advanced preparation, training, readiness, and awareness of your surroundings, is essential.

Yes, this decisive response may result in the death of the perpetrator, but that death should not be our goal. Rather, we should act to decisively stop that which is underway or about to start. That's it.

Let me dispense with the often repeated foolishness that we should shoot to wound, not kill. This is television melodrama, not the real world. Unfortunately, unlike what we observe on television or in the movies, a wounded person rarely stops their violent behavior. In fact they often become more vicious, and the situation more deadly and disastrous.

On television and in the movies, a person shot in the heart immediately falls to the ground, dead. In the real world, they might continue to stand, and have another minute or two to create mayhem and more death.

In my experience, it's the good people who fall down and give up when they are shot. More often than not, vicious criminals have the opposite reaction. Like a wounded wild animal, they tend to be cruel and brutal until their last breath.[95]

In real life, rarely does a single gunshot-wound disable the perpetrator, at least not immediately. So if we shoot to wound, thinking it is a more compassionate way to handle the situation, this is likely to result in more bloodshed and more injury to innocent people.

So what would I do? Absent other tactical considerations, personally I would shoot and keep shooting. I would continue to shoot the criminal until he (or she) is no longer a threat.

When I was a police officer I quickly learned that wounding a criminal may result in him killing his victim out of spite. Or, the criminal may kill to eliminate a witness, or seriously injure a witness in the hope that his opponents we will stop to give medical aid rather than continue.

In addition to this, shooting-to-wound has the capacity to create yet another big problem. If we shoot-to-wound in the midst of an unpredictable and quickly-changing fluid situation, the result is often a missed shot. And I do mean often. Occasionally these stray bullets injure or kill an innocent bystander. Therefore, we can't afford to miss.

As to ammunition, in my view it is essential that we utilize jacketed hollow-point (JHP) or frangible (fragmentation) self-defense bullets. A well-designed jacketed hollow-point or frangible self-defense bullet has several advantages.

Jacketed Hollow-Point (JHP) Bullets: A well-designed jacketed hollow-point bullet will almost double in diameter while still maintaining integrity as a single projectile. This feature is significant for two reasons. First, this makes it possible for the bullet to release all of its kinetic energy inside the human target, thereby increasing its stopping power. Second, because it is designed to hold together, it can often remain relatively intact after penetrating the window or side panel of a vehicle, or a wood fence or wall. As a result, it can still effectively stop a criminal who is hiding on the other side.

When unimpeded by an obstruction, the best hollow-point bullet designs will penetrate a fully-clothed human torso, but not exit the body. They will penetrate vehicle glass or the body of a car, and still be able to incapacitate a person who is behind these obstructions. Another benefit is that a jacketed hollow-point (JHP) bullet is less likely to ricochet than is a standard full-metal jacket (FMJ) bullet.

Frangible Self-Defense (FSP) Bullets: These 'fragmenting soft point' bullets are made from a blend of metals or nontraditional materials. Some can penetrate automobile glass or the thin sheet metal of a car's body, but many brands will not retain sufficient form to be lethal to a human target afterwards. Nonetheless, when a *high-velocity* frangible self-defense bullet impacts only a human or animal target, though it may not penetrate deeply, it can nevertheless deliver immense shock to the target's nervous system. This high shock-value is designed to cause incapacitation. The other key benefit of many of the frangible bullets is that they are generally the type of bullet which is least likely to ricochet. They are also less likely to penetrate the interior walls of a house and accidently strike someone on the other side. For a handgun used exclusively at home, this may be a significant consideration. (Visit the 'Resources' page at www.TXRFA.com for test results).

What Do Law enforcement Agencies Use? Most police and sheriff's departments use jacketed hollow-point bullets. They see these as being effective in more types of shooting situations. For them, they may encounter a violent criminal face-to-face, in a vehicle, or behind a wall or fence. They need a bullet-design that is a good compromise for all of these shooting situations. Exceptions include law enforcement officers who routinely operate onboard an aircraft, or in other environments where ricochet and secondary penetration are an overarching concern.

Note: 'Frangible bullets' are not the same thing as 'frangible self-defense' bullets, also known as 'total fragmenting soft-point' (FSP) bullets. Ordinary frangible bullets are often used on gun ranges as they can provide greater range safety, and some are supposedly more environmentally friendly. However, these are generally not a good choice for self-defense use.

* Most U.S. law enforcement agencies utilize JHP bullets. Overwhelmingly the most popular handgun cartridges in use by large police and sheriff's departments are these four:

> *Gold Dot,* made by Speer;

> *Golden Saber*, made by Remington;

> *Hydra-Shok,* made by Federal, and

> *HST,* made by Federal.[96]

> Probably the best frangible self-defense cartridge (FSP bullet) is manufactured by RBCD. It is often difficult to find, but it is available and can be found packaged under various brand names, all of which should indicate RBCD as the manufacturer in the fine print on the box.

Ethical Considerations: Why am I including this information about bullets in this book? It is because jacketed hollow-point (JHP) and self-defense frangible (FSP) bullets are more destructive than conventional bullets, so some people claim that they should not be allowed and that their use is reprehensible. Some opponents even claim that it is immoral to use this type of ammunition because these bullets deliver a massive and potentially fatal shock to the human nervous system, and they are more destructive to human flesh than is a standard FMJ bullet.

For some readers, the highly-destructive nature of these bullets may sound gruesome. However, if stopping the threat is our biblically-justified goal, this is an important feature. There is nothing immoral about using a bullet which delivers superior stopping power. Further, since these bullets can also reduce danger to innocent bystanders who might be harmed as a result of secondary penetration of the bullet, this added benefit alone would justify their use.

We need to keep in mind that the term 'knock-down power' is a misnomer. Any of the standard handguns used for self-defense will probably not deliver a knock-down punch unless the bad guy is already off balance. Being hit by a handgun bullet feels like being hit hard by a carpenter's hammer. It hurts, but it does not throw you to the ground. However, if you are hit repeatedly by handgun bullets in quick succession, this can be debilitating, just as it would be if you were hit multiple times with a hammer.

Determined criminals, as well as mentally ill people or those who are high on drugs, can continue to function despite multiple bullet hits. I once saw a criminal hit 5-times center-chest with a 9mm, and he still ran nearly a block before he dropped dead. This is why it is important to shoot and keep shooting until the threat has been neutralized. A single shot, or even a couple of shots, may not stop the threat.

It's important to understand that a standard full-metal jacket (FMJ) bullet rarely expands. Therefore it fails to release all of its energy inside the target. This not only delivers less stopping-power energy or neuro-shock power into the target, it can also create yet another dangerous situation. A FMJ bullet can fully penetrate the body of the criminal you are trying to stop, and after passing through his body it can strike someone else. In my experience, a FMJ bullet is also more likely to ricochet off of a bone or any hard object, and veer off in an unpredictable direction with the potential to injure some innocent person. This is why most police departments, and informed civilians, use ammunition with a jacketed hollow-point (JHP) or self-defense frangible (FSP) bullet.

If your firearm is a 9mm, be aware that the shape and high-velocity of these bullets makes them particularly susceptible to the problem of over penetration. Selecting a well-designed hollow-point bullet is additionally important if you are using a 9mm pistol, or using any high-velocity ammunition.

Further, most rifle calibers present this same over penetration problem. Conversely, a shotgun loaded with buckshot or slugs has the best stopping power of any firearm, but without the over-penetration problem of a rifle.[97]

On one SWAT call, my partner and I were assigned to guard the back of the suspect's house. For an action oriented guy, this was a disappointment, but even more so once the action started. On this occasion my partner and I spent the entire incident sucking grass; making ourselves as low as possible as we lay flat on the backyard lawn. Once the suspect started shooting at the police officers in front of his house, and the officers shot back, the bullets from my fellow officers passed through the entire house. They went through the front window, through two interior sheetrock walls, as well as the stucco exterior wall at the back of the house, and then continued to whizz past us. The 9mm bullets from the guns of my fellow officers would have still been lethal, even after penetrating the entire house.

For more about specific ammunition brands, tests, and ammo selection, visit the resources page at www.TXRFA.org.

A possible exception to the use of jacketed hollow-point bullets is if you are using a gun caliber that is smaller than 9mm or .38 Special. Small caliber self-defense handguns in calibers such as .380, .32, .25, and .22 are really not adequate for self-defense. I once saw a person get shot with a .32 ACP pistol at point-blank range. The bullet hit the victim in the foot, just behind the toes. Even though he was only wearing socks, the bullet failed to penetrate his foot. With this in mind, if you intend to use a self-defense gun in one of these lightweight calibers, you might want to carry FMJ ammunition to improve penetration. Or, if your gun is a high-quality steel model manufactured after 1970, you might want to experiment with a cartridge that uses a frangible self-defense (FSP) bullet. Better yet, trade in your handgun and get a new one in a larger caliber (9mm/.38 Special or larger).

No matter what caliber gun you are using, remember that when you miss the bad guy, that bullet can penetrate walls, cars, or travel a substantial distance. Given the right conditions, a bullet can travel more than a mile.

Even seasoned, well-trained police officers routinely miss with some of their shots, and they are typically trained to shoot at center mass (the torso). This is yet another reason why shooting at the middle of the chest, in the vicinity of the lower sternum, is generally the best option.

Keeping in mind the possibility of missing the target or over-penetration, we have a moral and legal responsibility to consider the backdrop. We need to ask ourselves the question, "What is behind the person I am about to shoot?" Of course when a shooting incident develops instantly, we may not have time to do anything but respond by shooting, but if we do have time, it's a good idea to pause and think tactics.

If necessary and possible, we should change our position to reduce the likelihood of injuring innocent bystanders. Often it only takes a slight change in position to increase public safety. Sometimes this can be accomplished by moving our position a few feet to the right or left, or it might be achieved by kneeling, or by lying prone on the ground so that we are shooting upward.

These considerations are additionally important if you engage a criminal inside your home or within your place of business. It's a good idea to select zones of fire in advance. Think about where it is safer to shoot, and also identify those areas in your house (or business) where it would be particularly unsafe to shoot. You don't want bullets from your missed shots, nor do you want the criminal's bullets which miss you, to penetrate an interior wall and hit a loved one or innocent person who is in another room. So in advance, take a walk through your home and workplace, and identify those areas where it is safer to engage a bad guy.

Unfortunately you often can't pick your battleground, but if you do have the opportunity don't just respond, think tactics. For example, you might be able to wait at a safer spot and let the criminal come to you. Or, the best tactic may be to advance rapidly to a safer zone for the encounter, or backtrack to a safer and more protected area. It's often not possible to control your environment like this, but if it is, try to utilize this and all other tactical advantages.

Shoot for 'Center Mass' – *the Torso.*

Why are police officers trained to shoot for center mass? (Center mass is the center of the torso; the largest, most vital part of the body.) It's because center-mass shots have a higher likelihood of stopping the criminal act by disrupting the heart and other vital organs. And, the police officer is less likely to miss if he is shooting at a moving target. Remember, bullets which miss the intended target still travel somewhere, and you don't want stray bullets to hit an innocent bystander.

If you are ever called upon to use deadly force, I implore you to use it to decisively stop an act of violence that cannot otherwise be stopped. And please, never think that the welfare of the perpetrator is more important than the Rights of the innocent victim.

Morally, our first priority is to save the victim and to protect the innocent bystanders in the vicinity. It's not to protect the criminal.

Another common moral misconception has to do with violent perpetrators who are mentally ill. After all, they are ill, not evil, right? Though this may be true, the circumstance we are considering is one that requires decisive action to stop an act of violence. It's not a time for counseling. It's a time to stop a serious or violent criminal act.

As discussed in the chapter on revenge, we are not judge or jury. Similarly, in the midst of a life or death situation, we are not psychologists or counselors. Our moral duty is to be a peace-*maker*.

The innocent person who hasn't done anything wrong is who should survive the altercation; not the one who is committing the serious crime. The offender may be mentally ill, but they are still the perpetrator; the initiator. It's not our job to discern motives or mental health. At this point it doesn't matter if you are a Nobel Prize winning psychologist or pastor. Your primary responsibility is to safeguard lives, to protect the weak against vicious oppression, and the peaceful against violence and anarchy.

In the real world, if a violent crime is occurring, it's irrelevant if the perpetrator is mentally ill or had a terrible childhood. What matters at that moment is the innocent victim(s), and stopping the serious crime or preventing it from escalating. If the use of deadly force is necessary, it's necessary.

If time allows, it's generally best to call the police and leave enforcement action in their hands. But in reality, if you ever encounter a deadly-force situation, there is a good chance that there won't be time for the authorities to arrive and intervene. You may need to act. If you fail to act, expect very bad things to happen to good people. Oftentimes, situations escalate to the deadly-force level in seconds, not minutes. This is why being armed, and being trained and ready, is essential.

If the situation is dangerously violent or about to become deadly, and you can't get timely law enforcement assistance, it may be your duty to personally take action. Or, if the police or sheriff's deputies are outgunned or overwhelmed and they need your help, it is your duty to help them. (If you find yourself in the vicinity of a criminal incident where the law enforcement officers need help, be sure that the officers know that you are a good guy before you attempt to get involved.)

Research tells us that every year in the U.S. there are 162,000 incidents where a gun was used to almost certainly keep another person from being killed. Annually, U.S. citizens use guns to frighten away a home intruder about 498,000 times each year. Statistically, 42% of Americans will be the victim of a completed violent crime (aggravated assault, rape, murder, etc.) in their lifetime.[98]

God expects us to act to protect ourselves and others. This isn't an optional assignment.

> *"Who will rise up for me against the wicked? Who will take a stand for me against evildoers?"*
>
> Psalms 94:16 NIV

> ***King James Version***
>
> *"Who will rise up for me against the evildoers? or who will stand up for me against the workers of iniquity?"*
>
> Psalms 94:16 KJV

If you ever encounter a violent situation and you aren't adequately armed and prepared for action, you will have to live with that failure the rest of your life. You will know that you could have saved someone's life, but you didn't, or couldn't because you weren't armed, prepared and ready.

Rules of Engagement:

You have probably heard the term *'rules of engagement'* to describe acceptable military behavior during wartime, but probably not in regard to individual citizens. Nevertheless, for those who are concerned with issues of morality, it can be useful to develop your own rules of engagement.

Developing your own 'rules of engagement' can help you define when you should, and shouldn't, use your firearm. It's not necessary to formalize this by putting it down in writing, but it is worth thinking about in advance, because this process can bring added clarity when you face a firearm-use situation.

So what are 'rules of engagement' (ROE) for a civilian? National and local laws may dictate some of this, but beyond legitimate legal concerns, we need to make moral decisions now when we have the luxury of time and no stress.

What I am suggesting here is that you define your own parameters regarding the use of your firearm. This will include when you *will*, and *will not* use deadly force. These rules aren't about results, nor are they just about what is legal. They should be designed to bring greater clarity to what is moral, so that you are prepared to respond to a critical incident faster and more responsibly.

Our 'rules of engagement' should cover various conditions and circumstances, and help us respond in the best way possible. When we have greater clarity, we can respond more appropriately. In the process, we are more likely to avoid mistakes and regrets.

Here are my standard rules of engagement. Before you establish your own, be sure that you understand your local laws.

1. Since I have a license to carry a concealed gun, I will routinely carry one wherever I go, so that I am able to use it if it becomes necessary.
2. I will train regularly using human-shape targets to help condition me for the real-world.
3. I will maintain myself in a state of readiness, and remain vigilant.
4. If I find that it is necessary to intervene with a firearm, if possible, I will position myself in a place where I can shoot from cover, and where missed shots will not hit innocent bystanders.
5. I will only use my gun to stop a criminal who is engaged in, or about to engage in criminal behavior which is likely to cause grievous bodily injury or death, or to rescue a kidnapping victim, stop an armed robbery, home invasion, carjacking, etc.
6. I don't fire warning shots.
7. I won't shoot a fleeing criminal in a property-only crime unless there are other extenuating circumstances which make it appropriate.
8. Further, I don't point my gun at anyone unless the situation already justifies my use of deadly force against that person.
9. Through diligent practice and the development of muscle memory, I will keep my finger off of the trigger until I am ready to shoot.
10. If I find it necessary to shoot, I use my sights (if possible) to carefully aim for center mass or the neutralization zone.
11. Absent other factors which dictate a different approach, I will shoot at least two (2) shots rapidly into the center mass of each assailant.
12. I will keep shooting until I have decisively stopped the violent criminal act, and there is no chance that the criminal can reengage with further violence.

What are your Rules of Engagement (ROE)? What are the applicable laws which need to be incorporated into your ROE plan? What are the moral implications of your engagement strategy?

As you answer these questions, I encourage you to jot down your thoughts, and then return to this topic in the weeks ahead to make sure your ROE covers the key aspects of '*shoot, don't shoot*' decisions for various circumstances. Consider it a work in progress, amending it as you gain greater insight and clarity into the moral implication of the use of deadly force.

If you've not yet worked through the issue from both a biblical and legal perspective, I urge you to not use deadly force to stop an illegal arrest or property-only situation.

Chapter 12

The Law:
What is Legal in Regard to Firearms?

Laws regarding firearm ownership, where you can have a gun and what is required for open carry and concealed carry of a firearm, vary greatly from nation to nation, and state to state. Before you attempt to acquire a firearm it is essential for you to know and understand both your national and local laws. This explained, the below information pertains primarily to the United States.

In the United States, each State and local municipality have different laws in regard to weapons. Significantly, in regard to firearms and what is legal, I've never seen a reputable gun store or sporting goods store offer a weapon for sale that is illegal to possess in that community. However, if you purchase a firearm in a State or municipality which is different from where you live, work, or where you will possess the firearm, you can easily get into trouble. Be aware of this potential problem. In advance, learn your local firearm laws before getting a gun.

If you buy a gun from a store which has a Federal Firearms License (FFL) it's a pretty safe bet that it's a legal firearm. However, buying a gun from a private party can be a problem, particularly if the owner "built" a *tactical* or short-barrel shotgun or rifle from a sporting gun or parts, or added a for-end grip (extra handle) to a handgun. A modified or home-built gun is a warning flag that you need to confirm legality.

All legal firearms have an intelligible serial number stamped into the metal of the gun, usually in the vicinity of the trigger. However, just because it has a serial number does not mean that it is a firearm that you can legally own.

For those who own a hunting shotgun that they don't use, some are tempted to use a pipe cutter or hacksaw to shorten the barrel, or to cut-down the stock. Don't. This is a quick way to get into serious legal trouble.

Whether the gun is new and purchased from a legitimate dealer, or you are buying a used gun from a private party, it is your personal responsibility to make sure that the gun is a legal firearm.

- - - - - - -

Note: The information contained in this chapter, and in this book, is not to be construed as instruction in the law, nor is the author providing legal advice. Also, this information may be out of date when you read this, so be sure to check with the U.S. Bureau of Alcohol, Tobacco, Firearms and Explosives (www.ATF.gov) before modifying a firearm. And, check with your State Attorney General, and Department of Public Safety (or equivalent), about what is legal in your area.

- - - - - - -

Answers to Frequently Asked Questions (FAQs)

Unless you have a special federal permit (National Firearm Act permit, also known as an NFA tax stamp or Class-3 license) issued by the ATF,[99] in the United States a shotgun must have a barrel that is at least 18-inches in length and an overall length of 26½ inches. A rifle must have at least a 16" barrel. Pistols can have a long barrel, but they cannot have a for-end grip (extra handle) or a shoulder stock. Most firearm manufacturers exceed the minimum size requirement by 1/10 – 1/2 inches as a safeguard against frivolous prosecution and authorities who don't know how to properly measure a firearm.

For more information on what is and isn't legal in the United States, read the government publication, "*National Firearms Act Handbook*." If you have an Internet connection, Visit the 'Resources and Links' page, at: www.TXRFA.org for a free PDF download of this ATF publication.

Of the many laws which relate to the modification of firearms, reducing barrel length, reduction in overall length, the addition of a stock or adding a fore-end grip to a handgun, and owning a silencer (or any noise reduction device for a firearm), are common but serious violations of the law. In the United States, these customized weapons and silencers (noise suppressors), and all fully-automatic firearms (multiple shots fired with one depression of the trigger), require a special license. This license must be obtained in advance from the U.S. Bureau of Alcohol, Tobacco, Firearms, and Explosives (aka/ ATF, BATF, BATFE; ww.ATF.gov). Weapons such as these are not necessarily illegal to own, but they do require a special license.

Federal law is strict and unforgiving when it comes to modifying weapons. If you want to adapt a shotgun that you already own, it is best to purchase a replacement barrel or stock made by a reputable company. Reliable online companies include Brownells (www.Brownells.com) and Midway USA (www.MidwayUSA.com). However, by the time you add up the cost of a new barrel, stock, and magazine extension tube, the cost of your purchases will likely rival the price of a new tactical shotgun. Don't assume that converting a hunting shotgun will be cost effective.

If you are determined to make your own modifications, be sure that you understand the law. The website for ATF, the primary federal law enforcement agency which deals with firearms, is a good place to start: www.ATF.gov. Keep in mind that this agency is extremely aggressive, and ignorance of the law is not an excuse, so be sure that you know what you are doing before you start modifying any firearm.

Though it would seem to be an obvious duty of ATF to provide easy-to-understand details of what the law requires, they apparently do not agree. It took me more than 6-months to obtain a PDF copy of the ATF handbook on the National Firearm Act which is distributed to law enforcement officers. This ATF document is now posted on the website for my firearm self-defense school, Texas Republic Firearms Academy (www.TXRFA.org). The 'Resources' page at www.TXRFA.org contains a wealth of helpful information.

If you are interested in purchasing a short-barrel tactical rifle or shotgun, you must *first* pay the NFA tax and obtain a special permit from ATF. For many people, this is best accomplished by creating a legal trust. One of the most economical ways to undertake this process is to use the legal services of a company such as *U.S. Law Shield's* Trust Department (www.lawshieldtrust.com). Expect to pay at least $300 to establish an NFA trust, plus another $200 tax which you pay to the federal government. There may also be state and local regulations and fees. The NFA process usually takes about 6-months to complete. If you are interested, I recommend that you undertake this soon as the current administration is trying to make this process more difficult.

If you use the legal services of U.S. Law Shield or Texas Law Shield, enter the Promo Code ***TXRFA*** to obtain expeditious help.

Legal Protection: I strongly recommend that you join U.S. Law Shield or at least a service which helps with legal services or costs.

Even if you are not interested in a specialized firearm (NFA) or concealed carry, I encourage you to become a member of *U.S. Law Shield* (www.USLawShield.com) or a similar firearms legal defense program. U.S. Law Shield and similar programs are expanding nation-wide to meet this need for specialized legal assistance in our age of legal harassment. If services such as this are not yet available in your state, the U.S. Concealed Carry Association (Self-Defense Shield), and National Rifle Association (Self Defense Insurance) programs are better than nothing.

As a point of clarification, membership in U.S. Law Shield is different than registering for their NFA program. U.S. Law Shield's *"Firearms Legal Defense"* membership program is designed to provide its members with an attorney who will come to their aid 24-hours a day / 7-days a week if they are ever involved in a shooting or firearm incident. It is not just an insurance-like reimbursement program, but rather a legal service which literally comes to the aid of its members. (See, www.USLawShield.com for details.) As a member of this program myself, I have also appreciated their seminars and the periodic legal updates which they send via email.

Speaking as a former police officer, I can tell you that this assistance will likely be a godsend if you are ever involved in a shooting.

Even if you were justified to use your firearm to protect yourself, it is still a big plus to have an attorney in your corner, helping you navigate the complexities of the legal system.

U.S. Law Shield has attorneys who specialize in this area of law, and this highly-knowledgeable experienced counsel can be invaluable. Membership in U.S. Law Shield can provide you with free legal counsel and representation, but be sure to visit their website for details. In my opinion, just knowing that you have this legal assistance available to you 24-hours day / 7-days a week, is worth every penny of the membership fee. If you travel outside your state be sure to register for their multi-state option. For more about their services, call or visit:

U.S. Law Shield, phone: 877-448-6839, or visit:
www.USLawShield.com.

* If you use the *Optional Promo Code* **TXRFA** you will receive two free months of membership.

Even if you don't intend to carry a concealed handgun, if your State has a licensing procedure for concealed carry (*CHL* – Concealed Handgun License, or *CCW* – Carry Concealed Weapon license), it's a good idea to get this State-issued license. Plus any training that goes along with it, as this can help you better understand the firearm laws of your State. Perhaps equally important is that if an emergency situation or disaster happens, and you have a Concealed Handgun License, you can legally carry a firearm.

It's worth noting, too, that many States have reciprocal agreements with other States. These agreements make it legal to carry a concealed handgun when you are traveling in those areas. For example, at the time I'm writing this, if you live in Texas and have a Texas CHL, you can carry a concealed handgun in Texas—*plus 30 other States.* But keep in mind, even if you are well versed in the firearms and concealed-carry laws of your State, if you carry in another "reciprocal" State, you also need to know and obey the laws of that State. You need to obey the laws of the State that issued you the license, and also the laws of the State you are visiting.

Disclaimer: None of the information contained in this book should be construed as legal advice or instruction in the law. The purpose of this book is exclusively to help readers understand the biblical, moral and spiritual ramifications of the issues covered. It is specifically not legal advice or counsel. The author is not an attorney, and is not providing legal advice or counsel.

Chapter 13

The Law: The U.S. Constitution Trumps Other Laws

Periodically I hear someone claim that we have a God-given legal right to own a firearm. Since firearms didn't exist during Bible times, this statement generates a lot of confusion. Nevertheless, there is a solid basis for the argument.

Chapter Summary:

Gun ownership is considered by many to be integral to our God-given Right to self-defense. Since a person without a gun cannot protect themselves from a person with a gun or another deadly weapon, it's an argument of equivalence (or an *'a fortiori'* argument) that we have a God-given Right to own and carry a firearm. In other words, if we can't defend ourselves without a firearm, then a firearm is necessary for self-defense.[100]

It is a well-established biblical principle that our Creator has given all people the Right to defend themselves. No competent Bible scholar disagrees. In the United States this concept is codified in many federal and state laws, and is affirmed by the U.S. Constitution.

Since constitutional law trumps all other federal and local laws, this is the primary legal basis for pro-gun and pro-carry arguments. Absent successfully evoking the constitutional amendment process,[101] the U.S. President, Congress, nor the courts—not even the Supreme Court, can trump (triumph over, or overrule) the Constitution. Since the 2nd Amendment says, *"the right of the people to keep and bear Arms, shall not be infringed,"* that's the end of it. Or, at least it should be.

Today, various legal-eagle *Progressives* suggest that the Constitution is a "living document" and subject to revision and modern interpretation. This is a common but unethical sleight-of-hand contrivance without legal basis.

On the other hand, a 'Constitutionalist' or 'Originalist' looks to the writings of the nation's Founding Fathers to determine *'intent'* or *'original meaning.'* This is the only objective and just method for understanding and interpreting laws, whereas 'Progressive' attorneys seek to manipulate the words to invent new meanings.

Thankfully, when it comes to firearms and the 2nd Amendment, anti-gun arguments immediately lose all foundation once the writings of the Founding Fathers are consulted. Nevertheless, the anti-gun crowd continues to manipulate the words of the Constitution and the 2nd Amendment, or use various inane or emotion-charged arguments in a flagrant attempt to eliminate our legal protections. These arguments are usually based on an emotional argument, not truth or facts.

Details: ***If you are not interested in better understanding this topic, skip ahead to the next chapter.***

In addition to the Constitutionalists (original intent) and Originalists (original meaning), and the Progressives (manipulation of the text to accommodate a radical political agenda), there is also a growing number of people who identify themselves as Strict Constitutionalists. Some of these argue that a court actually becomes "rogue" if it reinterprets the Constitution in opposition to the Founding Fathers original intent.

Rather than manipulating the words of the Constitution to give it a new or different meaning, or using the decision of a judge who offered an opinion in a prior court case, Constitutionalists, Originalists, and Strict Constitutionalist all agree that we need to use a more objective method to apply the U.S. Constitution and the Rule of Law. They look to what the nation's Founding Fathers actually said in their writings, and what these writings tell us about what they were trying to accomplish when they penned the Declaration of Independence, the Constitution and its Bill of Rights. Clearly, this is the only reliable basis for making legal decisions.

When we interpret the law and use those interpretations to make legal decisions, rather than focusing on the law itself and the meaning of the words, chaos ensues. Moreover, equal administration of the law is lost when unnecessary complexity is allowed to develop and confusion is exploited. This is the natural outcome when shyster attorneys are allowed to rule in the courtroom. As a result of these maneuvers, our judicial system has been co-opted by those with self-centered or Progressive agendas.

'Case law' is what is commonly used for decision making in our courts today. Case law is based on the outcomes and rulings of courts, rather than the law itself. This can be valuable when it adds clarity to a law, but when it is used to confuse or misuse a law, justice is thwarted. Today our judges and juries are led down rabbit-trails by abusers of the system who pave their legal arguments with case law. Rather than circling back to the law itself, they intentionally misuse the law to achieve their own goals. As a result, justice becomes elusive. Add professional attitudes of elitism and egocentric pride, or motivations based in power-grabbing and greed rather than equity, along with tactics based on confusion and charisma, and justice can be circumvented.

Over time these abuses have become routine. Though justice sometimes prevails, and there are still many honorable judges and attorneys, our limping legal system now seems to have become permanently crippled by these abuses. Yet, the judicial branch of government still carries a big stick. It tightly controls every walk of life.

In the eyes of our present legal system, an unconstitutional decision by a court is never considered "rogue," "invalid" or "illegal." According to the way the laws are actually administered in the U.S. today, there is no "loss of authority" by a court—it is just a violation of the defendant's constitutional rights, for which the law provides a remedy.

These court decisions may be wrong and "unconstitutional" according to the words of the Founders who wrote the Constitution, as well as by an honest reading of U.S. history, but they are not "invalid" in connection with the way the laws are enforced today. Instead, the Supreme Court has the last word on the subject, and anyone who acts contrary to it may be arrested, prosecuted and convicted. Though the court may have lost its legal authority in the eyes of some people, perhaps even the public at large, its decisions are nevertheless enforced using the full power of the government.

Today it is not unusual for judges to be ridiculed for acting as if they are a "god" rather than a public servant. This is sometimes just an immature response to authority, but other times these complaints are based on legitimate concerns. Elitist attitudes by those in power have weakened the legal foundation which is provided to us by our Constitution. This is a big part of our current problem.

For example, when I was a police detective, it was not unusual for me to encounter judges who fabricated their own applications and interpretations of the law. As a result, prior to making an arrest in a major case, a group of detectives and prosecutors would often meet to discuss what we thought the law, and case law, would be at the time the case got to court. Due to judicial arrogance, it wasn't enough for us to act lawfully according to the law as it was currently interpreted. We had to make an educated 'guess' as to what case-law would be when the case was finally tried in court. This was necessary because the criminal trial for of a major case was oftentimes held many months after the arrest.

As an illustration of the god-complex of our judiciary, I'll insert an example to show how this can create a dangerous, subjective environment—and a legal system where justice is not just illusive, but impossible.

When I was a police detective, I had a case in which the judge agreed with the defense attorney's baseless argument. As a result, the judge threw out the suspect's confession that I had legally and appropriately obtained.

In this particular case, the suspect had agreed to waive his Miranda rights before he made his confession, but the judge held that it was not admissible as evidence. Why? Not because I had done anything wrong, but because the police interview room was austere, and in his view, excessively intimidating. There was case law to support the concept that intimidation could be used to violate a suspect's 5th Amendment rights even after being Mirandized, so he subjectively applied this principle.

However in this case, the 'intimidation' was only in the form of gray steel furniture and white walls. Based on the defense attorney's argument about the intimidating surroundings where the interview took place, the judge threw out the confession. In his mind, this decision was simply an expansion of the justification used in a case decided by a higher court.

In this situation, the judge upbraided me about the construction of the police department building (which had been built many years before I became a police officer), and told me that I should have offered the suspect a cup of coffee and a cigarette—to make the surroundings less intimidating. This imperious judge told me that if the interior decorating had been more pleasant, or if I had offered coffee and a cigarette to counteract the effect of the room, I could have avoided the problem.

Even though the interview was recorded, and it was agreed by everyone that I had not personally intimidated the suspect, his confession was made inadmissible as evidence. This was solely because the judge agreed with the defense attorney, that the interview room was itself intimidating. (The prosecutor reminded the court that the interview room was no different than thousands of government offices around the country, but he was unable to sway the judge.) Unfortunately, the story doesn't end here. This wasn't the end of the craziness.

A few months later, in another case with a different judge but a similar set of circumstances, I had the confession of that suspect thrown out, too. Why? It was because I followed the instructions of the prior judge.

In this subsequent case, the defense attorney argued that because I had offered the suspect coffee and a cigarette, I used *hospitality* and *friendliness* to manipulate the suspect into a confession that he would not have otherwise made. This was a different defense attorney, but he used the reverse side of the same, earlier argument. He maintained that I had violated the suspect's 5th Amendment Right which protects him from self-incrimination, and that I had used *friendliness* to accomplish this intimidation. The attorney used a convoluted parade of case law to justify this claim. Using this logic, he convinced the judge that my actions had coerced the suspect, forcing him to witness against himself.

Agreeing with this convoluted argument, this demigod judge threw out the confession.

Risking being cited for contempt of court, after the trial I walked up to the judge and asked him to clarify what I should do in the future. I respectfully explained the dilemma that he and the other judge had created by their conflicting standards. His answer was to shrug his shoulders, saying that he was not in a position to control the standards set by another judge. In other words, he was not concerned with justice and equity. He was only concerned with his own turf, which he ruled over as if it was his private kingdom.

Because of these aristocratic judges, I, as a police officer, had no reliable standard to use for enforcing the law; and yet he didn't care. The presumptuous rulings of these two judges made it impossible for me to fairly and uniformly enforce the law.

Do you see how the prideful arrogance of those in our legal system, and the use of strings of case law rather than the pursuit of justice, has created a major problem? And, how ignoring the original meaning of the law to make decisions in court, has brought us to this point? It's no wonder we are witnessing this expanding trend toward redefining the U.S. Constitution.

To be fair, I need to repeat that there are many fine and honorable attorneys and judges. However, despite the efforts of these conscientious true professionals, the downward trend continues. Truculent attorneys and capricious judges, and now a growing number of social-engineer attorneys and activist judges, are intentionally redefining the Constitution to support their agenda. They have wrestled control over our judicial system. It's a runaway train.

Regrettably, there isn't an operational check and balance system that is correcting these abuses. It's getting worse, and nothing significant is happening to correct the problem.

The other two branches of government (*Legislative* - Congress and Senate; and *Executive* - the President) are supposed to provide this 'check and balance' function, but they don't. Why? One obvious explanation is that a disproportionate number of our legislators and recent presidents are lawyers. Since the end of World War II, 40-50% [102] of these representatives have been attorneys. Their careers in law have instilled in them an acceptance of the system as it currently operates. Though perhaps unintentional, by nature and as a result of their legal education, they are predisposed to accept and propagate the defects of our legal system.

Adding to this setback, just as in other branches of education, the faculty members of law schools are almost entirely self-proclaimed liberals or Progressives. As a result, young attorneys are inculcated with an understanding of the law which demeans justice, and a legal philosophy which promotes social engineering.

Are my courtroom examples real but ridiculous? Yes. Are the problems they illustrate real and honest? Yes, absolutely. These were my cases, and this is what I personally experienced in court.

Are situations such as these unusual? Unfortunately, no, they are not. The details of the courtroom antics change, but travesty of justice prevails and is now commonplace. Justice isn't just elusive, in many courtrooms it is no longer even considered relevant.

The ridiculousness of the legal arguments in my examples is unusually clear, so they provide an easy-to-understand illustration of the problem. More typically, the usual judicial abuses involve more finesse but equally ludicrous justifications based on case law. I assure you that such manipulation of the law and justice is not unusual.

Today, many higher court judges interpret the law according to their own rapacious and self-serving agenda, basing their verdicts on convenient decisions of other likeminded judges rather than the law itself. They have become managers of the law rather than advocates for justice. For many attorneys and judges, truth, fact, sound reason, and moral scruples are considered archaic concepts, replaced with a legal philosophy based on relativism. For them, truth and morality are negotiable concepts, and irrelevant when making legal decisions.

As a result, justice is being thwarted because our courts are no longer dedicated to the concept of justice as their first priority. Attorneys and judges look to case law which was created by their peers, rather than the law itself and the original meaning of the law as it was passed by the legislature.

It is important for us to remember that it isn't just our Constitution which is being neutered. All of our laws have become targets of these self-serving maneuverers.

The problem grows each year as our elected officials add literally thousands of new laws, and government agencies add countless new regulations for us to obey. This complexity becomes fertile ground for intentional manipulation and legalized corruption.

Of course, there are other facets to the problem. This is just an overview, but this background is essential if we are to understand our current predicament.

Why am I going into all of this in a book about God and guns? It's because we can't effectively protect our 2nd Amendment Rights, and our God-given Right of self-defense, if we don't understand the underlying problems.

Today, the "guts" of firearm defense involves more than being action oriented, and willing to stand up against a vicious assailant. It also includes having the guts to stand up against a broken legal system, and suffer all sorts of abuses from the government which is supposed to protect us.

Therefore, we also need to understand the problem so that we can be shrewd in formulating our responses. New "concealed carry," "open carry," and "stand your ground" laws may be helpful, but they are not going to solve the problems we are facing.

Our legal system is broken and getting worse. Not only is it filled with egoism, it has become unnecessarily complex; a bureaucratic black hole which captures time and money, and darkens justice. This complexity helps feed the egos and elitist attitudes of the attorneys and judges who often act as if they are a legal priesthood, expecting us to bow and then stuff their wallets.

It's not unusual for good people to be intimidated and abused by anti-gun prosecutors and judges. These officers of the court have been armed with a glut of conflicting and esoteric laws which disregard our 2nd Amendment Right. Not only are these laws used to maliciously persecute gun owners, they effectively discourage people from using guns. With increasing frequency, people are even fearful about using their God-given Right to self-defense.

Rather than be commended, individuals who have used a weapon to protect themselves, or someone else, are often prosecuted for some arcane or nitpicking violation. Even when a person is legally justified in their use of deadly force, they often need to hire an attorney to defend themselves against politically motivated or malicious criminal prosecution, or a frivolous civil lawsuit. This is expensive, and the process is abusive.

Even simple legal matters have become so complex that they require the involvement of an attorney and payment of lavish legal fees. Since everyone is aware that victory often goes to the person who can afford to hire the best team of attorneys, assistance is always expensive. Justice may prevail, but the victim often pays a high financial and emotional price.

If the honest citizen didn't have the foresight to purchase a membership in a legal defense program such as U.S. Law Shield,[103] or at least an insurance or reimbursement plan such as offered by the U.S. Concealed Carry Association or the National Rifle Association,[104] they are in a difficult position. It is easy to get lost in the morass of our legal system. As a result, good people are often victimized a second or even third time, by our abusive and excessively expensive legal system which has abandoned justice.

In our law schools today, young lawyers are specifically taught that their objective should not be justice. They are told that it is the prosecutor's job to seek a conviction, or to free-up the court schedule through the use of plea bargaining. Similarly, that it is the duty of a defense attorney to do their best to get their client acquitted. It's not about conducting a fair trial. It is no longer about justice and the purpose of law as it was written.

Thankfully, there are attorneys and judges who give serious attention to justice, and to what the lawmakers were endeavoring to accomplish when they established a law. Unfortunately, there seems to be a dwindling number of these valiant men and women, and the opposing forces are becoming increasingly formidable and influential.

When I was a police detective, I found myself a block away from the location of a potential crime in progress. Reported by a neighboring business, the dispatcher described an "unknown type disturbance" at an optometrist's office located in a strip mall. Since I was close, I responded. As I entered the office, I found a 12-year old boy straddling the lifeless body of the receptionist who was prostrate on the floor. In one hand he was holding a knife dripping with blood, and with the other hand he was rifling through her purse.

As soon as he saw me enter and draw my gun, he immediately dropped the knife. After apprehending the kid and giving medical aid to the nearly-dead victim, I transported the young man to the police department. In route, he boasted to me that nothing would happen to him because he was a juvenile. Several months later, he was proven right. The case never even went to trial.

It's no wonder our legal system is broken: We no longer protect victims and law-abiding people. Since our courts don't focus on justice, nor do they apply the law based on its intent, it's no surprise that our legal system fails to achieve equity, fair treatment, and just and moral rulings.

Importantly, when the law is misused to provide excessive protection to criminals, or misused to intimidate good and honest people, then lawlessness and tyranny has arrived. Without morality and the quest for justice, we cannot expect our society to achieve conformity to reasonable standards of behavior. We can no longer preserve civil society.

Our Founding Fathers were well aware of this inclination, warning that if the federal government became too large, tyranny was inevitable. The below motto was almost adopted for the Great Seal of the United States, and was so enthusiastically endorsed by Thomas Jefferson that he used it on his personal seal:

"Rebellion to tyrants is obedience to God." [105]

In my view, law-abiding sensible people who carry a gun are heroes; cut from the same cloth as our Founding Fathers. Just as the British government tried to disarm the people of the American colonies, many of our rulers are once again attempting to disarm the American people. The motivation for their anti-gun maneuvers is also exactly the same.

As a result of these anti-gun forces and their abuses, it has become a heroic act to acquire a concealed handgun license and carry a gun. As it was for our Founders, today it is heroic because it demonstrates a willingness to courageously stand against evil, as well as be subjected to the malicious attacks of the manipulated legal system and media. Anyone who is prepared to use a firearm today understands that they might suffer serious harm both in the incident, and again by the actions of the government. Having the guts to do the right thing can come with a high price, just as it did for our courageous and selfless Founders.

As the degradation of the justice system is applied to constitutional matters, it's easy to see how our Rights evaporate. As a result we are in a jurisprudential (philosophy of law) crisis; and we as citizens are subjected to the cruel effects.

Today, in the view of some Strict Constitutionalists, when one of these 'Progressive' courts sidesteps the intent of the highest law of the land, the U.S. Constitution, the decision of that court becomes invalid (or illegal). But this is not how the system actually works today.

Many argue that this is what *'We The People'*[106] must resolutely change. We need to demand reform.

Some advocates of the historic view of constitutional law, maintain that a court has lost its legal authority if the judge's decision does not align with what the Founding Fathers sought to accomplish.[107] They assert that fundamental change is needed to fix this systemic problem. If we can't fix it from inside the system, we nevertheless have a duty to restore justice.

Let me put this viewpoint in a familiar context:

During the era of Martin Luther King, Jr., there were a number of court cases in which a police officer arrested an African-American citizen based on a local law which dictated segregation. Eventually the Supreme Court ruled that laws which forced segregation are illegal, and overturned those convictions.

This same principle applies to actions taken by any State court or federal court. It's not unusual for a decision of a lower court to be reversed by a higher court, or the Supreme Court.

By a logical continuation of the same principle, some Strict Constitutionalists assert that an unconstitutional decision made by the Supreme Court can be overruled by Congress exercising the balance of power as provided in the Constitution. And, it can be overruled *by the people themselves,* too.

According to these reformers, "We The People" [108] have the right to declare a decision made by any court, including the Supreme Court, to be unconstitutional if it clearly violates the original meaning and intention of the Founders who penned the Constitution. They assert that the Founders bestowed the ultimate power of governance to the People, not to the President, Congress, and the Courts. As Patrick Henry[109] said, *"The Constitution is not an instrument for the government to restrain the people; it is an instrument for the people to restrain the government."* [110]

Police officers and judges (and congressmen and presidents), must all adhere to the U.S. Constitution first, federal law next, and then state and local laws. No lower body of governance can violate a higher law. According to this argument, since the U.S. Constitution is the highest law of the land, even the Supreme Court, President, and Congress can be considered "rogue" if any of these branches of government takes an action which violates, ignores, or attempts to reinterpret the Constitution in opposition to the Founders original meaning.[111]

Of course, in some matters there is a lack of clarity in the law or Constitution, so it is the responsibility of the court to make a determination. However, if the original meaning of the Constitution, and the intent of the Founders is abundantly clear and the court ignores it, proponents of this viewpoint assert that the court can be considered *rogue* and citizens have no obligation to obey that decision.

At this point, this argument has entered dangerous territory. The full power of the United States government may be used to back the action of the Supreme Court, President, Congress, or a government agency. So if anyone ever believes that this high standard has been met, and the action of the Supreme Court, President, Congress, or government agency has become rogue, they need to consider the cost before disobeying.[112]

On the practical side, our current government holds to a very different position than that of these Strict Constitutionalists. Our current government maintains that the courts rule the land supremely, and that the courts can overrule the People and Congress. Though not the stance of the nation's Founders, this is the viewpoint of our current government establishment, and this is what they enforce by wielding the crushing power of government.

Therefore, any person who bases their actions on a Strict Constitutionalist argument may be right, but they may still find themselves in jail, or worse. Those who contemplate this must be prepared for the consequences.

Our current situation is very complex. There is no easy solution.

Even though possession of firearms is legal in the United States today, the courts, legislature, or the president by Executive Order, or even a government agency like the Department of Justice or Environmental Protection Agency, may declare them to be illegal tomorrow. Regrettably, this is no longer the stuff of conspiracy theorists. *Rights* which have been recognized by the courts and legislature for more than 200-years are being circumvented today, and the courts have been duplicitous by upholding these incremental violations of our Rights.

Today it is a simple matter for congress to pass new unconstitutional anti-gun laws, or enter into an international treaty which makes what is legal today, illegal tomorrow. As one Progressive strategist said,

"We must exploit every tragedy to implement our agenda." Therefore, the next tragic mass shooting event may be used to manipulate public opinion at a time when emotions are running high. Overnight, this emotional outcry can be used to sweep into place a bevy of unconstitutional laws and policies.

Regrettably, the public is dangerously uneducated on constitutional matters. No longer seen as inviolable, many see the Constitution as archaic or malleable, or simply a hurdle to overcome. The protections of the Constitution, and the clear original meaning of the words are ignored by many, and this has already caused disastrous results. Whether as a result of an organized strategy or unintended fiat, the protections of the Constitution are being openly challenged. The greater danger may take the form of subtle erosion through government regulations, but reversal of Supreme Court decisions which protect our Rights are now only one or two votes away from being lost.

Consider this scenario: What if the U.S. Supreme Court came to the conclusion that the 2nd Amendment does not protect an individual citizen's right to own a gun? Who is going to stand up and say that the Supreme Court is wrong? Isolated individuals? What will they do? Even if their viewpoint is widely held, how will they be able to enforce their position?

Ideally, dissenters would invoke the Constitutional amendment process,[113] and use it to *"clarify"* that the 2nd Amendment does in fact recognize such a right. But that is a difficult process, and it would take billions of dollars and many years to accomplish. Sadly, it is becoming increasingly obvious to many that even a temporary loss of this Right might usher in a time of expanded government controls, long before the Amendment process could be completed.

With good reason, the citizens of the United States no longer trust their government. Sadly, there are many well-established reasons for this distrust. In a poll [114] conducted by the Gallup organization, 4 out of 5 Americans said that they do not trust their government. Incredible. When 80% of U.S. citizens don't trust their government, just a *perceived* shift toward tyranny can erupt into social unrest. At that point, even a relatively minor incident has the potential to tip the scale, spilling us into a time of widespread social upheaval. If even minor incidents of rebellion develop, unintended and very negative consequences can easily and quickly expand into chaos.

Further, even if a constitutional amendment was enacted, since the Court would have already defied the Constitution on this point, what guarantee is there that it will not do so again in the future? Trust is already a problem.

Since many citizens already distrust their government and the courts, what will happen if this trust in government and the courts erodes further? If this downward spiral continues, at some point we will encounter a tipping point where this distrust will cause a backlash or public revolt.

In practical terms, if *"We The People"* declare that the Supreme Court is inexcusably wrong in a legal decision it makes, it will likely launch a domino effect with catastrophic results. For many, this is a hypothetical situation which is farfetched, while others think it is likely. There are many knowledgeable and sane experts who think that we are on the edge of just this sort of tyranny.

What do you think?

In an important matter such as the 2nd Amendment, isolated instances of dissent would certainly bring about the arrest and imprisonment of those who make that "declaration," but massive civil disobedience and armed conflict can easily be the outcome if it becomes widespread. If the governmental authorities are perceived as overreacting to the situation, this will fuel the flames of opposition and garner the support of the undecided. Either way, the situation can easily escalate.

You may think that this scenario is totally preposterous. Maybe it is. But the federal government doesn't think it's farfetched. They are actively planning for it.

There are volumes of evidence documenting that federal and state agencies are preparing for this eventuality. My point is that this isn't some far-fetched conspiracy theory. The U.S. government thinks that this is sufficiently likely that they are spending billions of dollars to prepare for it. If you doubt this, read President Obama's *Executive Order* of March 16, 2012 which is available on the White House website, www.WhiteHouse.gov. Or, the 'Resources' page at www.TXRFA.com. It is a staggering-in-scope major expansion of a similar overreaching emergency-powers Order which was authorized by President Bush. (For more about this, read the editorial in the appendix of this book, "Signs of the Times.")

Morally, biblically, and legislatively, we are obliged to obey the law. Yet, presidential Executive Orders are not authorized by the Constitution, and these, along with government regulations not authorized by law (even though they have become de facto laws), are not authorized by the Constitution. So how do these relate to the biblical injunction regarding obedience to the law?

Many experts assert that we have no obligation to obey any law which does not come from a constitutionally authorized source—especially those which were intentionally created outside of the bounds of authorized lawmaking. Yet, these 'laws' are nevertheless in use today, and they are enforced using the force of government.

Notwithstanding, the supreme law of the land is still the U.S. Constitution. The government and our courts are only mechanisms for administering laws which are passed by congress. Therefore, these experts point out that our biblical requirement of obedience is to the Constitution, first, and then to those laws passed by the legislature. Further, we do not have an obligation to obey laws made by Presidential Executive Order, or other branches of government outside the legislative process.

Our first obligation is to obey God's law, then the laws of the land as long as they don't conflict with God's law. Similarly, when the action of a court or the requirements of a lesser law, conflicts with the Constitution, our moral and biblical responsibility is to follow the Constitution. It is the higher law. The Constitution trumps all other manmade laws and government regulations.

A news story comes to mind in which a child fell from a bridge into a lake. A teenage boy who was with friends on the shore saw it happen, and jumped into the reservoir and swam to the drowning child and rescued him. Later, the heroic teen was issued a citation because of a law which forbids swimming in the lake because it's the city's water supply. Should he have obeyed the law and left the child to drown? Of course not; thankfully he possessed the judgment and character to respond appropriately. For us today, this incident serves as a simple reminder that sometimes it is necessary to disobey the government, so that we can obey a higher law which protects life and liberty.

Yet, our responsibility *according to our government* is to obey the government and its courts. So there can be a conflict. Notwithstanding, for anyone who holds God's law and the Bible's instructions above manmade laws, this dictates obedience to God first, then the Constitution as the highest law of the land, before all of the government's courts (the mechanism for administering the law) and its other laws and regulations.

To be clear, simply not liking a law is *not* justification for disobedience. Moreover, any attempt to manipulate the Constitution, or to engage in wordplay to concoct a different meaning for its text, is not acceptable. The only reliable standard for interpreting the Constitution is the original intent and meaning of the Founders words, not a personal contrivance. Further, God-given Rights are those which are articulated in the Bible as a whole, not by using individual verses which are cherry-picked and misapplied to justify a personal viewpoint.

According to moral law and Bible standards, we still must obey a law we don't like, including one which we think isn't fair (as long as it doesn't violate a higher law such as God's law or the Constitution). We can work to change any manmade law, including the Constitution, but we need to obey even offensive laws until they are repealed. This obedience is the price we pay for a peaceful, orderly society. However, there is more to it.

In an organized society like the United States which is founded upon the consent of the people, and upon a Constitution adopted and ratified by the people and regarded as the foundation for that civil society, the situation is very different from other types of government. By law, *We The People* are also the source of the government's power.

American citizens have the power of the ballot box, and recall elections if necessary to remove legislators and presidents from their position of power.

But what if a group, government entity or official helps perpetrate, or facilitate, election fraud? What if they use fraud to tip an election, or they 'stuff' the ballot box to get their way? What then?

Historically, Americans consider government employees to be respected civil *servants*. But the practical reality is that many government workers are now attracted to power, and even addicted to it. They believe that the People have the duty to serve the government and the government employee's own concept of the Common Good, not the other way around.

So what happens when government workers, or a government entity, ignores or seditiously distorts the Constitution? It will eventually be seen for what it has become, a rogue entity that contravenes the basic laws that rest on the consent of the people.

What happens when the government itself becomes increasingly lawless? What happens when presidents flaunt the law and ignore due process, and repeatedly violate the Constitution? What happens when the courts, and the even the U.S. Attorney General, flagrantly subvert laws or refuse to enforce laws they personally don't like?

These abuses will continue to be tolerated for a while. Firing an occasional bureaucrat who is embroiled in a scandal may forestall the inevitable, but it won't stop it. Absent major reform, eventually we will come to a breaking point.

When the government abandons the Constitution and the rule of law, it has lost what the political scientists call *legitimacy*. People are not morally required to obey an illegitimate government; i.e., one founded on force rather than consent of the people.

As soon as citizens justifiably stop feeling an obligation to obey the government, bad things start to happen. At least in the short term.

When an individual *disobeys stealthily* (in private actions), this cultivates dishonesty, and a social attitude that it is okay to be a lawbreaker. As it becomes acceptable to disobey one law, then it becomes easy to disobey others.

When an individual *disobeys openly*, this will result in criminal prosecution. In the process, good, ordinarily honest people are subjected to great injustice and abuse. These government excesses will eventually cultivate public anger, an increase in stealthy disobedience, and more acts of open rebellion.

When an individual *disobeys openly en masse with others*, the result is civil disorder. Riots, acts of violence in various forms, and armed conflict are the result. If the government acts to crush this disorder, civil war can easily erupt. Conversely, if the government fails to adequately act, legitimate civil disobedience will be comingled with those who simply enjoy lawlessness and this can become an incubator for anarchy. Either way, economic disaster will probably become part of this melee.

None of these options are good. Yet, at some point these actions might be justified, and necessary, to stop the development of widespread tyranny which is an even bigger problem.

Sadly, the strength of law abiding people can also be the source of their greatest weakness. It is the obligation of members of a civil society to obey all the laws, including those they don't like. But unchecked obedience emboldens tyrants and would-be tyrants, and it paves the way for the downfall of a society. So, dissent needs to emerge in time to stop domination.

At what point do good people refuse to obey? When does a government become illegitimate?

Political action is the first path of action, but what happens when that fails? What happens when the political process has been subverted by special interest groups and voter fraud? What happens when the political process has been preempted by those in power? At that point, other actions become necessary to avoid disaster.

Unfortunately, law abiding people display weakness when they allow their non-confrontational attitude to be exploited. Additionally, since they are generally busy with their own affairs and are not meddlesome, they often procrastinate in regard to public affairs. As a result they fail to initiate timely corrective actions. Though this is understandable, it is in direct opposition to Jesus command for us to love our neighbors as ourselves (Mark 12:28-31). To love our neighbor involves a commitment to be engaged in the betterment of our community, our nation, and our world. We need to be people of appropriate action.

When it comes to charity, too often we think only of helping the poor, or donating to some worthy cause when we think about Jesus' command to love our neighbors (Matthew 22:36-39). Yet, though these acts of charity might be wonderful, they aren't enough. There is more to "loving our neighbor" than just kindly gestures.

When we delay the full application Jesus command to love our neighbor, social and cultural problems grow, and corrective action becomes far more difficult. When good people fail to take decisive action in time to avoid harmful developments, the results can be beyond serious.

***"The only thing necessary for evil to triumph,
is for good people to do nothing."***

-- *Anonymous,*
but often incorrectly attributed to
Edmund Burke

As this popular truism reminds us, throughout history, busy productive people often wait for the pendulum of government excesses to naturally swing back to a center point. Unfortunately, many of these discovered too late that the pendulum didn't return to the middle, it crashed and toppled the pillars which support civil society.

We are now facing this type of danger. The cost of our inactivity will be enormous if we don't act now, and make this a top priority.

A few years ago, when actor Charlton Heston declared at the annual NRA convention, *"[The anti-gun crowd] is going to smear you as the enemy. He will slander you as gun-toting, knuckle-dragging, bloodthirsty maniacs who stand in the way of a safer America. Will you remain silent? I will not remain silent. If we are going to stop this, then it is vital to every law-abiding gun owner in America to register to vote and show up at the polls on Election Day. [Pause] So, as we set out this year to defeat the divisive forces that would take freedom away, I want to say those fighting words for everyone within the sound of my voice to hear and to heed, and especially for you, Mr. Gore: 'From my cold, dead hands.'* (Referring to a slogan popularized by the NRA, *"I'll give you my gun when you pry it from my cold, dead hands."*[115])

Heston was right about the need for us to be involved in the political process. However, a growing number of experts now claim that the control of the three branches of government has been largely wrestled away from the people.

Are there still honest politicians and honorable public servants? Of course.

Many if not most U.S. politicians do want what is best for their country. Still, that goal can involve very different perspectives on what is 'best' and what needs to change. Herein is the crux of the problem.

Many things do need to change, and many changes are reasonable – as long as they don't conflict with the Bible. When we abandon our Bible base, we lose much more than a book and our national history.

When the structure of our nation moves away from the rock-solid foundation of the Bible, and exchanges it for one that is built on shifting sand, our national stability disappears. An economic quake, or some flood of adversity, can cause it to collapse. Our biblical foundation isn't just 'nice,' it is foundational to our form of government, equality, and justice.

We've all heard of the 'Salem Witch Trials' which took place in 1692-1693. These trials are often touted as an example of why religion needs to be kept out of public life. However, what the modern history textbooks fail to communicate is that it was three pastors who went to the governor of Massachusetts, and they used their Bibles to show him that these trials were wrong. They pointed out to the governor that rather than follow the biblically mandated rules of evidence and due process, the judge in these trials was using the methodology of the European legal system.

Armed with this information, the governor immediately confronted the judge who was in charge of the witch trials. Using these same Bible passages, he convinced the judge that the trials were a travesty of justice. He didn't base this on his own viewpoint, but on the Bible. As a result, the judge immediately stopped the Witch Trials.

The following Sunday the judge stood up in front of the congregation of the church he attended, and repented for his sin. The governor called for a day of prayer and fasting, asking that the people of Massachusetts pray, and ask God for His forgiveness. Statewide they acknowledged that they had been doing things man's way rather than God's way. As a result, the people repented for the unjust killing of 27 people during the infamous witch trials, and a new standard of justice was implemented.

During this same period in Europe, witch trials were also underway. Unfortunately, in Europe they continued to use their secular (unbiblical) legal methods. The Europeans put to death more than 500,000 people in their witch trials, but we never seem to hear about that detail. The application of the biblical approach brought justice, whereas the secular approach used by the Europeans brought injustice.

So even if you aren't a particularly religious person, this abandonment of biblical standards should still concern you. If you doubt the magnitude and powerful influence of the Bible on early American life, including the principle of self defense and the right to bear arms, this is easily established. Even a cursory study of some of the thousands of documents written during the period of the nation's founding, as well as the writings of the Founders themselves, makes this clear.[116]

The United States was intentionally built on biblical principles. This was because the early settlers and the nation's Founding Fathers came from countries where other standards had been tried, and these had failed miserably. The Bible formed the bedrock on which the U.S. government and society, and the judicial system, was based. This is what made it possible for the United States to grow into a prosperous and highly respected nation.

Precepts such as integrity, justice for all, individual freedom, personal responsibility, equitable taxation and free enterprise, are all concepts which are found in the Bible. The Bible 'Way' even provides protections for the people who identify with other religious and belief systems. It also guarantees equal rights for the rich and poor, and opportunity with freedom for all. It's these biblical principles, built into our public life, which made the United States unique. This is what led to greatness.

When French historian Alex de Tocqueville toured the United States in 1831-1832, he coined the term "American exceptionalism" to describe the unique character of the country and its people. He had a lot to say about religious life, and also about the Bible applied to public life.

In de Tocqueville's book "Democracy in America," he talked about the Bible's influence on American society, especially in matters such as the effect of faith on community, parenting, marriage, public morality and justice. Yet, the "Abridged for the Modern Reader" version of his book which is used in our public schools today, eliminates the parts of the book which address these topics, and deletes de Tocqueville's observations on the positive influence of the Bible on society. De Tocqueville was not a particularly religious person, but he did recognize that the Bible brought something unique to life in America.

Revisionist history has become a big problem for those who want to understand the truth about the law, the U.S. Constitution and the 2nd Amendment. Most modern history books are full of inaccurate information, so we need to explore the original writings of the nation's Founders, and read the history books which were written before the modern wave of disinformation.

If we are to understand and stop those developments which are subverting the Constitution, we first need to gain an accurate understanding of the history of the United States ourselves. Furthermore, we need to identify the false information so that we can isolate the problems this has created—so that we can design solutions. We need to also separate the revisions which are the outcomes of poor scholarship, from those which were intentionally fabricated to influence the nation's laws and politics, and to manipulate the American people.

The core concept that we must remember throughout this process is that the basis for justice and fairness, respect for truth and virtue, care for the poor and disadvantaged, and the freedoms articulated in the Constitution and Bill of Rights, all find their basis in the Bible. Therefore, even non-religious people, and people who are adherents to other respectful religions, should find it unsettling that there are people who want destroy this historic orientation.

Unfortunately, an increasing number of influential leaders are looking to fundamentally transform the United States. As you probably already know, there are now a large number of politicians, judges, attorneys, government workers, lobbyists, educators, media people, entertainers, corporate leaders and others, who are committed to the task of securing the complete abandonment of the biblical principles on which this nation was founded.[117]

This isn't just a tacit rejection of the tenets of the Christian or Jewish faiths. It is a well funded, deliberate, and multifaceted campaign. The goal is to fundamentally change America by abandoning its founding principles, facilitated by hacking away at its historic spiritual roots. It's not an agnostic approach which is seeking concessions; it's a Crusader-like movement which demands surrender to their viewpoint. These people operate with religious elitism like the Taliban.

Fortunately, as a whole the American people still believe in the core principles on which the nation was founded. Notwithstanding, the group of usurping dissidents and deluded people is growing rapidly.

What is it that makes these people hate the Bible, and the Jewish and Christian people who are the people of the Book? Why is it that this anti-Bible crowd is consumed with rabid hate for anything which reminds them of the spiritual heritage of the United States? These are important questions.

There are a number of reasons, but chief among them is the Bible provides an external basis for moral behavior and operating principles for life and governance. This objective standard is beyond their ability to control, so they don't like it.

On a personal level, it can simply be anti-authority belligerence. They don't want to acknowledge that there is a 'Creator' who has jurisdiction over them. Like truculent children of Eve, they want to be like God or become their own god. They are full of pride and self-absorbed. For others, it is a fundamental shift in how they interact with the world and humanity.

How should we respond to this?

Ordinarily I'd say, "Fine, let them dig their own grave. Let them go their own way." Sadly, they aren't willing to tolerate other viewpoints or beliefs. Bigots to the core, these pretentious people are blind to truth and don't want to be bothered with facts. Lacking reason and rationale for their viewpoints, they resort to name calling, deception, manipulation, threats and now even violence to get their way. Like spoiled children, they demand that everyone must dance to their tune.[118]

I'm pointing this out because we need to understand that the root of the opposition to the Constitution and the 2nd Amendment is not simply a different viewpoint. It's something much bigger, and far more insidious.

To further advance these anti-God anti-Bible beliefs, these same 'secular progressive' special interest groups are actively working to replace historic justice and fairness with laws and regulations based in their humanistic and other secular philosophies. Some of these "Progressives" have an ideology of elitism which is re-packaged fascism; others are into socialism and the redistribution of wealth, while others seem to be motivated by avarice, greed, and jealousy. They want to discard the Bible, and replace it with a philosophy of secular humanism which, at the core, is simply a refined way of saying 'survival of the fittest.'

These people have made a religion out of atheism. To understand their approach, and their atheistic evangelism quest, we need to keep in mind the four orientations they have toward life. Together they form the political viewpoint which they themselves often describe as "Progressive."

First, 'Post-structuralism' which insists that there are no transcendent values; that everyone can decide for themselves what is right or wrong, and that the 'greater-good' is more important than the rights of individuals. Their orientation is to focus on groups, and to assign individuals their worth based on factors such as race, sex, or genetic value. For them, the concept of family should be replaced by community. They see patriotism as selfish, and see themselves as more progressive because they identify as citizens of the world. Therefore, the U.S. Constitution is irrelevant except as a tool to manipulate the masses.

The second tenet of this anti-Bible religious faith is 'Modernism,' which sees our modern world and intellect as superior to the people who lived in the past. The Modernists see themselves as smarter and more discerning; more enlightened than our Founders and other historical figures. Just as scientific knowledge and progress builds on prior discoveries, they think of themselves as having evolved to a higher level of humanity.

Therefore, Modernism finds the study of history to be irrelevant. Nevertheless, if history is to be understood it must be studied in the framework of our own modern environment. For example, many of the Founding Fathers were members of the Unitarian Church, which today does not recognize the Bible as the Word of God. Using their logic, they conclude that the Founders did not believe in the Bible. They ignore the fact that the Unitarian Church has changed significantly in the last two hundred years, and that in the era of the Founders it was more like today's Baptist Church or independent Bible Church. Similarly, they label George Washington as a Deist, and insist that he wasn't a Christian because he used terms such as 'Providence' and 'Divine Creator' rather than 'Jesus Christ.' The 'Modernist' ignores that this was the vocabulary used in the Geneva Bible, which was the English translation of the Bible used in that era.

Third, 'Academic Collectivism' looks to contemporary 'experts' for truth, rather than to the original sources. This bubble-like orientation propagates errors and becomes group-think.

In the justice system, this results in an orientation toward 'case law' which favors the legal precedent set by another court. They contend that the opinion of another judge is more relevant than the wording of the law, and more important than the intent of the legislature which formulated and passed the law.

When this same *academic collectivism* is applied to science, it stifles breakthroughs and demands adherence to current thinking rather than building on new discoveries. Integrity and innovation in science languishes. Those scientists who fail to stay in lock-step with their brethren are blackballed.

In history, this same 'Academic Collectivism' promotes ignorance and error. Those who are willingly infected with this group-think ailment perpetuate all sorts of factual errors. These lead to false conclusions, corrupted education, and a misinformed electorate. It also leads to a dismissive attitude toward the U.S. Constitution.

A good example of Academic Collectivism is the life of Thomas Jefferson, principal author of the Declaration of Independence and third president of the United States, and signer of the U.S. Constitution. He is often used as the 'poster child' of the Progressives, to help them document that the Bible and faith in God had no significant role in American independence and the formation of the nation. They suggest that he had vague deistic beliefs, but nothing more. They claim that he is typical of the Founding Fathers who sought to develop a secular government, and that they didn't actually believe in the Bible.

As a result of these efforts, today's public school students and 95% of law school students[119] are taught that Jefferson didn't believe in a supernatural God. Furthermore, he didn't believe in the miracles of Jesus, nor did he believe that Jesus was divine. They learn little about Jefferson's life, but they do learn about the 'Jefferson Bible' and that he didn't have a traditional belief in God.

Students are taught that Jefferson literally cut-up the Bible to remove everything supernatural and divine from the text, to form his own version of the Bible, know today as the 'Jefferson Bible'. This has now been repeated so often, and is contained in so many textbooks, that it has become an undisputed 'fact.' However, it's simply not true.

This is the kind of false information that is perpetuated by Academic Collectivism. In the process, it deceives people, misleads our leaders and courts, and it manipulates legislators, judges, and voters.

The truth is that Thomas Jefferson not only identified as a Christian, he wholeheartedly believed in the Bible—including the miracles and all of the other supernatural elements. 'True,' he did cut-up the Bible for a project, but this wasn't to create the so-called 'Jefferson Bible.' He didn't do this so that he could remove the parts which talk about the divinity of Jesus. Nor was it to remove the miracles and supernatural aspects, as has been assumed by the majority of our present day historians who lack integrity in their scholarship.

Today, most of our academics get their facts, and the answers of "why?" from other historians. Even when it's something important, like this incident with Jefferson, they don't bother to research the details—especially if the group-think conclusion furthers their secular agenda.

They make an assumption which fits the narrative they want to promote. Then they share their ignorance with each other, they write textbooks and teach their classes, and our history suffers distortion. The truth is ignored and buried; their secular agenda is advanced.

What's the truth about Jefferson? His pastor sought out Jefferson's help to develop a summary Bible for use by their local Indians. For these Native Americans, English was a 2nd language and reading the Bible was difficult. Missionaries to the Indians had found that the Bible was seen as a big book that contained a lot of difficult words, so they avoided reading it. In 1804, Thomas Jefferson accepted the challenge to help the Native American people become Bible literate.

Similar to our present-day Bible story books for children and the untrained, Jefferson cut up the Bible so that he could assemble a summary of the Gospels. This synopsis included the key events and teachings of Jesus life, as well as the miracles Jesus performed. This small book also included the incidents when Jesus raised people from the dead, when He cast out demons, His teaching about our need for reconciliation with God, and the reality of heaven and hell. From beginning to end, it bears no resemblance to the "Jefferson Bible" which scholars talk about today.

Additional proof about Thomas Jefferson's faith and his traditional view of the Bible is also ignored. For example, Jefferson was a life-long member of the Virginia Bible Society. While involved in leadership in that organization, he learned that some families in Virginia couldn't afford to purchase a Bible. He responded to this discovery by making a substantial donation to the Society to pay for the printing and distribution of the Bible to these families. This distribution project was of the whole Bible, including both the Old and New Testament in their entirety. Furthermore, in Jefferson's own family, as each of his children and grandchildren learned to read, he gave them a copy of the whole Bible. These aren't the activities of someone who doesn't believe the Bible.

The fourth tenet of Progressivism is "Deconstruction,"[120] which includes the art of re-telling history in a manner which advances a cause. It makes it possible to defame the heroes of the past, belittling their lives and selfless contributions to the nation. Deconstruction is also used to tear-down past successes and national virtue by fabricating "the other side of a story" which sullied accomplishments and sacrifice. This technique is also used to change historic emphasis, transforming some irrelevant tidbit into an important facet of the story.

Like an employee who stabs his co-workers in the back in an effort to personally appear to be more competent, Progressives artfully use Deconstruction. Using this technique they disparage the nation's Founding Fathers and other heroes of history, all in an effort to make their own lives and ideas seem more acceptable.

When a different slant on the facts doesn't work, a Progressive will make up a story and present it as fact. For the Progressive, the ends justify the means.

For example, during President Clinton's impeachment hearings his sexual peccadilloes made him seem 'slick,' and his unfaithfulness to his wife made him look untrustworthy. To help Clinton regain the support of the general public, historian Joseph Ellis jumped in to help.

Articles carried in the magazines "Nature" and "Science," reported that Ellis had new DNA evidence which confirmed that Thomas Jefferson fathered the children of his slave, Sally Hemings. This newly discovered 'fact' was carried by 221 news outlets in the United States, and it did help bolster support for Clinton during the impeachment proceedings. Six weeks later, these magazines were forced to print retractions when the DNA evidence was exposed as a fraud. Only 11 media outlets carried that story.

Despite being exposed as a fraud on several other occasions, Ellis surfaced again with disparaging claims against George Washington, and these were also widely published and heralded. Later, these assertions were also exposed as fraudulent, yet Ellis is still quoted today, and students are still taught these falsehoods in public school classrooms.

One of the problems of big government is that its size and momentum makes directional changes and correction difficult, and Progressives exploit this weakness to help them advance their cause. They use government like a monster truck to carry their agenda, to put power behind their avenues of action, and to run over their opponents.

Now that Progressives hold many positions of power, they are using government to steer the country toward more intrusive and controlling policies, and centralized control that can be maneuvered by an élite few rather than the people. This makes it possible for them become increasingly effective at crushing opposition and influencing the weak. As a result, our society is now undergirded with falsehood and misconceptions, and it is running on momentum rather than being fueled by substance. This can't last.

Our busyness no longer hides the truth. Society is sick. The Progressives have garnered most of the power, but they don't have a cure. Their solutions don't work in a democratic form of government, so that want to guide us to something different. As with the issue of gun control, they treat crime and social illnesses with new laws and more regulations. These they pile on top of those that have already failed. They tell the public, *"Just a little bit more,"* like the drug addict who is sure he can get well with one more shot of heroin.

Regrettably, the infection that their drugs and dirty needles have introduced is now systemic, and the cure will be difficult to administer. If the American people wake up and demand sweeping reform, and the downsizing of government and its pervasive influence, there is hope—but this is a fleeting hope. Many experts contend that we are actually beyond the point of no return. Yet, nothing is hopeless if the God of the Bible is brought back into the picture and we return to a nation of laws and justice.

In any case, this isn't a Democrat or Republican problem. It's a Democrat AND Republican problem that only the people themselves can fix with God's help. Politicians can't fix this. It can only be accomplished through the people themselves.

At this juncture, both Republican and Democrat presidents routinely issue "Executive Orders" and allow, or use government agencies (IRS, EPA, Dept of Education, etc.) to implement and enforce unconstitutional policies, encouraging them to engage in improper and prohibited activities. Both parties are treating symptoms because they are unwilling to embrace the cure which is a return to the Constitution and the rule of Law, and the biblical beliefs which made the U.S. strong and vibrant.

Unfortunately, the abuse of power has now become flagrant and habitual. This makes our illness far more difficult to cure.

Congress not only passes laws which are blatantly unconstitutional, they pass others which are so immense that the consequences are totally unpredictable. Compliance is often untenable, and obedience so difficult and costly that it cripples the very people the law is supposed to help. Ineffective laws are rarely repealed, and new laws are added by the thousands each year. The burden to society is incalculable.

Special interest groups are served while the citizenry is abused. The government has become like molasses to the gears of society, impeding the mechanisms of social health and liberty.

Many have concluded that all three branches of the federal government have become drunk with power and out of touch with the needs of the people. As accurate as this might be, merely complaining does not bring us a solution.

The problem is much larger than the 2nd Amendment, but the 2nd Amendment is probably the last wall of defense because it is a protection designed for individuals, neighborhoods and communities. Nonetheless, most Americans lack the guts to do anything productive in regard to curtailing the government's excesses, whether it is deficit spending, stopping the growth and intrusion of government, or social programs which produce slavish and submissive people.

As a culture we have become weak, so it's time to start exercising with our Constitutional rights and God-given Rights. It's time for *We The People* to flex our grassroots muscle, especially in our own towns, communities and States, and take a no-nonsense stand. Will you?

At this point we need sheepdogs, not just vocal sheep. As we work to educate, guide and empower the people of the United States who have become like sheep, and have been led astray, we need to also get serious about guarding our way of life and our biblical heritage. Remembering that a sheepdog is not aggressive except when the flock is at risk, we nevertheless need to become more assertive. Like a sheepdog we should not bare our teeth except to deal with the wolves at the door, but neither can we forget that God gave us those fangs for a purpose. (To learn more about the Christian sheepdog movement, visit: www.SheepdogGuardian.com).

If you believe that the Bill of Rights, particularly the 2nd Amendment, is the keystone for protecting our constitutional and God-given Rights, then it's time to get even more serious about living like a sheepdog. Yet, there's no benefit in a sheepdog growling if it's not also prepared to bite.

If you boldly proclaim that you won't give up your guns, you had better include this scenario in your contemplations. (For details on developing practical scenarios, refer back to the earlier chapter, "*Deadly Force: Literally a Grave Subject.*") We must always seek amiable solutions, but we must always be prepared for dissonant forms of action, too.

In regard to the wording of the 2nd Amendment, it is true that there is little which fits into the category of "vague." When we read the words of the Amendment, and review the other writings and speeches made by our Founders during that period of history, the original meaning and purpose is clear. When they wrote these words it wasn't to simply protect our ability to engage in hunting or shooting sports. It was to protect and facilitate our Right of self-defense, and to protect us from tyranny.[121]

It's important to understand that the 2nd Amendment was amply discussed when it was proposed in 1789,[122] so the original meaning and intent is clear. Nevertheless, even though the Constitution vindicates this pro-gun position, corrective action can still be difficult. As historians remind us, civil disobedience should not be the automatic response to injustice. Not only is it disruptive and costly, it can also be ineffective if it is not strategically implemented.

Today, many people claim that they are willing to lay down their life in defense of the 2nd Amendment. They consider it to be integral to their God-given Right of self-defense and liberty. They also remind us that the U.S. Constitution is the highest law of the land, and that it trumps any other law or regulation. This does validate their stance; yet, the day may come when there will be a high price paid for trying to maintain this Right.

What do you think? Would you be willing to make the ultimate sacrifice?

If you were alive in the days surrounding the signing of the Declaration of Independence, would you have stood with the Founders? Or, would you have supported the status quo, and with it the increasingly-oppressive government? At what point would you have decided that you had to revolt?

What does it take for a government to lose its legitimacy to rule?

When does a peaceful person abandon peace?

If you had lived in Concord, Massachusetts in April 1775, would you have surrendered your arms and ammunition as the government demanded?[123] Would you have been willing to fight to retain your Right to keep and bear arms?[124] How valuable is liberty to you?

Living in San Antonio, I often pass the Alamo. Texans consider it hallowed ground for a good reason. On March 6, 1836, after a grinding 12-day siege, 189 men from Texas and across the United States and six other countries, lay dead, having sacrificed their lives for the cause of liberty.

The defenders of the Alamo refused to scatter when they faced General Santa Ana of Mexico, and his overwhelming army of 3-6,000 soldiers. The poorly trained and inadequately equipped defenders, who were all civilians and civilian militia, took a brave stand against impossible odds. They knew what they were doing, and they understood the cost.

These defenders of liberty fought valiantly for nearly two weeks, killing 600 Mexican soldiers before the battle ended. The brave defenders died, but their heroic example galvanized the men and women of Texas. Weeks later, another group of Texans defeated the much larger and better equipped Mexican army. They re-won the freedom which Santa Ana had stolen from them when he suspended Mexico's Constitution.

What is noteworthy here is that the Alamo defenders could have escaped prior to the battle, but instead they chose to stay and fight a battle they knew they couldn't possibly win. They prayed, sent emissaries asking for help, and did what they could to secure assistance, but no one came. In each letter requesting aid, the Alamo commander, Colonel William Travis, signed his correspondence with his name above a bold statement, *"Victory or Death."* He lived up to that statement. He and all of the other Alamo defenders stood their ground. They died, but victory was eventually attained, largely because these men were willing to take a stand for Liberty.

Today more than ever, our votes need to be cast for the people, and in support of the laws, which protect the U.S. Constitution and advance a biblical worldview. Supporters of the Constitution and the Bible are not looking to form a theocracy; they are looking to restore our constitutional form of government and the rule of law.

It's not about imposing a personal viewpoint, it's about defending, affirming, and protecting life and liberty as defined in the timeless truths contained in the Bible and reflected in our founding documents. (You will find transcripts of the Declaration of Independence, the U.S. Constitution and its Bill of Rights in the appendix of this book.)

It's time for us to prepare ourselves for adversity, and the reality that a century of irresponsible leadership has eroded the foundation of the United States. Political activism may not be enough to fix the problems we are now facing. These words from the U.S. Declaration of Independence are becoming increasingly poignant as we consider our modern predicament…

> *"We hold these truths to be self-evident, that all men are created equal, that they are endowed by their Creator with certain unalienable Rights, that among these are Life, Liberty and the pursuit of Happiness. That to secure these rights, Governments are instituted among Men, deriving their just Powers from the consent of the governed, — That whenever any Form of Government becomes destructive of these ends, it is the Right of the People to alter or to abolish it, and to institute new Government, laying its foundation on such principles and organizing its powers in such form, as to them shall seem most likely to effect their Safety and Happiness. Prudence, indeed, will dictate that Governments long established should not be changed for light and transient causes; and accordingly all experience hath shewn, that mankind are more disposed to suffer, while evils are sufferable, than to right themselves by abolishing the forms to which they are accustomed. But when a long train of abuses and usurpations, pursuing invariably the same Object evinces a design to reduce them under absolute Despotism, it is their right, it is their duty, to throw off such Government, and to provide new guards for their future security…"*

What do you think? Will political action be enough to solve our problems?

Are you willing to accept your biblical responsibility to be a person of Constitution-supporting Rule-of-Law action? If we can awaken the American people and get them onboard with the tasks of demanding major change, we may be able to avert disaster. However, at this point it will take a miracle from God because such a large segment of U.S. voters has been bribed with government handouts. Our Founding Father's understood this inherent problem of democracy…

"When the people find that they can vote themselves money, that will herald the end of the republic."

- Benjamin Franklin [125]

Personally, I am actively praying for the United States, its leaders, and for spiritual and social revival. In regard to action, I've chosen to side with the Constitution as the supreme law of the land, and with the U.S. Founding Fathers' vision for a *land of the free and the home of the brave.*[126]

When the Founders signed the Declaration of Independence (see appendix), they knew that they might be signing their own death warrant. With this in mind, they preceded their signatures on the Declaration of Independence with this pledge…

"… with a firm reliance on the protection of Divine Providence [God], we mutually pledge to each other our Lives, our Fortunes and our sacred Honor."

- Excerpt from the Declaration of Independence

How about you? Are you willing to make this type of commitment to *liberty*, and to the practical side of *loving your neighbor as yourself?* [127]

In Summary:

Nationally, we need to return to the biblical principles on which the United States was founded. These principles encouraged responsible freedom and the Rule of Law; prosperity through free enterprise, greatness as a result of limited government and respect for life and individual liberty, and community well-being through responsible citizenship and personal charity.

Individually, we need to live according to these same principles, but for us as individuals this isn't enough. Biblical principles are powerful for a nation, but for individuals, the *Jesus of the Bible* needs to become *Jesus of the heart.*

Throughout this book I've urged action; having the guts to do the right thing. I've talked about the use of force and our need to be assertive in securing healthy reform and restoration in our nation and in our personal life. It takes guts to fight for cultural and social health, and it takes guts to pursue health of mind, heart, and soul.

Bold action is definitely needed and we can't delay. This is not, however, a call to be strident or shrill in defiance against those who govern. Our concept of government was designed by God[128] as a counter to tribal and feudalistic self-centeredness and anarchy. Founders Thomas Jefferson and James Madison discussed this at length:

> "Societies exist under three forms sufficiently distinguishable: 1. Without government, as among our Indians. 2. Under governments wherein the will of every one has a just influence, as is the case in England in a slight degree, and in our states in a great one. 3. Under governments of force: as is the case in all other monarchies and in most of the other republics. To have an idea of the curse of existence under these last, they must be seen. It is a government of wolves over sheep. It is a problem, not clear in my mind, that the 1st. condition is not the best. But I believe it to be inconsistent with any great degree of population. The second state has a great

deal of good in it. The mass of mankind under that enjoys a precious degree of liberty and happiness. It has it's evils too: the principal of which is the turbulence to which it is subject. But weigh this against the oppressions of monarchy [elitist government], and it becomes nothing. Malo periculosam, libertatem quam quietam servitutem. [Translated: "I prefer the tumult of liberty to the quiet of servitude."] Even this evil is productive of good. It prevents the degeneracy of government, and nourishes a general attention to the public affairs. **I hold it that a little rebellion now and then is a good thing, and as necessary in the political world as storms in the physical.** [Yet] Unsuccesful rebellions indeed generally establish the incroachments on the rights of the people which have produced them."

-- Thomas Jefferson[129]
Founding Father,
Principal Author Declaration of Independence,
3rd U.S. President

Just as the Founding Fathers of the United States realized, government needs to operate under biblical principles. Our experiences over the last century have demonstrated yet again that this is necessary for securing a righteous government that is committed to justice and the Rule of Law.

As citizen, we must remember that to defiantly oppose evil, including evil in government, is different than being defiant as a personality trait. One is akin to righteous indignation, the other to being self-righteous.

Defiance without both humility and a personal return to the supremacy of the God of the Bible, will only produce endless conflict. Defiance without surrender to God's Will and God's Way, will only produce perpetual animosity. Our goal should not be vindication of our principles, but rather the rebuilding of our national life, *and* the building of our personal life on the foundation which is the Rock of Jesus and the Bible.

It's a matter of focus: National focus, and our personal focus. Both. Moreover, both at the same time.

We can be fearless if we trust in God. But we will only be successful if we fear God. This isn't a dichotomy; it's the flipside of the same coin.

Today we are engaged in a fight. This fight is probably going to get more intense in the future. We cannot shy away from this fight just because it's uncomfortable or costly.

If we don't fight, we, and our families, will die as victims. If we fight according to our own insights, relying on our own power, we will go down after a fatiguing fight but still as losers. However, if we acknowledge the supremacy of the God of the Bible, and engage our foes according to the 'better way' of our Creator and humble ourselves before Him, we will win. Victory is assured.

> *"To God and posterity you are accountable for [your rights and your rulers]... Let not your children have reason to curse you for giving up those rights and prostrating those institutions which your Fathers delivered to you."*

-- Matthias Burnet,
Famous sermon preached to in
Hartford, CT, May 21, 1803

Disclaimer: In this chapter the author has attempted to report on the historic, contemporary, and future of the issues surrounding the subject of God, guns, and guts of firearm defense. None of the information contained in this book should be construed as legal advice or instruction in the law. The purpose of this book is exclusively to help readers understand the biblical, moral and spiritual ramifications of the issues. It is specifically not legal advice or counsel. The author is not an attorney, and is not providing legal advice, nor is he providing counsel.

Chapter 14

Political Action & Discerning Actions: Protecting our God-given Rights is a Sacred Duty

In the tradition of the U.S. Founding Fathers, today we need to have both the *guts* to assume personal responsibility and the guts to engage in responsible citizenship. This includes political and other helpful actions.

We need to also restore personal and public virtue, as well as fact-based history and civics education. We need to awaken Bible-believing people and insist that our churches provide serious Bible education. Beyond this, we need to have the guts to stand tall and demand that our leaders and government agencies obey the law and our Constitution. It's not about imposing our sense of morality on others. It's about restoring the rule of law and our national Bible-based tradition which includes obeying the Constitution and constitutional laws, respect for each individual person, justice for all, and liberty unfettered by excessive government control.

Being prepared, and prepared to responsibly and skillfully use a firearm, is only one facet of our God-given Right to life and the protection of life. Another aspect of protecting life is our responsibility to protect the Right of self-defense itself,[130] and the Bill of Rights as these are necessary for liberty.

We are at a crisis point in our nation's history so we need to redouble our efforts to defend our society from those who want to take away, or diminish, our God-given and constitutional rights. We need to give particular attention to restoring constitutional justice and the rule of law, and the restoration of a government which is worthy of our trust. The 2nd Amendment is our last citadel for protecting our republic, so we must refuse to let anyone, or anything to undermine it.

Protective action is a responsibility we must actively embrace. Each of us must actively pursue conversations, political activism, promotion of unbiased education, legislative action both locally and nationally, the defense of those who are wrongly persecuted, and other helpful proactive activities. Inaction, complacency and self-centeredness are not an option for those who seek to live according to the teachings of the Bible.

Whining about these problems isn't action; nor is talking enough. Each of us has different skills and abilities, and with a little creativity we can find ways to apply them to these tasks. Each of us has a role to play.

Today, even though there is a mountain of solid evidence which documents the merits of gun ownership for reducing crime and victimization, our gun rights are being systematically eroded. Responsible citizenship therefore cries out for our action. All of us need to be engaged and be part of the solution. Together we can demand a return to the rule of law and our constitutional form of government. We can change laws, regulations and attitudes, especially those that insolently defy God's law.

In the modern world, firearms have replaced the sword as the great equalizer. Like the swords carried in Bible times, a gun makes it possible for a weaker person to stand against a strong or violent oppressor. Though nonviolent resolutions are always preferable, the use of a weapon is still necessary when other options aren't viable.

When a friend was asked, "Why do you carry a gun?" His sage answer was, "Because I can't carry a police officer." It was a good answer.

One particular truth that we must clearly communicate is that a firearm is not something that is good or bad. It is simply a tool [131] to be carried in case it is needed. And, like any other tool, it can be both properly and improperly used.

We must champion the message that guns are not the problem; the problem is the decline of our society.

Yet for many people it's easier to blame neutral and lifeless objects such as firearms, rather than admit our society is unhealthy as a result of moral decline. It's more convenient to blame guns, rather than admit our need to restore biblical principles, personal responsibility, and God-honoring family life.

Another truth that is evident to any honest observer who is knowledgeable about history is this: *Our social institutions are not failing to make us safe due to a lack of laws, funding or effort. They are failing because crime and violence are the result of abandoning our nation's founding principles.*

This truth is obvious to most Americans. Unfortunately the professionals in government, law, education, and the mainstream media, refuse to acknowledge the elephant in the room, that their religious fervor for secularism is what has brought us to this point. We can't allow this to continue. Both sides can't win. With something like this there is no position of compromise. We will either be subjected to their fundamental change of America, or we will return to the biblical precepts which made America great and good.

Whether these self-proclaimed experts will admit it or not, we are in the midst of a moral crisis. It doesn't matter how much money we pour into making things better, we can't fix a problem that we refuse to acknowledge.

Despite what opponents say, neither the people nor the government of the United States has ever required individuals to adhere to the tenets of any religious faith. However, in the past our society did extol biblical concepts such as personal responsibility and integrity, honesty, truth and justice, as these are necessities for a healthy civil society.

Though the U.S. citizenry has never been perfect, in the past Bible-based ethics permeated American society. These principles were accepted as the standard for desirable behavior. Now, even though many are rejoicing that everything related to God, the Bible, morality, ethics and virtue has been forced out of public life, this rejection is nevertheless the root of our current predicament. This isn't politically correct, but it's still true. We can't afford to sidestep this truth, and we can't allow others to, either.

As the anti-gun advocates incessantly remind us, criminals and oppressors sometimes use firearms. Nonetheless, the gun isn't at fault when it is misused. If someone were to suggest that we should outlaw carpenter's saws because they are sharp, can cause injury and some people misuse them, we would laugh. But it's no laughing matter when people knavishly suggest that we should prohibit good people from carrying guns. They've missed the obvious; or more likely—they are refusing to admit to the obvious because the alternative viewpoint is uncomfortable.

Truth can be uncomfortable for each of us. Furthermore, personal responsibility involves personal work, and virtue is often costly, and the price we pay for it is sometime very high.

Our society needs to honestly embrace truth, too. The truth is that we are all in agreement on many key points.

For example, there are those who should not use guns and other dangerous tools. If a person is taking drugs, consuming alcohol, or even medicine which is labeled that it should not be used when driving or operating dangerous machinery, these people should not carry a gun. A firearm is a dangerous machine. True. Some people should not have guns. True.

Similarly, a person who is prone to fits of anger, road rage, abusive behavior, fighting, emotional outbursts, or emotion swings; or, has a physical impairment which makes it unsafe to handle a firearm; these are all "no gun" warning signs as well. We all agree on these points.

Another truth is that firearms are essential tools for use by the general public. This is because guns make it possible for us to invoke our unalienable Right to self-defense, and to protect life and the freedoms guaranteed by the Constitution.

Regrettably, in the guise of seeking the public good, misguided people, elitists, and shameless power-grabbers are actively working to deny us this God-given Right. This is where our disagreement rests; it's not in the topics listed above, even though that is all they seem to talk about.

For those who are responsible people, telling the truth, and being an advocate for the truth is required. To intentionally mislead is not acceptable; it's lying. As my British friends say, to be economical with the truth is still a lie.

This is a responsibility of citizenship: We must vehemently confront the anti-gun advocates who refuse to acknowledge that the problem isn't guns.

We need to all admit that the truth is this: The United States is suffering the effects of a malignant social disease. This malady has nothing to do with guns. Obviously we can't fix a problem we refuse to acknowledge. Avoidance of the truth is injurious to society, and this can no longer be tolerated.

Embracing the truth and seeking solutions is a requirement of citizenship; it's not solely the responsibility of the 'professionals' or those in leadership. For those who follow the teachings of the Bible, it is also a sacred duty to fight this battle.

Each of us has a responsibility to stop abuses of authority and power which oppose God's law. At the same time, it is also our duty to be involved in training our children and friends, to help the poor and disadvantaged become safe in our communities and around the world, to work with our fellow citizens to improve understanding and education; and to be responsible gun owners ourselves, armed and equipped with common sense, and well trained and skilled in firearm defense.

Personal integrity isn't enough.

As we engage in this fight, it is essential for us to respect the rights of those who disagree with us, however misguided they might be. Likewise we need to be winsome, not antagonistic. However, respect does not translate into weak-kneed responses which fail to stop the abuse of power, and fail to acknowledge the true cause of our social sickness.

We have a duty to be truthful ourselves, *and* to fight for truth in our society. We cannot allow anyone to steal human rights with impunity. These anti-gun activists are trying to steal human rights. Their arguments are empty, and they remain recalcitrant and refuse to accept what research has proven again and again—that guns in the hands of good people, reduces crime and victimization.

The truth is that more gun control legislation will not reduce crime, and it will not keep our children safe. In my experience, the only form of gun control that works is a common-sense citizen who is armed, and has a steady aim and smooth trigger pull.

Responsible citizenship demands that we become more assertive in opposing those who distort the truth, whether it is regarding guns, or any of our other God-given or constitutional rights. At the same time, we must speak the truth into people's lives shrewdly and fight strategically.

With those who are simply uninformed, we need to calmly and patiently engage in meaningful conversations. These individuals are often misguided and simply need to be educated. With these people it is essential that we respond with kindness, and without rude condescension. Plus, we need to look for new ways to educate the general public on these issues, and we need to vote our conscience not our Party.

For those power-grabbers who are seeking to 'reinvent' the Constitution, and demean the Bible truths which were used to form the foundation of this country, we need to become far more assertive. While our opponents preach to us about tolerance (a characteristic we endorse), they are intolerant as well as deceitful, and they have abused and exploited our commitment to respectful debate.

As the old adage reminds us, to do more of the same thing and expect different results, is foolishness. Therefore, we need to identify new and more effective strategies, and empower them with more forceful and assertive actions.

Inexplicably, as we watch God-given Rights of life and liberty disregarded by those who oppose the Constitution and hide the biblical foundations of this nation, a new tactic of strident and vitriolic, and even violent opposition has emerged. They now use bullying, the courts, and physical force via government agencies, to instill fear.

In the process they overuse the term "Constitutional Right" in an effort to jade and confuse the public, and to give more credence to their cause. These people are constantly misusing the terms "Constitutional Right" and "Rights" as a way to manipulate the public, and to validate their unscrupulous political agenda. The misuse of these words is not accidental.

For example, Congresswoman Nancy Pelosi made a push for expanding gun control laws,[132] urging other lawmakers to pass unconstitutional legislation by telling them that it was their duty. Her justification was that they had sworn an oath to 'protect and defend' the U.S. Constitution. What a disgraceful strategy. Not only was she advocating an unconstitutional law, she actually invoked the Constitution to do so. Her fellow lawmakers probably understood the doublespeak for what it was, but many uninformed citizens would assume she was literally taking the high road by supporting the U.S. Constitution.

We need to stop soft-peddling the truth. Truth is not a concept which is different from one person to another. Truth is truth. It's a facet of honesty.

It's time to expose the myth which claims that truth is just a matter of perception or viewpoint. It's time for us to clearly proclaim the truth. Those who peddle falsehood are liars and we need to call them out.

Since we have the truth on our side, exposing lies can be accomplished without unhelpful anger and without personal attacks. Our effectiveness resides in shinning the spotlight of truth on each lie with relentless determination.

There are times when it is important to be tactful, of course. Yet for most people the problem isn't a lack of tact, it's a fear of confrontation. Therefore we all need to do a little soul-searching on this topic. We need to make sure that we aren't using 'tact' to hide being spineless. Conversely, we can't let being 'direct' get in the way being shrewd and strategic.

It's our job to be purveyors of the truth. We can't let *tact* stand in the way of being forthright, nor can we let *directness* stand in the way of being shrewd. There is a balance.

> [Jesus said,] *"Behold, I send you forth as sheep in the midst of wolves: be ye therefore wise as serpents, and harmless as doves."*
>
> Matthew 10:16 KJV

Some circumstances require diplomacy while others require few words and direct exposure. Unfortunately, most people are so soft that they aren't even a bump in the road for those who bulldoze the truth. We're not all equipped to be a barricade to protect truth, but all of us can be a rock in the roadway to impede the progress of those who are trying to bury it.

Knowing the truth isn't enough. Our methods can be shrewd, but they *must* be forthright. Our opponents manipulate facts and people, but these techniques are not legitimate tools for defending truth. For us, the ends do not justify the means.

Using the word 'Right' and 'Constitution' inappropriately to advance political goals, no matter how wonderful they are, is inappropriate. It demeans us as it desecrates the meaning of these words. It's fraud. Not only is it trickery, it is a mechanism to cheat the public.

A God-given '*Right'* is something unique; it is part of God's law as articulated in the Bible. As such, it must be viewed in stark contrast to the machinations of even well-intentioned people.

The truth is that a 'Constitutional right' is not something vague or nice sounding, it is a protection articulated in the Constitution or Bill or Rights. Notwithstanding, these words are routinely misused by many of our leaders who are fully aware that they are being deceptive.

There are many admirable aspirations such as improvements in public education, jobs, housing, and other endeavors which are worthy of our effort. But these topics do not rise to the level of being "unalienable" Rights given to us by our Creator, nor are they 'Constitutional Rights.'

The Founding Fathers of the United States did an outstanding job of encapsulating our God-given Rights. In the Declaration of Independence they articulated the individual's Right to seek: "Life, Liberty, and the pursuit of Happiness."

Life, which was breathed into us by the Creator of life, is the Right mentioned first because it is the most important. This is a Right given to us by our Creator, not by government. The *Right* to life and self-defense, and our responsibility to defend the lives of others is an essential ingredient of this God-bestowed Right.

The United States government may affirm some of these God-given Rights in the Constitution or other laws of the land, but they exist even if they are not specifically acknowledged. Importantly, obedience to God's laws takes precedence over all other laws.

If any government or agency acts to take away (or limit) any God-given Right, or invalidate or restrict any of God's laws, that regulation is illegitimate. For example, we have a God-given *Right* to defend ourselves and our loved ones, so any human law to the contrary is trumped by God's law. God's law is above all human laws, and we are to obey God's law even if a gangrenous government punishes us.

When we have the opportunity, it is our responsibility to work to change bad legislation and regulations, not just ignore them. This is a duty of responsible community-minded citizenship, and it is also a requirement for anyone who follows the teachings of Jesus or the Bible.

It takes hard work, sound strategies, and "guts" to stand up for truth. It takes guts to be a responsible citizen and to do the right thing.

For anyone who cares to live according to biblical principles, one aspect of *doing the right thing* is to not just obey just laws, but to accept that we also have a duty to uphold them. Obedience is not enough.

Another facet of "obedience is not enough" requires similar fortitude, and also the guts to do the right thing: Though it might be difficult to countenance, sometimes the 'right thing' is to disobey an unjust law.

Our nation's legislators and jurists take an oath to protect and defend the Constitution of the United States of America. Many of them don't live up to that pledge. What about you? Are you willing to protect and defend the Constitution?

What would you do if the police, or some other representative of government, demanded that you register or surrender your guns in response to a new law or regulation? If you have a legal Right to have those weapons, and the Constitution's 2nd Amendment protects your Right, would you surrender them? Would you register them? It may sound like a minor issue, but is it?

Incrementalism is a technique used for subverting the truth and manipulating the public.

Using the technique of 'incrementalism,' rights are eroded one step at a time until their foundation collapses, and they are swept away. This technique has been a very successful strategy throughout history, and it is being used against us today.

Historically, banning certain types of firearms and gun registration have been first-steps toward confiscation. This is how it was accomplished in England and Australia—and Nazi Germany.

After World War I, the Treaty of Versailles brought about gun control measures for Germany which sounded completely reasonable. But later, this paved the way for Hitler's expansion of gun control, which became progressively more stringent. Eventually, the public was disarmed—but the Nazi thugs were well equipped and used their weapons to crush opposition.

In reality, *new* gun registration laws serve no legitimate purpose. Further, the banning of certain types of weapons, like the constantly attacked 'assault rifle' category of firearms, also serves no legitimate purpose.

In the United States today, when a new gun is purchased, or a used gun is purchased from a gun store, pawn shop, or gun show, the seller uses a computerized system to submit the buyer's identity information to the government for review. The store employee receives a message back from the government which indicates if the buyer is approved. If the buyer isn't approved, this stops the transaction. The Bureau of Alcohol, Tobacco, Firearms and Explosives (ATF.gov) is the federal agency which maintains this system. Like the F.B.I., it's part of the U.S. Department of Justice. All purchase information on firearms is retained by ATF, including the serial number of the gun.

Why do we need more? Why do we need new gun registration laws when we already have so many gun laws?

We don't.

When I was a police detective, it was a routine matter to track down who bought a gun, and to follow the path of ownership to the crime. So my experience affirms the research; that new gun registration laws will *not* serve a crime-solving or crime-reduction purpose. Yet, for many law abiding people, new registration laws and bans seem relatively harmless.

But are they? If we already accomplish background checks on the buyers of new guns, and register those guns in a national database, why is there a push for more gun registration?

The truth is that we now have volumes of research, including that undertaken by the federal government itself, which proves that *new* firearm registration laws will not reduce crime. These results are further validated by my own personal experience as a police detective. Similarly, new bans on certain types of guns, such as assault rifles and guns which have high-capacity magazines (clips) will not reduce crime. Nor will they help solve crimes. This is reality. This is an irrefutable truth.

- - - - - - - -

To be clear, I'm not suggesting that we should eliminate all gun laws. What we need to do is eliminate the thousands of ineffectual laws, and then enforce the remaining viable regulations.

- - - - - - - -

We already have laws designed to keep guns out of the hands of the mentally ill, but most of these are not enforced, and the federal government actually hinders the enforcement efforts. Therefore, we certainly don't need new laws to solve this problem. Adding new laws on top of what we already have will only bring more confusion and compliance hardships for law-abiding citizens.

Throughout history, 'incrementalism' has often been the strategy used by those who are power-hungry. The power-grabbing kingpins, who are pulling the strings of the gun-control crowd today, have become very adept at using this technique and manipulating the public. Typically they don't directly attack our freedoms; rather they shrewdly work to erode them. This gradual decline is a cunning step-by-step strategy. It's like walking down a flight of stairs; with each step our rights drop just a few inches, but over time we will find that we have descended into a place where our essential liberties are gone.

This strategy makes it possible for the power-hungry to impose their unwanted political agenda on a society that doesn't notice the decline until it's too late. Just as with the Nazis and others throughout history, oppression becomes inevitable when liberty is sacrificed. Increased safety is a ruse. It's a bold-faced lie.

The rope of truth which binds us to our freedoms is becoming weaker and weaker. Few seem to notice that the strands of truth and liberty are being cut a few at a time. Hopefully we'll start caring before the rope breaks. At the current rate of cuts to our freedoms and abrasion to our Constitution, this can't be far off.

It takes guts to demand truth, and to become an advocate for our Rights. Nevertheless, this is part of our biblical duty to uphold the law. The media and the masses, and even our friends, are often clueless but quick to believe these lies, and to ridicule gun owners and 2nd Amendment advocates. We are often referred to as having our priorities out of balance, or accused of being unbalanced "gun nuts" or some other baseless term of derision or ridicule.

What about you? Are you too busy to be an advocate for truth?

Are you silent when you hear anti-God or anti-Bible rants, or anti-gun rhetoric? Do you let people get away with citing half-truths and using misleading arguments? Or, do you take a stand?

Even when we are polite and shrewd, there is often a price to pay for doing the right thing.[133] Are you willing to pay the price of integrity?

It takes guts to carry a gun. It takes *guts* and *courage* to be prepared, and to be willing and ready to properly use a gun.

When I talk about these matters in our classes that include a section on the 2nd Amendment, thoughtful people often start asking specific questions about civil disobedience and resistance. "Should I get a gun even if ownership is illegal in my community?" Or, "Should I carry a concealed handgun even though the law prohibits it? After all, the Bible makes it clear that we can disobey a human law if it is in opposition to God's law."

We not only can, but we should defy any law or regulation that goes against God's law, but the questions of civil disobedience and resistance are not simple ones. We should not enter into such actions with cavalier bravado. These gun issues just aren't that simple.

Regrettably, civil disobedience and resistance is too complicated, and far too big of an issue to address here. Suffice to say that those who countenance such actions need to do more than just consider the biblical morality of the issue. They must also ask, "Is this issue so important that I am willing to go to jail for it?" And, "Am I willing to be killed, and kill, defending this Right to keep and bear arms?"

Personally, I believe this issue to be that important, but simple defiance of manmade laws may not be strategic. We need to be *shrewd as snakes and as innocent as doves* (Matthew 10:16) when we consider our course of action.

Extreme caution must be applied whenever we consider even minor resistance against the government. Yes, we must refuse to obey any law that violates God's law. That's a given. But our duty goes beyond this; we must be advocates for God's law, too.

Obedience is not enough; we have a duty to uphold the truth, and to maintain God's laws. Private or secret obedience is not enough.

At the same time, we must also remember that just because a law is extremely offensive, this does not automatically mean that it violates God's law.[134] We need to be sure of our footing before we start to run at a problem, particularly if it involves civil disobedience or resistance.

These things said, inaction is not acceptable, either. To do nothing is, in fact, a sin of omission.

Further, it is useless to get involved with ineffective groups and fringe initiatives which aren't biblical in approach. Poor strategies deplete our energy and treasure, and oftentimes they harm our credibility. Plus, they rarely make real headway in actually solving the problem.

The Bible teaches that we should be shrewd (Matthew 10:16). Yet at the same time, we need to act with haste because the anti-gun lobby is powerful and they are willing to lie and to use backdoor tactics, such as government regulations, to circumvent the law. The time for action is now. We can't wait to get active. Yet our actions still need to be astute, and our strategies discerning and ethical.

Fortunately, once again we don't need to do this alone. There are people, and organizations which have been fighting this fight for many years. Their experience is invaluable and they need our encouragement, financial support and participation. Of strategic importance is to support experienced organizations such as the NRA,[135] and the other national and state rifle and gun organizations which provide a cohesive strategy. Unity building and coordinated efforts are important.

Despite being viciously opposed and unjustly vilified, the NRA is still the largest and most effective organization for protecting 2nd Amendment Rights.[136] We may not agree with everything they do, but they are still worthy of our support as long as their tactics remain compatible with biblical truth.

If you are relatively new to this issue you may have some reservations about the NRA. If you do, this is likely the result of the anti-gun lobbyists who have run effective misinformation campaigns. I encourage you to examine what the NRA is doing (www.NRAila.org), and then get involved.

Why bother? It's because national revival and restoration is still possible. Seeking peaceful resolution is part of the process of reconciliation, and the Bible directs us to this type of engagement whenever it is possible.

Even so, we need to remember that reconciliation is something that happens after the conflict has ended. This war against our beliefs and rights is far from over. Now is not the time to compromise and appease; it's time to aggressively fight. Our previous unwillingness to handle the heat of conflict, and our spineless softhearted approach and 1960's-style confusion is why our rights are evaporating so quickly. We can't allow this to continue. To turn this around at this late hour we'll need to be very assertive and dedicated.

We do need to keep in mind our responsibility to seek peaceable resolution and reconciliation whenever possible (2 Corinthians 5:18). That said, before we focus on reconciliation, we must first accept our precursor responsibility for righteousness and justice, and our role as peace-*makers*. Before we concern ourselves with reconciliation, we need to heat-up the furnace so that we can forge peace.

We need to be forceful people of action. In the process, we can still be amicable. We need to prefer peace, but we need to accept the role of warrior, too.

As we consider strategy, we must avoid the unscrupulous tactics of our opponents. We can be wise, peace-loving bearers of truth and advocates for justice, and at the same time be shrewd and uncompromising in regard to our moral scruples.

Today, too many good people are flying the white-flag of defeat. We need to stop licking our wounds, get out of our foxholes, and get back into the fight.

It's time for shrewd strategies, effective tactics and alliances, and stamina, as we defend what's right and what's worth saving. It's time for us to engage in potent, partisan resistance. It's not time to sing the song *"Baby Jesus, Meek and Mild"*. It's time to belt out, *"Onward Christian*

Soldiers," and act like the warriors God created us to be.

This will be a difficult, protracted, and sometimes painful and costly fight, but we needn't succumb to discouragement. After all, Jesus did call us to be peace*makers*, and peace-making is an active process that is only needed during times of peril.

Adversity, and these times of difficulty, should not be a surprise as if they are something out of the ordinary. Historically, adversity is more common than comfort. Read the Bible's 'Book of Acts,' and then let's "cowboy up" and get it done.

We have a God-given Right and responsibility to defend ourselves and others against violence and oppression. And, we have the responsibility to take action to protect these Rights from abuse and dismemberment.

World history is full of examples of people who didn't defend their God-given Rights and allowed them to be eroded. Then, one day they woke-up and discovered that their freedoms were gone and their lives were in jeopardy. As the pro-2nd Amendment bumper sticker reminds us…

"The experts agree, gun control works, just ask
Hitler, Castro, Stalin, Chairman Mao, and Pol Pot."

Thankfully, we don't need to reinvent the right-defending process. Our nation's Founder's lived through stressful times and many abuses of their Rights. So in addition to the exploits of the heroes in the Bible, we need to also study the lives of our nation's heroes.[137] These men and women provide us with fitting examples of what to do and not to do, and models of courage.

The lives of these brave men and women should inspire us and give us renewed hope. Their trials and tenacity, and eventual success in spite of insurmountable odds, should encourage us.

The Founding Fathers of the United States took on the biggest, best equipped, and most experienced and highly trained army in the world—and they won. God was with them, as He is with us if we are seeking Him first and His righteousness.[138]

Noble efforts are worth the sacrifice. This book is also a call to action; everyone has a role.[139] How will you respond?

Chapter 15

36READY and the 6-P Code: Living a Life of Readiness

Jesus' teaching of Luke 22:**36** can be summed up by the words: *'Prepared'* and '*Ready'*. We need to be *prepared* with the physical resources needed to face adversity, and we need to be *ready* emotionally and spiritually, as well as adequately trained.

According to Jesus' teaching in this Bible passage, there are **3** facets of being prepared, and we can identify **6** facets which enable this preparation. This is why we talk about being **36**READY.

The 3 elements of preparation are: financial/economic, provisions, and being prepared for defense. According to Jesus, we need to do more than prepare for defense, we need to become wholly prepared to face changing times and any crisis. We need to be capable of caring for ourselves, and we need to be ready to serve our family, friends, neighbors and others.

Just as owning a football doesn't make you a football player, owning a gun doesn't mean that you are ready for defense. Similarly, having gold coins and a GO-Bag[140] does not mean that you are adequately prepared, either. It takes more than 'things' to become prepared.

In regard to firearms, before you contemplate using a gun to defend yourself or others, you need to train. And standard target-practice isn't enough if you want to be prepared as the Bible advocates.

To be fully prepared, you need to obtain instruction from a qualified firearms *self-defense* expert. This training isn't just desirable, it's important. And don't forget to schedule regular practice, too.

Better yet, make a lifestyle decision to live by the 6-P Code:

The 6-P Code

To be prepared and ready requires far more than just being armed and stockpiling supplies. It also involves contemplating various scenarios in advance—and then planning and preparing for them. Those who commit to being prepared and ready live by the 6-P Code...

I will diligently:

1. **P**lan for emergencies, and live as a vigilant and always-alert person.

I will acquire...

2. **P**ractical training to help me face plausible real-world challenges, including spiritual conflict, social and financial upheaval, and hazardous events.

I will...

3. **P**repare my body, mind, spirit, and family for healthy living today, and for future times of adversity.

I will assemble...

4. **P**rovisions and cache supplies of water and food, essential gear, GO-Bags, firearms and ammunition, cash and means of trade.

I will undertake...

5. **P**ainstaking logistics, and be systematic in my maintenance and management of the many different facets of preparedness.

Plus, I commit to engage in regular...

6. **P**ractice; both personal and family/group exercises.

Just prior to His arrest and crucifixion, Jesus told His followers that they need to be prepared financially, prepared with provisions, and prepared for defense (Luke 33:36)

This wasn't just a suggestion. Jesus didn't say that this is an important consideration. He wasn't simply advocating this as desirable, nor did He say that this is a responsibility of leadership or for some special, select group. Quite the opposite. Jesus was providing general instructions for all of His followers. The meaning of this Bible passage isn't obscure; it's a clear injunction for you and me. Obedience to Jesus, and living according to biblical principles, requires these three actions.

To download a PDF copy of the 6-P Code for printing, visit the 'Resources' page at www.36Ready.org

Chapter 16

Summary of Relevant Crime Statistics

Those with political and other social agendas remain active today, not just in their misuse of Scripture, but also fraudulently representing facts concerning firearms. In my view, the most useful and scholarly analysis of the effect of civilian use of guns on crime is the book, "More Guns, Less Crime" (Third Edition) by Professor John R. Lott, Jr. Notwithstanding, the below statistics were gathered from various other reliable sources, including the FBI's Uniform Crime Reporting program.[141]

- In a nationwide survey, it was found that over the previous five years at least 0.5% of U.S. households had members who had used a gun for defense during a situation in which they thought someone "almost certainly would have been killed" if they "had not used a gun for protection." A conservative estimate is that there are at least 162,000 such incidents per year. (This figure excludes all police, security guards, and military personnel.[142])
- Based on survey data published in the *Journal of Quantitative Criminology*, U.S. civilians use guns to defend themselves and others from crime at least 989,883 times per year.[143]
- A U.S. Justice Department study [144] found:
    - 42% of Americans will be the victim of a completed violent crime (assault, robbery, rape, etc.) in the course of their lives.
    - 83% of Americans will be the victim of an attempted or completed violent crime.
    - 52% of Americans will be the victim of an attempted or completed violent crime more than once.
- Over the past two decades, U.S. cities which have made handgun ownership illegal or difficult, have seen a significant increase in violent

crime, whereas cities which have made it legal for citizens to carry a handgun, have enjoyed a significant decrease in crimes of violence.

- The average murder rate dropped in 89% of the States after right-to-carry (concealed handgun license) laws were passed. Similarly, 81% experienced a significant decrease in the number of rapes. Other States either had an increase in these crimes or a substantially smaller reduction in crime.[145]

- In Europe, the country of Switzerland issues assault rifles and ammunition to its citizens. In that country, everyone is part of their national militia[146] and keeps their assault rifle in their home. As a result, Switzerland was the only European country not invaded by the Nazis.[147] Today, murder is rare and the violent crime rate is low.

- Europe has very strict gun control laws, and the U.S. media often reports that they have a much lower murder rate than the United States. This is true. However, what they fail to report is that in Europe the overall incidence of violent crimes (murder, rape, armed robbery, burglary, violent assault, etc.) is 300% higher than the U.S. (Adjusted for the difference in population size, crime rates are calculated based on the number of crimes per 100,000 people.)[148]

- Mexico has strict gun control laws and yet has more murders and violent crime than does the United States. Russia has had harsh and extremely tight gun control laws for decades, yet it has a murder rate that is twice that of the U.S. When compared to the United States, even Scandinavia which has a reputation of being one of the most peaceful places on earth, has 200% more crimes of violence.[149]

- Since the progressive Labour party came to power in the United Kingdom (England, Scotland, Wales, and Northern Ireland) in 1997, the crime rate has skyrocketed. During this period England has experienced a 77% increase in murders and crimes of violence. Long considered to be a national 'gun free zone' where even the police do not carry guns, this has all changed. England has become more violent than any European country, and more violent than the U.S. Per capita, it is a far more violent place than the United States.[150] Many British police officers now carry either Glock 17 pistols or H&K MP5 submachine guns.[151]

Chapter 17

Gun Control, Politics of Deception

Proponents of gun control legislation which outlaws certain types of weapons, or large-capacity magazines, routinely claim that these new laws will reduce gun violence. However, evidence suggests otherwise. In reality, assailants armed with "assault weapons" and high-capacity magazines almost always obtain these items through illegal sources. Yet, in spite of the availability through illicit markets, these guns are involved in less than three percent of U.S. homicides.[152] In fact, more people are murdered each year with fists and feet than with all rifles and shotguns combined (including assault weapons). Knives are used more than twice as often.[153]

Furthermore, most of the machineguns, submachine guns, and military hardware used in the commission of a crime were stolen or smuggled into the U.S. by drug cartels. Even so, these weapons were used in fewer than 100 of the 12,664 homicides which occurred in the U.S. last year.[154] These types of guns are already highly controlled or illegal, but just like any illegal commodity, smugglers find a way if there are people who are willing to purchase them. Since drugs are easily available on the streets of our cities despite all our efforts, there is little hope of stopping the flow of illegal weapons. This doesn't mean we shouldn't try; it just means we shouldn't expect this approach to be particularly successful.

Improved border controls will help, but if drugs are being successfully smuggled into a country, then illegal guns will also get through. Strict gun control laws have been tried in many States and they have failed miserably. So when gun control advocates claim that gun control will reduce crime, this is a complete fabrication. Not only does gun control not stop crime, it actually has the opposite effect. The result of strict gun control is primarily that honest people are unable to defend themselves.

Many gun control proponents claim that they are motivated by our need to protect children from gun violence. This is certainly a worthy goal, but we need to face the facts: research has demonstrated again and again that increased gun control does not reduce violence against children. It doesn't work.[155]

This isn't a new discovery. Not only is there a mountain of research which shows that guns in the hands of good people reduces crime, the opposite has also been proven. In those parts of the country which have had a long history of draconian gun control laws, these laws have not only failed to reduce crime, they have generally resulted in an increase in violent crime. As the saying goes, "When guns are outlawed, only outlaws have guns," and as a result, law-abiding people are unable to exercise their God-given Right of self-defense.

Strict gun control laws actually reduce child safety. This is because they hamper the ability of parents to use guns to protect their children. In the real world, "Gun Free Zones" serve to encourage gun crimes because the assailant knows that they will be the only one who is armed. So "yes," gun control is effective—but only effective in stopping good people from protecting themselves and others.

If gun control worked, then Chicago and Washington, D.C. would be the safest cities in the country. These cities have had the strictest[156] 'gun control' laws for many years, yet they also have the highest crime rates. When we compare the crime in these cities to other communities which have scrapped their anti-gun laws and have made concealed carry of a handgun legal, we observe that more guns actually result in less crime. For some people this is counter intuitive, but it is nevertheless true.

In the past decade, crime has gone down in the areas which have enacted laws which make it possible for honest citizens to carry guns. Yet, during this same period, violence increased in places like Chicago and Washington DC, which intensified their anti-gun efforts during this same period.

Nationally, as the ownership of self-defense guns has increased, the murder rate has dropped to an all-time low. [157]

Your help is needed to spread the truth about gun control. We need to make it clear to everyone that new gun laws and regulations will not stop criminals from committing crimes. But, they will seriously reduce the ability of good people to protect themselves and their loved ones.

The 2nd Amendment of the United States Constitution protects the citizen's Right to be armed with a firearm, but this Right is under constant attack. To stop these assaults on the protections afforded to us by the Constitution, we need to do more than correct fallacious assumptions about guns and crime. *We need to understand that these anti-gun efforts are based on a problem which is much bigger than emotion-driven flawed thinking and bad legislation.*

Gun Control is not really about 'public safety.' Gun Control is fundamentally about *people*-control. It's a power grab.

The wisdom of our Founding Fathers, and their concern for the misuse of power and people-control efforts of elitists, reminds us that these concerns are not new. These evils inevitably grow out of big government everywhere and in every era.[158] This danger is why our Founders added the 2nd Amendment to the U.S. Constitution. Lets read what our Founding Fathers had to say about this threat to liberty, and what they were thinking when they penned the 2nd Amendment:[159]

George Mason, Founding Father and author of the 2nd Amendment

> ***"[W]hen the resolution of enslaving America was formed in Great Britain, the British Parliament was advised by an artful man, who was governor of Pennsylvania, to disarm the people; that it was the best and most effectual way to enslave them; but that they should not do it openly, but weaken them, and let them sink gradually."*** [160]

Richard Henry Lee, Founding Father

> ***"To preserve liberty it is essential that the whole body of people always possess arms."***[161]

Federal Gazette, June 18, 1789

> ***"As the military forces which must occasionally be raised to defend our country, might pervert their power to the injury of their fellow citizens, the people are confirmed by the next article (of amendment) in their right to keep and bear their private arms."*** [162]

Noah Webster, Founding Father

> ***"Before a standing army can rule, the people must be disarmed; as they are in almost every kingdom in Europe. The supreme power in America cannot enforce unjust laws by the sword; because the whole body of the people are armed, and constitute a force superior to any band of regular troops that can be, on any pretence, raised in the United States. A military force, at the command of Congress, can execute no laws, but such as the people perceive to be just and constitutional; for they will possess the power."***[163]

Thomas Jefferson, 3rd President of the United States, principal author of the Declaration of Independence

> ***"Laws that forbid the carrying of arms. . . disarm only those who are neither inclined nor determined to commit crimes. . . Such laws make things worse for the assaulted and better for the assailants; they serve rather to encourage than to prevent homicides, for an unarmed man may be attacked with greater confidence than an armed man."***[164]

Alexander Hamilton, Founding Father,
Spokesman for the U.S. Constitution

> ***"[I]f circumstances should at any time oblige the government to form an army of any magnitude, that army can never be formidable to the liberties of the people while there is a large body of citizens, little if at all inferior to them in discipline and the use of arms, who stand ready to defend their rights and those of their fellow citizens."*** [165]

Patrick Henry, Founding Father

> ***"Guard with jealous attention the public liberty. Suspect everyone who approaches that jewel."*** [166]

Armed with the research which proves that more gun control laws will not reduce crime, the history of gun control leading to oppression in other countries, and that our nation's Founders actually anticipated this problem and provided protections, should encourage us. The facts are on our side.

So what is behind these anti-gun efforts? It's important for us to look deeper into this controversy.

Eric Holder's Department of Justice fiasco, *"Fast and Furious,"* was *not* a law enforcement debacle. Although it was originally conceived for a legitimate anti-crime purpose, it was co-opted so that it could be used as a tool for political maneuvers. In this case, *Fast and Furious* was transformed from a law enforcement operation into a political strategy. The goal switched from crime reduction to 'people control.' It became a scheme to increase political power of those who regard themselves as Progressives.

Unfortunately, in recent years it has become commonplace for government agencies to be used for political purposes. As a former law enforcement officer myself, it pains me to acknowledge that these abuses of power have now infected the Department of Justice and the

Department of Homeland Security. Importantly, these misuses of power are not the result of bureaucratic blunders, nor are they the result of poor judgment or accidental violations. They are intentional, and they are designed to achieve political objectives.

Individual instances of corruption have historically been present in every organization, everywhere, but thankfully these corruption problems have been relatively infrequent in the United States. This has now changed.

Yet today's corruption problems are not primarily financial graft, but based in a quest for power. These schemes use the muscle of government agencies to achieve social and political goals. These strategies often use government regulations, and the manipulation of legislators and the simpletons in the media, to achieve their agenda. Therefore, this form of corruption dupes the public as the true objective is clouded by volumes of unrelated detail.

What makes this even more confusing is that when there is more than one accomplice involved in the scheme, the various participants may each have different objectives. This makes corruption more difficult to recognize. The lack of transparency in government often makes discovery impossible unless the observer has insider information. Nonetheless, if something doesn't pass the "smell" test there is usually a reason, but evidence is often impossible to obtain externally. Transparency in government, and limited government, is the only way to stem this rising tide of corruption.

Even government reports and statistics are often filtered to provide the desired effect. Therefore we need to use care to discern the truth amidst the rhetoric. In the past, official government statements and reports were regarded as the most reliable, but this is no longer true. Now, with all research reports and statistics, we need a healthy dose of skepticism if the results are surprising. We also need to always look at the details; not just conclusions reported by the media, or statistics cited by a government official.

For example, while doing research for this book, I sought statistics from the ATF regarding the purchase of self-defense firearms. Oddly, though they are the agency tasked with monitoring gun sales, this information was not readily available. As a result, I had to laboriously tally the sales of relevant types of firearms, line by line, to come up with the total. All the data was in ATF reports, but the important details were buried in volumes of data and laborious to exhume.

Unfortunately, annoyances such as this are not the main problem. In recent years, even the most senior law enforcement officer in the land, U.S. Attorney General Eric Holder, routinely misused his office to advance his political agenda. For example, Holder stopped local police and federal agents from enforcing border protection and immigration laws. He actually stopped them from enforcing the law, and he used Department of Justice lawyers to sue States that were enforcing laws he didn't like. Incredible. He also instituted policies and paved the way for programs which violate federal law and constitutional law. For him, apparently the law is irrelevant and unbinding unless it matches his personal agenda.

However what's even more incredible is that he got away with it. We have moved away from justice and the Rule of Law, to the Decrees of the Powerful.

When the nation's top law enforcement officer brazenly disobeys the law, we can expect this mind-set of corruption to influence the conduct of local law enforcement officers, and the courts as well. Without respect for the Rule of Law by those who are sworn to uphold and enforce it, we are in serious trouble. This development doesn't bode well for the future of the United States, especially since these abuses are flagrant and frequent.

It's all the more ominous when we see that once abuses are exposed, the perpetrators not only escape punishment, they usually aren't even held accountable. Oftentimes exposure doesn't even stop the conduct. Occasionally a low-level operative is thrown under the bus, but those who are doing the throwing usually escape with impunity.

If you think I'm overstating, take a close look at the *Fast and Furious* program. Take a look at what our federal law enforcement officers did—and the results of their 5-year *Fast and Furious* gun-walking campaign.

In this covert operation, the U.S. government allowed more than 2,000 weapons—including massive long-range .50 caliber sniper rifles—to be purchased by drug-cartel employees. With the full knowledge and assistance of Department of Justice federal agents (ATF), these guns were smuggled into Mexico and used to build-up the arsenals of Mexico's drug cartels; people who would obviously use these weapons for criminal purposes.

Why? The Department of Justice's hidden objective was apparently to provide a graphic example to the American public that more gun control is needed; specifically that 'assault rifles', 'black rifles' and all military-style firearms should be confiscated from American citizens. The goal of the operation was to manipulate public opinion, and convince lawmakers and voters to believe their gun-control 'public safety' nonsense.

Crime statistics clearly show that there isn't a U.S. crime problem with these weapons, so they decided to create a crime problem. With *Fast and Furious* they orchestrated a series of incidents; crimes of violence which would provide graphic photos and news stories. The American people would naturally respond with horror and demand new gun control laws. When emotions run hot, at that point it doesn't matter if the new law is unconstitutional.

In essence, with *Fast and Furious*, key people within the Department of Justice manipulated a Mexico crime problem, so that they could manipulate U.S. public opinion. This elaborate scheme was conceived to advance a Progressive political agenda.

Since crime statistics did not support their gun-control (people-control) objective, they needed to manufacture justification. The already established *Fast and Furious* operation was the ideal front, so they overhauled it for this new purpose. They simply retooled the program so that it would produce the results they needed. If it hadn't been exposed by honest federal agents, they would have used it to convince the American people that military-style weapons shouldn't be in hands of civilians, even though the U.S. Constitution specifically protects this private ownership—and despite the fact that honest statistics prove that these legally-owned weapons have no negative impact on crime. But as tyrants know, these guns can be used to stymie the efforts of those who seek to take power away from the people.

What was the result of *Fast and Furious*? U.S. Government federal agents became criminal co-conspirators when they intentionally facilitating the perpetration of violent assaults, kidnappings and murder, including the murder of one of our own law enforcement officers. These reprobate federal agents engaged in a whole series of serious crimes. Yet none of them went to jail. No one was arrest. No one was even fired.

This is not just a lack of accountability; this is intentional criminal conduct. It is abandonment of the Rule of Law on which this country was founded.

Fast and Furious redux was literally designed to help smugglers get weapons into Mexico, a friendly neighbor already plagued by drug cartel violence. Then, our government feigned horror that this was happening, so that they could publically exploit these crimes which involved assault rifles and military-style guns from the United States.

This illicit campaign was either conceived by the leadership within Department of Justice, or it was accomplished with their full knowledge. Either way, they understood that these weapons were being used to arm violent criminals in Mexico.

They also knew that these guns were intensifying drug cartel and community violence. They knew that innocent people were being injured and killed. The success of their strategy depended on this result.

The 'Fast and Furious' debacle wasn't just a few corrupt government employees who used a federal program for their own ends. This entire program was a government-sanctioned criminal conspiracy.

What was the result? What happened when the honest agents exposed the scheme, before 'Fast and Furious' could be stopped?

Many innocent people died during the years of this federal crime spree. Fortunately, the illegal activities of our government were eventually exposed. There are honest people inside our Department of Justice and the ATF. Yet, unrepentant Eric Holder, the U.S. Attorney General, kept his job and he continued to flout the law, unabated.

If Eric Holder was upset about this criminal enterprise within his department it wasn't evident. He didn't do anything about it, nor did congress or the president. Thankfully, this 'Fast and Furious' scheme failed. Unfortunately, other reprobate strategies are ongoing in this federal agency, and in others.

This state of affairs is shameful and discouraging. Today the American people can't trust their top law enforcement officer, the U.S. Attorney General, to be forthright and honest. This is unfortunately part of a trend toward lawlessness within our government. The Rule of Law is being ignored.

On the positive side, we now understand the extreme measures these people are willing to use to disarm the American people. Apparently nothing is off-limits to their tactics, including the death of innocents. As I write this it seems impossible that our government has fallen this far, but the facts speak for themselves.

We have repeatedly seen that the anti-gun crowd exploits tragedies like mass shootings and terrorist incidents for political gain. But now we see that they are even willing to manufacture incidents, like 'Fast and Furious,' which are designed to cause the injury and death of hundreds of innocent people. They are willing to facilitate violence and create tragedy, just to advance their political and social agendas. This is more than sobering.

A clear understanding of the history of gun control in the U.S. and around the world can help us better understand what is happening today. People seeking power and control isn't a new phenomenon.

Since the 2nd Amendment is clear, and the intent of our Founding Fathers is easy to establish, and since statistics on gun violence do not support their agenda, these Progressives and anti-gun groups need a different strategy to garner power.

The Progressives who are aligned with the political Left and other special-interest groups who will benefit, are endeavoring to manufacture a groundswell of public opinion to advance their anti-gun people-control agenda. This in turn paves the way for their other plans. Gun control is not their ultimate goal. Firearms in the hands of the public is simply an impediment to achieving control over their social, political and economic objectives. Exerting authority over the population and public life is essential if they are to attain their Progressive goals. An armed population has the potential to thwart these plans, so gun control has become an important stepping stone.

These alliances are an application of the Arabic and Chinese proverb, "The enemy of my enemy, is my friend" (at least for now). This ancient battle strategy is being used today to bring together people who have different agendas, but are united in their desire to fundamentally change America.

This doesn't require some elaborate conspiracy. They all recognize the need to disarm Americans if they are going to succeed with their goals, thus anti-gun cooperation becomes necessary and obvious. It's a mutually-beneficial alignment. There may be collusion, but the alignment doesn't really require secret back-room meetings. It's simply an alignment of strategies.

Empowered by public opinion rooted in emotion and false 'facts,' these anti-gun collaborators are working to pass unconstitutional laws and regulations by manipulating public opinion. This expansion of government includes not only new laws, but also regulations established by unelected officials in government agencies, all in an effort aimed at restricting gun ownership and use. Since people-control is their aim, and because armed resistance is their concern, their emphasis is on military-style weapons and high-capacity magazines which would be more effective for armed resistance.

This might sound bizarre to some, but it is nevertheless true. If you have doubts, I invite you to look into this yourself. These details are under-reported, but the facts can be gleaned even from mainstream media sources and the websites belonging to these organizations.

The ultimate goal of these power-grabbing people is beyond the scope of this book, but their gun-control objective is easy to discern. It is clearly an effort for these élites to increase control over the citizenry of the United States. They want to have the ability to impose changes without the fear of a significant public backlash.

At the very least, since people will not have the capacity to protect themselves, the population will demand increased protection from the government. This shift away from personal responsibility, and away from the ability to be involved in personal and community safety, would also play right into their plan for bigger government and increased control.

This shift alone would grow government (and taxes) significantly, and reduce personal freedom as emerging leaders gain new heights of power. In the process, new technologies will continue to be applied which limit freedom and intensify government control. As we increasingly surrender our liberty, these *benefactors* will be in the position to quell opposition as they progressively increase their control and power. Increasing taxation (and economic hardship) is also useful tactics for increasing control, as people are so busy trying to stay afloat that they don't have time to rebel.

Irrespective of their motivation, as we observe their strategies we see that they will do whatever it takes to get their way. They are unscrupulous and willing to manipulate public opinion, circumvent the legislative process and coerce law makers, create fraudulent reports, utilize activist judges, dupe weak-minded reporters, spearhead machinations of government agencies, break the law, and anything else that will help them advance their cause. Several of their leaders[167] have even made public statements about inventing disasters or tipping us toward economic collapse, to orchestrate events which will move the country toward accepting their agenda.

It's a *"the ends justify the means"* mentality, and these groups are becoming increasingly devious. These people are willing to brazenly break the law, and they have become increasingly astute in their tactics. Their strategies are shrewd and multifaceted in approach, and they are adept at using backdoor attacks to advance their agenda. (Backdoor gun-control attacks that have been used, include attempts to use the Environmental Protection Agency to control the lead and smoke 'emissions' of guns, insurance regulations to penalize gun owners, and V.A. hospitals to disqualify veterans for gun ownership.) They have learned that two steps forward and one step back is still progress.

This confederation routinely use tragedies like mass shootings as a fulcrum to launch new attacks, introduce new laws, and to institute incremental regulations which make gun ownership more difficult. Increasingly, they are seeking advocates from among the Hollywood set, musicians, and others who are respected by young people. These tactics overwhelm the naive and uninformed, and they have a profound effect on influencing voters.

It's worth noting yet another aspect of their anti-gun strategy: *They pretend to actively promote the Constitution, and they talk as if they are trying to protect our Rights and the Constitution.*

Yet, as they talk about protecting the Constitution, they insert terms such as *"living document."* For them, 'living document' is a code word for another track of their strategy, which is to convince the American people that the Constitution is fluid and adaptable. Once this concept is accepted, they will have the ability to reinterpret the U.S. Constitution whenever, and however, they think it is useful.

At the same time, to add credence to their "living document" approach, they use public schools to intentionally besmirch the reputation of our nation's Founding Fathers. They talk about the nation's founders as if they were uneducated, somewhat primitive people, slave owners who had mistresses, and they use an assortment of other demeaning and misleading 'facts' to discredit the foresight and wisdom of the nation's Founders.

Since the Constitution is the test to validate or reject all laws and government actions in the United States, these people understand that they need to change it, so that it will support, or at least not prevent their political agenda. If they can discredit the dedicated and insightful people who penned the U.S. Constitution, then they can also discredit their original intent in regard to what the Constitution says, and what the

Founders were communicating when they wrote it.

If the Progressives and the Left can convince the American people that the Constitution is now old and out-of-date, and the authors disreputable or at least ancient and irrelevant, they will have damaged our defenses. If they can convince people that the U.S. Constitution needs to be adapted to the modern world, then they have won a decisive battle.

Next is the implementation of Phase-2 of their strategy, which is already well underway. In this gambit they don't just present the concept of the U.S. Constitution being a *'living document,'* they start treating it as an irrefutable fact that it is a living document. As this lie is repeated again and again by those in authority, the uneducated public increasingly accepts this misleading concept. Once this is widely accepted, the Constitution will be subject to change whenever they consider it necessary. There will be no need to invoke the constitutional amendment process. (Most people don't even know that this legal process exists, anyway.)

As this mental shift is accomplished, the anti-Constitution forces are in a position to win the war. Whether due to ignorance or intent, the mainstream media, courts, and education system are assisting these efforts. As this transition is accomplished, these organizations and leaders will be able to progressively restrict gun ownership.

It's likely that the most significant gun restrictions and de facto-seizures won't be implemented by sweeping new laws, at least not initially. The anti-gun crowd will keep trying, but they know they can't win using this approach—at least not yet. They continue to try to win sweeping new legislation, but this is primarily a distraction and a way to suck money out of organizations like the NRA. As they distract us, they make real progress using their more subtle divide-and-conquer approaches.

For example, they might make it increasingly difficult and expensive to own a hunting preserve. However, most hunters don't hunt on a preserve, so few will come to their aid. Divide-and-conquer works.

They also initiate actions designed to drive up the cost of gun ownership, and reduce opportunities to practice by making ammunition and practice increasingly expensive. Even when they fail to "win" with broad, sweeping legislation, they nevertheless win with their back-door tactics.

Using the Environmental Protection Agency (EPA), the anti-gun crowd is striving to expand laws on lead contamination which the EPA interprets as applicable to gun ranges. (There are also efforts underway to use the Toxic Substance Control Act and other EPA regulations to ban ammunition generally, due to the gases released by the gunpowder when a gun is discharged. Even if this scheme is unsuccessful at banning ammunition, it is likely that new controls will be implemented which will drive up the cost of ammunition and limit the number of manufacturers who have the capability to meet the stringent new standards.) Using the Occupational Safety and Health Administration (OSHA), the anti-gun crowd is seeking to increase safety regulations, so the facilities of gun ranges must become more elaborate.

When new regulations only impact a small group, such as the range owners in this example, most gun owners are oblivious to the impact and therefore not motivated to intervene. This strategy is working.

As it becomes more costly to operate a gun range, many ranges are being forced out of business. New gun ranges find it increasingly complex to open. As a result, it is becoming more and more difficult and expensive for gun owners to practice. At some point we can expect to see new regulations which force gun owners to have gun insurance. Over time, time insurance companies will begin to require professional training and frequent practice to maintain the policy. The cost of increasingly expensive practice, and the reduced number of gun ranges, will make compliance difficult or impossible.

What we are seeing is a very slick approach. Gun owners are being hit with higher range costs, higher ammunition costs, higher insurance costs, and other controls which restrict ownership. As a result many will be priced out of gun ownership, while others won't bother because the web of requirements is too complex. The poor, who are often the ones who need a gun most due to high crime rates in their neighborhoods, will be unable to afford gun ownership. This is tragic.

The 2nd Amendment may remain intact, but citizens will find it increasingly difficult to invoke it. You've got to hand it to the anti-gun crowd, they are clever.

At the same time, the anti-gun crowd is increasing harassment of gun owners using sympathetic prosecutors and criminal courts, and they are seeking to expand civil liability. More and more we are seeing the courts used to attack and financially ruin honest law-abiding gun owners. As these developments receive publicity, many gun owners will become increasingly fearful of these mercenary courts and government agencies. These abuses will result in gun owners voluntarily getting rid of their guns. Support for the 2nd Amendment will dwindle.

Intimidation of gun owners is yet another technique being used. Police SWAT teams and federal law enforcement agencies are being used to 'raid' the homes of honest, law-abiding citizens. It's become routine for black-masked military-equipped officers and agents to kick in the doors of homes during the middle of the night to search for contraband. Parents and children are thrown from their beds, and submachine guns are pointed at their heads as the house is searched. Most often there is no intelligence to support these tactics, and oftentimes no significant contraband is found. In 1985 there were 3,000 "no knock" raids such as this in the United States, but by 2011 this number had grown to 80,000. An Orwellian police state has apparently arrived.[168]

What is the objective? If gun owners are made to live in fear, they are more likely to voluntarily surrender their firearms to avoid these confrontations. Secondly, these unwarranted and unconstitutional searches will eventually lead to armed resistance, and just like with Fast and Furious, the anti-gun zealots will create excuses to clamp down further on the public and the citizen Right to keep and bear arms. It's additionally unfortunate that police officers and federal agents are being duped, and participating in violating the Constitution that they have sworn to uphold. To combat this misuse of power, organizations such as Oath Keepers[169] (www.OathKeepers.org) are springing up to support the officer's rights to refuse these unlawful orders.

In the process, we can expect to see the incremental confiscation of firearms using 'public health' justifications. These might include prohibition of gun ownership, and seizures of guns from veterans. To disarm these skilled gun users and potential firearm instructors, they might use a combination of financial incentives and new definitions of mental illness.

Sad cases of Post Traumatic Stress Disorder (PTSD) will likely be used to make it easier to claim military veteran benefits. Veterans will be encouraged to apply, and monthly stipends will become easy to acquire. Then, the axe will drop. Veterans will be prohibited from gun ownership based on a 'mental health' clause in the law.

Beyond this, new definitions of mental illness will likely be used to disqualify large segments of the veteran population from gun ownership, particularly those with combat experience as they *might* have a propensity toward violence.

Other segments of the population likely to be similarly targeted are divorced or separated couples, especially those who have children. The authorities will claim that this segment of society is prone to emotional outbursts and may suffer from a repressed but potentially volatile mental state.

New frontal-attack gun seizure laws will probably not be passed until a large part of the voting population has already been excluded from gun ownership. They will keep trying, and mass-shooting events will continue to be exploited to try and pass sweeping laws, but these high-visibility laws are not necessary for the anti-gun crowd to reach their objective.

By frontal attacks, by cunningly regulations, by intimidation and increased financial liability, and by campaigns which exert social pressure, gun ownership will become increasingly difficult. The anti-gun crowd will do whatever it takes to achieve their disarmament objective, and they are cunning adversaries.

At some point, you can also expect prohibitions and seizures which focus on certain groups. Bible-believing people, Christians, and other people of Faith are an obvious target.

Do you think that this is highly unlikely? If you haven't been on the inside of these schemes you'll probably think all this is farfetched. But it isn't.

Where do we Americans get the arrogance that we will avoid persecution? The United States has been blessed by God due to our past faithfulness to the precepts of His Word, the Bible, but how can we expect this to continue? As a national policy we have allowed the United States to demean God and His Bible, so why do we think that God's hand of protection will remain with us? If Christians and Jews in the rest of the world are suffering persecution, which they are, why do we think that we will continue to be exempt?

Walk through this with me. Let me show you how this could be accomplished.

This won't happen tomorrow, but I have personal knowledge from insiders that the rabid anti-gun crowd is actively working on various divide-and-conquer strategies, and one of these is to single out Christians and other people of Faith. These plans may not develop exactly as I describe here. To be clear, I've not included the following scenario as a prediction, but rather to illustrate how this divide-and-conquer strategy is being used to target specific subset groups of gun owners.

Over time and absent nationwide revival, I think that the disarming of people of Faith can easily be accomplished using a shrewd and patient strategy such as this:

If a person has ever been associated with a Bible-believing church or conservative religious organization, or if they have expressed belief in the Bible or biblical principles on a social media site, etc., these people may one day find themselves disqualified for gun ownership.

How is this possible? As we move down this road of disarm-America strategies, it is becoming increasing probable that government authorities will label Christian organizations and Bible-believing people as intolerant and guilty of 'hate crimes,' and Jews as dangerous Zionists, just because these people don't agree with politically correct attitudes on various social and political issues. (For example, homosexuality, marriage, abortion, euthanasia, Israel's statehood, etc.) As a result of these beliefs or associations, people of Faith could individually be considered guilty of 'hate crimes' based solely on affiliation or beliefs, not on any act or action.

Before or after this pronouncement, it would be a simple matter to pass a law which disqualifies a person from gun ownership if they are guilty of a hate crime. Think about it. Pastors in Canada are already being charged with hate crimes just for preaching on what the Bible has to say about homosexuality and marriage. Why is it such a stretch that this could also happen in the U.S.?

Who would oppose a law which bans members of an extremist group, like the neo-Nazi party, from gun ownership? It would be easy to pass a law such as this, especially after a domestic terrorist incident happened and a group like the neo-Nazis was responsible. After this new 'hate crime' law is passed, administrative policy could start adding groups which are also considered to be guilty of hate crimes. This isn't legal, but the Department of Justice is already doing things such as this. (This is another example of why we need to return to the Constitution and the Rule of Law.)

Initially, the Department of Justice (DOJ) might add members of obvious groups, such as the people who are included on the FBI's Terrorist Watch List. Later, this could be expanded to include any hate group. At that point, it wouldn't be a leap for the DOJ to administratively apply the 'hate group' gun ban to Bible-believing Christians. It's a slippery slope, and we're already started to slide.

What do you think? Is this plausible?

As the gun-control strategy becomes increasingly successful, we will see transitional techniques like this develop. In addition to government manipulation, we will see efforts directed toward the development of new social values which include anti-gun ideals. This might take several forms, but it will probably be a new 'peace' or 'global citizen' movement.

At this stage it will become a simple matter for the nation to willingly accept an expansion into extreme gun-control laws, including seizures. Overt and subliminal media campaigns will be used to influence those portions of the population which are not personally affected by a proposed gun ban. At some point, willing disarmament will be touted as 'patriotic' or 'responsible.' Or, that Americans need to cast-off their gun fetish and lead the world to a new era of 'peace,' and that we need to lead by example. Those who resist will be ostracized as Neanderthal and anti-progressive.

As techniques such as these are implemented, these power-hungry people will begin to adapt the Constitution to support their other ambitions, as well. As gun ownership dwindles, these 'Progressives' and self-proclaimed "Brights"[170] will be able to persecute opponents without risk of reprisal, because they will have effectively disarmed the population. Anyone who disagrees with their agenda will be marginalized, or worse.

Yet, gun control is only one aspect of the 'control' strategy. Another part of the strategy is to misuse, and overuse, the term "Constitutional Right." The objective of this strategy is to desensitize people so that they will no longer think of the Constitution and the Bill of Rights as something special.

For example, advocates of the *"Patient Protection and Affordable Care Act"* (Obama Care) are promoting health care as a *Constitutional right*, when the Constitution has nothing to say about it being the government's duty to provide universal health care. You may like or dislike Obama Care, but we all need to understand that it isn't defensible as a constitutionally protected right. To do so is pure sophistry.

Also, it's important to understand that pro-gun advocates may be legitimately concerned with hunting or gun-sport rights, but this is not the reason we have the 2nd Amendment in our Bill of Rights. Pro-gun people sometimes argue that this is why we have the 2nd Amendment, but this isn't accurate. The 2nd Amendment was added to the Constitution primarily to protect our God-given Right to self-defense and liberty. It gives us the ability to protect ourselves against criminals, and from other threats to liberty, both foreign and domestic. Yes, it does protect hunters and sportsmen, but it wasn't included in the Constitution for that purpose.

Our nation's Founders understood the importance of gun ownership to counter tyranny. Based on their personal experiences in England and Europe, they recognized that the growth of an oppressive government is inevitable when the people are disarmed. That's why this is such an important issue for all of us today, even for those who don't want to own a gun.

As a result of a wide array of shrewd strategies,[171] as well as happenstance occurrences which are exploited, today we are seeing the United States government, and local governments around the country, usurp the power of *"We The People."*

How is this happening? As my history-professor father was fond of saying, "It isn't just one thing, it's a multi-causation problem." In other words, it's a number of things happening at the same time. For example, this usurpation of power is made possible by a dumbed-down electorate.[172] This is the result of the elimination of meaningful history and civics education in our schools,[173] it is nurtured by a mainstream media that is politically motivated, and a public which is poorly educated, self-absorbed and distracted.

It's also facilitated by voter fraud (allowing people to vote in elections without government-issued photo ID, the Department of Justice's failure to prosecute voter fraud, voter intimidation, etc.), the fostering of entitlement attitudes, government spending designed to solidify and broaden political support among blocks of voters, open immigration which bolsters the political base of candidates who appeal to these groups, the elimination of standards of morality, a mainstream media which is ideologically in lock-step with a 'Progressive' and anti-God ideologies, the creation of a false understanding of the separation of Church and State (which, by the way, isn't in the Constitution), a judicial system oriented to case law rather than justice, etc.

On and on and on goes the list of reasons. Each one individually significant, but together they create a downhill-rolling snowball effect that is growing in size and speed. Each contributes more momentum and expands the magnitude of the problem. As a result, we are quickly tumbling toward a crisis.

Political agendas now permeate and control our society at every level. Truth, honesty, and justice have been thrown on the garbage heap as if they are antiquated concepts. Attacks on the family, church, and other institutions which resist, are intensifying. But at the core of these conflicts is not politics, but warring worldviews. One worldview has the Bible at its foundation; the other is contrived by the beliefs of people such as Sigmund Freud, Karl Marx and Charles Darwin.

In regard to gun control, the conflict will not be resolved by doing a better job of articulating the 'facts' about crime and gun control. The anti-gun people are not swayed by the truth. Many of them are controlled by emotion, but all of them are guided by their worldview. And their worldview has more to do with elitism, and survival of the fittest, than it does public safety or protecting children. Only when we understand these motivations can we work to defuse these unhealthy social and political time-bombs.

Gun control should not be our only concern, nor should it be the sole focus of our activism. But gun control may be the most important contemporary issue because of the ramifications, and because it is winnable. The general public is not onboard with the *Progressive* agenda, but many are duped by it.

No matter what the anti-gun crowd says, we need to keep in mind that gun control is *not* about public safety; it's about power and *people control.*

Regrettably, there are a lot of good people in the anti-gun camp who are being duped by wonderful-sounding rhetoric. These people are not part of the inner-circle of the anti-gun power brokers, so they fail to see what's really going on. In a sense, they are also victims of these schemes.

Every day, nice well-meaning people are conned by the anti-gun leadership who talk passionately about crime control and community safety. We need to remind these beguiled people that if it was truly about crime reduction, then relevant gun and crime statistics would vanquish their anti-gun arguments. Instead, the anti-gun advocates respond with character assassination, mean-spirited comments, and emotion-based arguments; then they wait for the next tragedy so that they can use it to manipulate public opinion.

We need to hammer away using the truth, explaining that the capacity of a gun's magazine to hold more cartridges, assault rifles in the hands of sane civilians, and other gun control measures have no noteworthy effect on crime. (Keeping guns out of the hands of criminals and the mentally ill, is a good thing. But laws which hamper good people are not helpful, nor are they Constitutional.) Interestingly, we already have an abundance of laws to keep guns out of the hands of mentally ill people, but most of these aren't enforced. What does this tell you about the real objective?

The real issue at play is not just political supremacy, but power, and we need to remember this fact. The social elites think that they are smarter than everyone else, that they know what is best for society, and that people who have a religious faith are weak minded and need to be tranquilized or subjugated. Their idea as to what is 'best' is for the population to slavishly obey; or at least be subservient to their enlightened benefactors.

Importantly, just as a violent criminal can be thwarted by an armed homeowner, these elites understand that they can't control, and force their agenda on an armed population. This is the crux of what inspires their antigun agenda, and it is precisely this that our Founding Fathers sought to prevent when they penned the Constitution and the Bill of Rights.

What most people don't realize is that we already have literally thousands of gun laws on the books. Just like failed social policies, the reaction to these failures isn't to admit that these anti-gun strategies (and philosophies) don't work, but to keep piling on new laws.

Just as we have failed social programs on top of failed social programs, we have gun laws upon gun laws. We have thousands of gun laws that don't reduce crime but are nevertheless costly and burdensome. This is why many gun-owners resist new gun laws. The content of a proposed law might seem reasonable, but the volume of laws has made it nearly impossible to be law abiding. We don't need to add more laws—especially when they will be ineffectual laws for crime reduction.

On the other hand, this abundance of gun laws does have a very real effect: *It intimidates and impedes honest people from owning and using guns, and from exercising their 2nd Amendment Rights which are guaranteed to them by the U.S. Constitution.* This isn't an accident. It's all part of this power-grab strategy.

By definition, law abiding people don't want to violate the law, even unintentionally. They certainly don't want to unknowingly tread on one of the hundreds of obscure gun laws, because they also know that the legal world is full of complexity. So given the option, they will often sidestep the whole issue to avoid the complexity of the law and the potential for accidently violating some arcane legal statute.

Combine this with our era of professionalization fused with government growth, and we observe that many people feel that they don't need to own a gun, anyway. They observe that we have well trained police officers to protect us, and a government that wants to take care of us, so they think they can avoid personal responsibility.

As a result, personal responsibility becomes increasingly rare, and liberty crumbles. The "Nanny State" is able to secure more and more control over our lives.

It is important to remember that there are many 'good' people, including Christians, who are simply duped by the emotional rhetoric of the anti-gun activists. Unfortunately, these good people are exploited to further the goals of the élite—an élite who believe that the ends not only justify the means, but an élite which consists primarily of *predators.*

Schooled in Darwinism, they easily justify their 'survival of the fittest' methods. They even make it appear to be laudable, and they promote their worldview as 'progressive' or 'enlightened.'

Setting aside all talk of conspiracy theories, at this point we have cause to pause. In my view, at this juncture it is almost irrelevant if an organized conspiracy exists. Frankly, I don't really care at this point.

What I do care about is that if we aren't diligent, this is going to become an even bigger problem in the future.

Consider what is quietly happening all around us. Think about gun control in relation to these current-day developments:

In an era of deficit spending and staggering government debt, the United States government is going to extraordinary lengths, and initiating a staggering amount of new spending, to prepare for domestic upheaval. If this upheaval does strike, we, as individuals, will need to be well armed and well trained, and we will need to be prepared, just as Jesus teaches us in Luke 22:36.

Why is the government preparing for this upheaval? Are they simply engaging in appropriate but general contingency planning? Or, are they actually anticipating something which is more specific?

I don't know, but obviously our government is going to great lengths to prepare for social unrest. That is obvious. (For details, read the following chapter, "Signs of the Times.")

There are those who see a link between these government preparations and gun control. Maybe, maybe not. The truth is elusive in this regard, and many people have different theories on the subject. But there are a couple of things which we can know with certainty:

We know that gun control is relevant today, and it looks like it will be an even more important freedom to protect in the future. Facts which are obvious are...

1. Gun control is an organized effort to disarm the American people.

2. This is happening at a time when, more than ever before, we need to be armed. Our government is obviously planning for, and anticipating, social upheaval. It would be foolish for us to ignore their massive planning efforts. Unfortunately, gun-control efforts are gaining public support at a time when we can least afford it. It has never been more important to be armed.

Not only do we have a biblical and moral duty to oppose gun control. Not only do we have a Constitution-supporting reason to defeat gun control. It is now more important than ever to support pro 2nd Amendment Rights groups like the National Rifle Association,[174] and to use our networks of friends to educate the public on the truth about gun control, and to undertake other strategic actions. In addition to all these worthy things, we also need to renew our own efforts to prepare for uncertain times.

At this point, the only form of new gun control
we should endorse involves…
a strong stance, smooth trigger pull, and proper sight alignment.

***"Those who would give up essential Liberty,
to purchase a little temporary Safety,
deserve neither Liberty nor Safety."***[175]

**- Benjamin Franklin,
Founding Father**

Chapter 18

Signs of the Times

At the start of each of our firearm self-defense classes we ask our students, *"What motivated you to take this class?"* In the past their answers have been straightforward. They are there to learn how to protect themselves or their loved ones, from becoming a victim of crime. Either they had personally experienced some criminal incident, or some friend or news story had prompted them to gain instruction.

Three years ago the answers to this question began to change significantly. Today, more than half our students are seeking firearm self-defense training in response to changing signs-of-the-times.[176]

So what are the signs-of-the-times? What has changed?

As I review our classroom surveys, I can bundle our student's answers into two summary motivations:

1. They observe a sharp increase in economic instability, both nationally and internationally.

2. They see various indicators of an increase in social instability, and indicators of impending adversity, social upheaval or the breakdown of services. Further, that there is a very real possibility that these may combine to create a major calamity, or at least a crisis event in the not so distant future.

The potential to become a victim of crime is ever present, and our students still identify "protection from crime" as one motivating factor somewhere on their list. However, it is the combination of other signs-of-the-times which was the primary motivation for them to attend class.

In our surveys, each of our students prioritizes their list somewhat differently, but each agrees that they want to be prepared for the disastrous times which they believe are coming. While most people just gripe about their concerns, these men and women[177] want to make sure that, like the ant mentioned in the below Proverb, they are being proactive. They want to prepare. For them, a firearm self-defense class is just one component of their preparation. I agree with their conclusions.

There is a well-known Bible passage in the Book of Proverbs which is often quoted as a description of lazy people, but if we take a closer look at the entire passage with signs-of-the-times in mind, we see that the intended meaning is much deeper.

Modern English Translation:

> *"Take a lesson from the ants, you lazybones. Learn from their ways and become wise! Though they have no prince or governor or ruler to make them work, they labor hard all summer, gathering food for the winter.'*
>
> *"But you, lazybones, how long will you sleep? When will you wake up? A little extra sleep, a little more slumber, a little folding of the hands to rest—then poverty will pounce on you like a bandit; scarcity will attack you like an armed robber."*
>
> Proverbs 6:6-11 NLT

———

King James Version:

> *6 Go to the ant, thou sluggard; consider her ways, and be wise:*
>
> *7 Which having no guide, overseer, or ruler,*
>
> *8 Provideth her meat in the summer, and gathereth her food in the harvest.*
>
> *9 How long wilt thou sleep, O sluggard? when wilt thou arise out of thy sleep?*
>
> *10 Yet a little sleep, a little slumber, a little folding of the hands to sleep:*
>
> *11 So shall thy poverty come as one that travelleth, and thy want as an armed man.*
>
> Proverbs 6:6-11 KJV

———

As this famous Bible proverb suggests, we need to wake up. If we dig deeper into what this passage is telling us, we'll see that it's not just about individuals who spend too much time in bed, but rather an issue of focus, priorities, and big-picture preparations. As we consider our current signs-of-the-times, these signs seem to indicate that we are coming to the end of the "harvest" season referred to in the proverb. Are we diligently preparing for the "winter" when scarcity will be upon us?

Given the opportunity, most people look to leisure when their employer isn't directing their activities. In their free time, whenever possible, most people turn to relaxation and diversion. Not that a little R&R is a bad thing;[178] it's just that our responsibilities need to include more than just living in the present. We are to diligently prepare for the future, and this isn't just building a retirement fund. We are to have 'faith' in God's care, but He clearly tells us that we have a responsibility to personally do what we can to prepare.

As this proverb reminds us, scarcity will attack us like a robber if we don't respond to the signs-of-the-times with astute preparations.

In the Old Testament, God used a king's vision to provide Joseph with the wherewithal to prepare for a famine that would last for seven years (Genesis 41-45); and in the New Testament, Jesus made it clear that we are not to take unnecessary risks. Risk-taking isn't faith in action, it's insolence.

To take unnecessary risks is to arrogantly try to force a test upon God, a behavior which is essentially an attempt to manipulate God. This is an evil misapplication of faith (Matthew 4:5-7). Moreover, 'faith' isn't an excuse to justify laziness, either. The attitude that *"God will take care of me so I'm not going to prepare"* is not faith, its foolishness. God does not promise to protect us from the effects of being idle.

Jesus' injunction which is chronicled in Luke 22:36, actually requires us to be prepared. What did Jesus say, specifically? Jesus told us to prepare financially, prepare with provisions, and prepare for defense. So working on preparedness serves an important purpose, and it also demonstrates that we are being obedient to Jesus' instructions. To fail to prepare is actually a sin – not a sin of commission (something we do that is wrong), but a sin of omission (something we should do, but don't).

This book has focused on the issue of firearm defense, but I would be remiss if I didn't point out that this is only one track of preparation. Being prepared for defense is one of our most basic needs, but there is more that needs to be done.

We also need to *prioritize* our tasks of preparation. More to the point, we need to be balanced in our approach so that we are thorough, and *painstakingly complete* in our preparations.

Having an orientation toward becoming prepared does not mean we should become "*the-sky-is-falling*" doomsday-ers. It's simply that we need to be prudent. We need to live full, vibrant lives today, while also preparing for the future.

Responsible people who are able, prepare for retirement. They also buy insurance for their vehicles and homes, and they obtain medical insurance in case they become sick or injured. Similarly, we need to do what we can to prepare for living life in the future; a future which will probably look very different than today.

This has always been true, but now, since there is an increasing number of disturbing signs-of-the-times trends which have serious implications, we need to ratchet-up our preparations. Because of these signs, our preparations need to be undertaken more earnestly.

I'm not recommending that everyone quit their job and build a bunker at a rural location, but I do think that we need to prepare as if disaster might strike tomorrow; as well as plan diligently with a second-tier of more elaborate preparations. We need to utilize a most-important-first strategy that will take a year or more to accomplish, and then continue to refine and improve. I think we need to prepare for natural disasters, and also for unprecedented un-natural disasters.

If this signs-of-the-times discussion is a relatively new concept for you, I suspect that you will recoil at what I've compiled in this editorial. Nonetheless, I encourage you to use this as an opportunity to digest what I've said, and then start compiling your own list of "signs." When we prayerfully reflect on our lists, and read and talk with others who are knowledgeable, we pave the way for a reasoned response.

Your conclusions may be very different from mine, but as iron-sharpens-iron,[179] together we can calmly and prayerfully prepare for the future. My recommendation is that we don't focus on survival, but for changing times. Integral to this is our need to prepare for new opportunities. Major changes will also bring important new opportunities to serve others and our Creator.

In my opinion, absent revival and the restoration of God's blessing, some form of significant economic collapse of the United States, the UK, Europe and perhaps a large portion of the world, is inevitable. Our financial situation is simply unsustainable. Like a family who is using new credit cards to make payments on their current credit card debt, as well as to buy groceries for today, our nation's financial house of cards will collapse at some point. Our current national debt, habitual borrowing and out of control spending, isn't sustainable.

Due to federal and local government debt, unfunded liabilities and deficit spending, plus the downward spiral of the value of the dollar, coupled with a society which has an ever increasing appetite for government entitlement programs, portend disaster. The inevitable major increase in taxes will stagnate the economy, and at some point, sooner or later, we will probably experience some form of economic collapse. This may take the form of an extremely difficult period for a few years or it may be catastrophic in magnitude, but the change will be substantial. Corrective action is unavoidable.

This isn't just my opinion.

Our government is actively preparing for major social upheaval. Contingency planning is the duty of responsible government, certainly, but these current preparations seem to go far beyond normal preparations. Executive Orders such as the 2012 *"National Defense Authorization Act"* (March 16, 2012),[180] are staggering in scope. But that's not the end of it.

If this was just routine contingency planning, it is unlikely that they would put to paper odious and unconstitutional presidential executive orders which offend liberals and conservatives alike. But even more significant is that in this era of budget crisis and deficit spending, we are devouring billions of dollars on these preparations. This isn't crony politics, and it isn't pork barrel allocations, it's a unified and comprehensive, major strategic undertaking.

We are observing joint military and police actions in every major city in the U.S.; "war games" with scenarios which purport to use terrorism as the reason for the exercise, but don't really have a credible relationship to terrorism. These exercises are unconstitutional, and they are scaring the American public who get caught-up in these exercises, and yet they do not provide anyone with a political benefit. Even the notoriously liberal Huffington Post reports that the president "quietly placed the United States on a war preparedness footing." [181]

We also see that innocuous government agencies such as National Oceanic and Atmospheric Administration (NOAA), which have no security or law enforcement function, being armed with SWAT gear and military equipment. Why do NOAA and similar agencies need SWAT teams?

At the same time, the Department of Homeland Security is buying thousands of military tank-like vehicles (MRAP – 'Mine Resistant Ambush Protected' armored military trucks) and war equipment for use here at home. I've seen the purchase order. Each major urban center and FEMA region will have hundreds of these MRAP tanks cached for immediate use. These actions aren't secret, this all 'public record' information.

As the name implies, the Department of Homeland Security was established to provide increased security and safety inside our nation's borders. It isn't part of our military. Yet, they have apparently issued purchase orders for more handgun and rifle ammunition than was expended in several years of war in Iraq. Ominously, this ammunition is of a type which is illegal for our military to use; ammunition which is particularly destructive against soft targets (human flesh). [182]

What's going on? This is far more elaborate, and extensive, than just routine training, disaster-prep stockpiling, or what is needed to secure discounts by placing large orders. It is unprecedented in scope.

On the local level, we are seeing federal funding of military training for law enforcement officers, and the delivery of advanced weaponry and military equipment to state, county and local police departments. This includes funds to expand the number of local-police and federal police SWAT teams, funding for even small communities to purchase armored vehicles (in addition to the MRAP tanks), military-style body armor and tactical gear for police officers, the distribution of high-tech surveillance drones equipped with FLIR systems which can look through the walls of buildings, and the nationwide delivery of inefficient off-road capable SUV police vehicles which are replacing energy-efficient and more maneuverable police cars, even in places where it never snows.

We are also observing the construction of regional refugee camps, which the government is calling 'Residential Centers' or 'Internment and Resettlement' (I/R) Centers. Each of these is surrounded by guard towers, and walls within walls of barbwire and razor-ribbon fences facing inward. (Inward facing barbed wire is an indicator that the perceived threat is inside the fence). A majority of these are being built under the supervision of the Federal Emergency Management Agency (FEMA), while others are apparently funded by the U.S. Centers for Disease Control and Prevention (CDC) and other state and federal agencies.

Some of these facilities are FEMA owned, but most are either constructed using land at closed military facilities, or fully owned and maintained by private corporations under contract to FEMA, CDC, or the Department of Homeland Security. Therefore, most of these facilities are not included in the list of government properties which is maintained by the General Services Administration, so reliable factual details are scarce. Yet, irregardless of creative accounting practices, each documented Residential Center or I/R camp is clearly designed for either the incarceration or forced-quarantine of thousands of people.

It's estimated that there are as many as 800 of these camps being prepared within the U.S. If you doubt the reality of this development, note that for several *years* the U.S. Army has been actively recruiting staff for these I/R facilities. Further, you can read about the concentration camp-like design and management procedures in U.S. Army publication, FM 3-39.40 "Internment and Resettlement Operations."[183] This government publication provides specifics on the design, layout, and the management of these domestic facilities once they are activated.

Photos and some information about these camps is publically available, yet the purpose of these emergency camps remains somewhat obscure. Nevertheless, the serious nature of the planning is evident, additionally so as photos of a government leased storage facility in Georgia have surfaced which document a stockpile of 500,000 plastic coffins—just at that one location.[184]

These are just a few of the many preparations which are happening all around us. Much of this is clearly part of a unified strategy. Is it simply out-of-control contingency planning for disasters, or is it something else? What do you think?

None of this is secret information. It's just under reported by the media.

To accomplish these elaborate preparations, the U.S. Government is borrowing billions of dollars at a time of fiscal crisis, when the federal government is borrowing $ .46 of every $1.00 they spend. Therefore these preparations must be in response to a credible threat to justify this level of spending during a budget crisis. With this factor in mind, if this is such a high priority for our government that they are borrowing money to finance these preparations, then maybe we ought to get serious about getting prepared, too.

It would be guesswork to put a finger on a specific point on a graph, and say that our economy will crumple on a specific date. Nevertheless, a radical change must occur in the near future. We will either voluntarily make these changes now, by making difficult decisions and accepting deep-cutting austerity measures; or, involuntarily, as the result of a disastrous economic crash sometime in the not-to-distant future.

Optimistic to a fault, the American people and most Western countries do not exhibit the willingness to voluntarily enact austerity measures. This delay will likely cause a larger, unmanageable crisis.

Either way, we can expect that those who have become government dependent will continue to demand what the government can no longer deliver. As has occurred in Greece, Spain and elsewhere, social unrest will inevitably occur. For the U.S., our situation is both national and international in scope and effect. For us there won't be a European Union, International Monetary Fund, or a government-funded bailout to help us recover. As a result, at some point I expect social unrest and lawlessness in the United States to be rampant, and magnified in intensity because there won't be anyone to help bail us out.

The fires of social unrest will also be fueled by moral decay which has stripped away conscience and a sense of right and wrong. As a result, when this happens we can expect many of our urban centers to be literally consumed by riots and anarchy.

It's important for us to understand that this destabilizing set of circumstances will likely not be very predictable. We will not be able to identify a specific day of reckoning by charting these events on a timeline. More likely, there will be a "tipping point" brought about by a cascading series of unrelated events, or some unrelated major incident.

We have a natural tendency to think about economic and social decline as a trend which we can chart on a graph, and then try to extrapolate to a date when things will fall apart. Unfortunately, our current situation is not that predictable. Just as the fall of the Soviet Union was a surprise to everyone, so it will likely be for us when a series of events suddenly snowball into an unstoppable force that brings radical change. If we are fortunate, this rebalancing of our economic system will last for a decade or two. However, since the situation is declining rapidly, recovery may take a very long time.

Some Christians expect Jesus to return before things get too bad. Maybe so. But the Bible does not provide us with any guarantee that we won't suffer serious adversity before that happens. Though we may not be here for the Great Tribulation as described in the Book of Revelation, that cataclysmic time will likely be preceded by an escalation of adversity.

Are you willing to gamble with your family's health and welfare? Do you think that a major crisis is unlikely? What if you are wrong?

Even if we consider signs-of-the-times such as national debt, moral decline and other key economic and cultural indicators, it will likely be some other event, or the domino effect of several unrelated events which will tip the balance. In other words, a "tipping point" that drops us over the edge into an era of radical social and economic upheaval. This tipping-point might be reached due to economic decline, but more likely it will be financial instability, *plus* something else. Like a house of cards which suddenly collapses, our social structures can crumble relatively quickly. Like that final card which adds too much weight and instability to a house of cards, various events, in combination with other factors, might cause a sudden crash.

This tipping-point might be reached as a result of something simple, such as added stress to the system. This could be brought about overnight by something like a natural storm or another major disaster which impacts a large portion of the United States. Or, it might be the result of a progressive drought over a period of months which gradually diminishes food and water supplies; or within a few weeks as a widespread epidemic or antibiotic-resistant pandemic develops; or as a result too many weeks of an ongoing nationwide labor strike or political upheaval; or a multi-city terrorist incident or EMP attack, or something as simple as computer hackers or a crippling computer virus that shuts down our power grid, which would force our banks and businesses to close for weeks or months.

Or, it could be the result of dozens of other potential occurrences, big or small. Even a series of relatively minor events can become like a rolling snowball, producing increasingly dangerous effects as it builds and rolls along. Any combination of events, such as these, could instigate a cascade effect which leads to a major collapse. Our current situation is precarious.

If the United States economy and culture was still strong, the country would be able to withstand a lot of stress to the system. However, if the U.S. is hit now by a major event or a cascading series of small events, it can easily falter. As a result of our weakened condition, it would not take a lot to tip us into a crisis.

Further, we Americans tend to think of ourselves as friendly and peaceable people, but there are people and nations who hate us. We do have enemies, and our enemies are already aware of our weakened condition. If they are given the chance, we can expect them to exploit our vulnerabilities.

If this crunch-time happens soon, it's probably better as it may not be as devastating. If it happens ten years from now, and we have not undertaken a massive overhaul of our debt and spending problems, restoration to life-as-we-know-it-today may actually be impossible. This may sound like doomsday talk, but an honest appraisal of the facts supports this viewpoint. Either way, major collapse or minor crunch, there are many indicators which make it clear that we are headed toward trouble. When our nation stumbles as a result of these developments, we must be prepared to face it.

Our government is actively engaged in preparing for this type of major upheaval. We can too—and we'd better.

If anything like this happens, the need for firearm defense may take on a whole new meaning. Desperate people do desperate things. We need to be prepared for defense today, and for tomorrow, too. This means that we need to also prepare to respond to a whole new set of moral dilemmas.

As a whole, even if our nation is devastated, individually, and as families and cadres of friends, we have the opportunity to prepare to weather the coming storm. If we are adequately prepared, we will also be ready to experience a time of unprecedented opportunity. If equipped for it, we will be able to serve as the hands and feet of Jesus to need-filled communities and neighbors. And, we will need to be active as peace-makers. (A valuable network of resources is being developed at: www.SheepdogGuardian.com).

What exactly will happen as a result of the coming crunch? We can only guess, and anyone who claims to know is delusional. Due to many interrelated factors of multi-causation crisis, there are many scenarios which might play out. There are hundreds of interrelated causal factors in the physical world, and also in the unseen spiritual realm, and both will come into play.

Various combinations of these different circumstances would produce different results. However, we can nevertheless diligently prepare physically and spiritually.

First, we need to prepare *broadly* as we can't predict exactly what we will encounter. Fortunately, there are common threads of preparation which run through the center of each likely scenario. For example, we can broadly prepare for physical defense, water, food, shelter, health, defensible space, and long-term sustainability. These are the places to start. Only when we have completed these universal preparations should we give much attention to individual scenarios.

When economic or social collapse happens, the American people will have the opportunity to pull together and weather the storm. If we do, we will emerge stronger and more quickly. But more likely, due to moral decay and a social attitude of entitlement, we will experience large-scale acts of theft, rioting, animal-like violence, rampant lawlessness and anarchy. Due to the magnitude of the problem, we cannot expect the government to cope. Therefore, we need to prepare as if help isn't coming. If help does arrive, that's great. If it doesn't, we need to be ready to go it alone with a cadre of family and friends. It will be impossible to do it alone.

Keep in mind that if the coming crunch lasts longer than 2-3 weeks, which is very likely, many who are honest and good citizens during 'normal' times will become violent when they (and their children) become hungry. Therefore, we need to be prepared to retreat to a place where we can ideally be unseen, while remaining vigilant and cautious.

Do you have friends who live in a rural location who would appreciate your help? Make arrangements now, and prepare the location with provisions, etc. The best location will be 200-300^{+} miles from a major urban center and at least 10-miles away from a major highway.

The best firearm defense is to be ready to use your gun, but to settle in a place where you likely won't need to use it. Hope for the best, prepare for the worst.

People we trust today may not be trustworthy during these times. We must keep this in mind. We need to also keep in mind that if people start starving, even if we give away all of our food and starve our own family, our act of 'kindness' will likely not accomplish anything. We are talking about preparing for extremely difficult circumstances and new moral choices; occurrences and decisions which are *far* beyond anything that most of us have ever faced.

For some, a circumstance of this magnitude sounds impossible. Yet, I urge you to give serious consideration to these possibilities. If it turns out to be something less serious, you'll be well prepared for that eventuality, too. However, just like the government and their contingency planning, we need to prepare for the worst case scenario.

Furthermore, if nothing big ever happens, your efforts won't have been wasted. The odds are high that at some point you will utilize these same preparations to respond to a natural disaster.

If a serious crisis does occur, the police and other government agencies will quickly be overwhelmed. This is well understood, so now, for the first time ever, federal agencies and the military are preparing for major offensive and defensive operations in our local communities. Again, this is not just my personal viewpoint. The government is now spending billions of dollars to prepare for this type of collapse.

The federal government's contingency plan includes the option to 'quarantine' hotbed areas to keep violence (or disease) from spreading. If this is implemented in your area and you have failed to leave, you will be cut-off and completely alone. Help will not be coming anytime soon. Therefore, it may be far safer to abandon your home and city early, and 'bug-out' to a pre-arranged rural location in advance of the closure.

During this time many good people will be victimized by both rampaging criminals and by government neglect. FEMA camps and other refugee areas will be established. However, if the problem persists, these areas will become sites of even greater disaster.

Since I have been involved in government and community contingency planning for disasters, and personally experienced several, this is an area in which I have some experience. I encourage you to think this through yourself, but I'll share with you one scenario which I think is likely:

Even now when we are living in a time of peace, consider that the inside of our prisons are literally controlled by the inmates. Consider that V.A. hospitals which are government run and well established, are feeble and inadequate. So imagine what will happen inside hundreds of government refugee camps set-up for this crisis—when preparations have been made quickly and are ad hoc? You don't want to go there.

If you think I'm overstating, take a closer look at what happened in the Louisiana Superdome after hurricane Katrina in 2005. Since the Superdome had previously been used as an emergency shelter on two prior occasions, the government had it pre-staged with emergency supplies and equipment. Yet, it still became its own disaster area for 20,000 people, much worse than the devastation experienced by those who remained outside its gates.

Unlike a FEMA compound which would be a temporary facility and minimalist at best, the Superdome was well-built and well-designed to handle thousands of people and security. Not only was it stocked and prepared to serve as an emergency shelter, the authorities had extensive prior experience using this facility for this specific purpose. Nevertheless, and despite the presence of 550 National Guardsmen inside the Superdome, it quickly became a combat zone controlled by gangs and criminals who robbed, raped, and spawned an atmosphere of unrestrained violence and cruelty.

Unfortunately, it won't be safe outside the FEMA camps and emergency shelter areas, either. For those who try to make it on their own outside the quarantined areas, when you combine the loss of freedom due to martial law with inadequately trained or stressed government forces that will periodically over-react, we can expect to see the citizenry become increasingly frustrated, angry, and violent. They will eventually push-back using force.

If survivors keep their heads down, and work at remaining unnoticed by the government and marauding gangs, there is a good chance for survival. If you are part of a self-sufficient group, and prepared for sustainability, you will probably be okay. However, large independent and visible self-reliant groups, and well-equipped communities might become targets for federal government seizures and forced population relocation (already authorized by presidential Executive Order),[185] as well as looting by organized criminal gangs.

In the United States, no region has experienced this level of disaster because prior incidents have been localized, and the rest of the country was available to render assistance. However, if the incident affects more than 15% of the population, the response will look much different. In fact, in many areas help will effectively be nonexistent.

Therefore, Christians and churches that are prepared will have unprecedented opportunities to minister to those in need. The cultural gods of materialism, pleasure, fame, technological achievement, and traditional power, will be recognized as empty. As never before, people will become open to hearing about the real hope and peace that can only come through a personal relationship with the God of the Bible.

Once culture crumbles, the general populous (unprepared Christians and churches included) will be in crisis. Many people will lose all hope quickly, and countless will commit suicide. Between being victimized by crime, falling prey to disease and lack of adequate sanitation, starvation, unsafe drinking water, and being victimized by spiritual despair, as many as 317 million people will likely die within the first few weeks of a nationwide disaster. Widespread death, living life amidst adverse conditions and constant danger, unreliable communication networks and destabilizing uncertainty, missing family members, coupled with social upheaval, will breed more hopelessness–and also more disease, which will likely progress unabated.

Hopelessness and fear will drive many people to irrational responses. Likewise, the response of most unprepared people will be ineffective and unhelpful. What we would today call "mental illness" will become a widespread problem. People will do many things that they never would have considered doing in normal times. Defense will become a priority.

Again, at this point Christians and churches will have the opportunity to respond by being the hands and feet of Jesus, serving others as Jesus did during His life on earth. If revival takes hold, things will start to get better. Otherwise, the decline may level off in its intensity, but things will continue to spiral downward.

Only God knows how this will play out. We may be spared by the rapture[186] at some point during all of this, or it may not happen in our lifetime. Many Christians anticipate that this event will happen soon since Bible prophesies have essentially been fulfilled or are imminent, but this does not mean that God will intervene immediately. It just means that it is possible at any time.

Fulfilled Bible prophesies means that the time is at hand, but like Jesus' parable of the bridesmaids who were waiting for the bridegroom;[187] we may still have an extended wait. Therefore, we can't sit back unconcerned with an attitude that it doesn't matter because we won't be here, anyway. It does matter. And Jesus expects us to do what we can to prepare;[188] and when it happens, to be His representatives. He expects us to do more than look to our own well-being, He expects us to take an active role in making things better. This means we need to be peace-makers and a whole lot more.

Just like the parable of the three stewards,[189] we need to be diligent and invest our time wisely. We also need to be shrewd as serpents, but harmless as doves,[190] both now and in the future.

I don't have the benefit of divine revelation here, but it seems consistent with God's nature and the history of His intervention in human history, that He will let things get quite bad before we depart for heaven. This isn't because He doesn't care about our suffering, but because these dark days will be an unprecedented time of opportunity to spread the Good News,[191] and we will be able to engage in incredibly meaningful service. Many people will cry out to God. I suspect that we will still be here so that we will have the opportunity to introduce them to Jesus, and help them learn to live in hope as His disciples.

So what should we do? We should live as if our departure from earth is imminent, but also prepare to survive an extended period of dark days and years. We need to become prepared for what is coming, not just so that we can survive, but so that we can thrive—in ministry and service.

Each of us can have a role as a peace-maker, but more than this, each of us has different spiritual and physical gifts.[192] So we need to re-evaluate our gifting in light of what is coming. We need to take whatever steps are necessary to adapt our skills and ready our spiritual gifts for the days ahead. It takes preparation to become fully equipped for these new opportunities of service.

Additionally, we also need to organize and align with other discerning followers of Jesus. This won't be a time for a Lone Ranger approach. We are not in this alone; it is the unified-in-purpose Bible-believers who will respond effectively. It won't be individuals or individual families. Therefore, we need to establish cadres now, and join together in both individual and group preparations. Frankly, we probably won't survive it we try to do this alone.[193]

If revival comes soon we might be able to avoid the worst of the dark days ahead. God's hand of protection and blessing can still return to this land, and this crisis can be averted. This, too, is what we should strive for, letting Jesus use us as His hands and feet today as well as tomorrow. We need to be busy now with activities of Bible-centered outreach, discipleship, service, and other forms of activism; but not only these activities. We need to diligently observe the signs-of-the-times, and prayerfully prepare for all aspects of a future that will look very different from today.

It may be facing rocky days or major change, but significant change is inevitable. It's time to get ready.

We need to pray for revival, and for the awakening of His sleeping Church. Of course. But we also need to prepare physically, mentally, and spiritually for the days ahead.[194]

We were born into this time not by accident, but by God's design.[195] He has a purpose for us today, and especially in the days ahead.

He has tasks for us to fulfill today, and He has birthed-us into this time to serve Him in the dark days ahead. This is an honor. It's not a time for fear; it's a time for faith. If we pray, look to God and study the Bible, He will give us the strength and faith to be victorious.[196]

Let's get busy.

> *"God has not given us a spirit of fear, but of power and of love and of a sound mind."*
>
> 2 Timothy 1:7

> *"Be on guard. Stand firm in the faith. Be courageous. Be strong. And do everything with love."*
>
> 1 Corinthians 16:13-14

To read the author's blog on disaster and preparedness topics,
visit: www.36READY.org

Author's Post Script

Things are not getting better. Unfortunately, just the opposite seems to be the case.

If one day you wake up and find that you need a gun for family or personal protection, and you don't have one, it will be too late. Get it now. Similarly, if your jurisdiction issues concealed handgun licenses, get one. Even if you don't plan to carry a gun, if you have a license you will have the option to carry if circumstances change and you find it has become necessary. Don't wait.

If you need firearm training, don't delay. Make arrangements to receive training from a competent firearm self-defense instructor, now. Most firearm training focuses on target practice. This isn't enough. You need serious training, ideally in self-defense handgun, as well as tactical shotgun and rifle. Train with what you have; get what you don't have but need. Make it a priority. Don't procrastinate.

If you have read this book you should have enough information to make an informed decision on firearm self-defense and the use of deadly force, but this is only the starting point. If you are going to own a gun for the purpose of defense, you need to have ready access to the appropriate weapon(s). And, you must become adequately trained in safe and tactical use. You will always need more practice and training. Firearm defense is a perishable skill.

If your desire is solely to protect yourself or your family at home, a tactical shotgun may be your best choice. For more on this topic, visit Amazon.com to download my book, "Family and Personal Protection: What is the best gun for self-defense at home?"

However, if you are interested in protection in an urban environment while away from home, your best self-defense weapon is probably a concealable handgun in 9mm or larger caliber. On the other hand, if your primary concern is protection in a rural environment, such as in a wilderness area or on farmland or ranch property, a high-power rifle is probably your best tool for defense. Whatever firearm you select, be sure to have a quantity of ammunition, magazines and other essentials. Safe use, and safe storage, is mandatory.

In regard to firearm selection, the best place to start is to answer these questions:

A. Where will I be, and under what conditions will I most likely find myself needing a firearm?

B. What are my anticipated environments-of-use? (work, home, walking the dog, jogging, driving in a car, in a shopping mall parking lot, camping, etc.)

C. How will I carry it? (Open-carry in a holster on my belt? Concealed under my shirt or jacket? In my purse or briefcase? Using a sling and carried on my shoulder? Collapsed and contained in a backpack? In the trunk of my car, or in a closet? Etc.)

D. What will be the circumstances that I will most likely need to overcome? (Armed robbery? Burglar inside my home? Rape? Kidnapping? Car-jacking? Animal attack? The aftermath of a terrorist attack? Cattle rustling, or what?).

After you've asked yourself these questions, identify what type of gun best meets these needs. Is it a large handgun, mid-size, or one that is small and ultra concealable? If it will be fired from inside a pocket or purse, it needs to be a revolver. (A revolver holds fewer cartridges, but it is less likely to jamb when it's in contact with fabric and other objects.) If you will be outdoors and won't need to hide your firearm, your best option might be a tactical shotgun, sporting rifle or assault rifle. You need to consider the merits and drawbacks of each.

Regardless of where you start the process, able-bodied, mentally competent and financially-able Christians will ideally have ready access to at least four firearms. If financially able, it is desirable for each household to have at least one gun in each of these categories:

1) A handgun (9mm, .38 Special, or larger caliber);

2) A tactical shotgun (18-20 inch barrel, 12-gauge, loaded with 00-Buck or #4 Buck for self-defense (not #4 Shot), plus bird-shot shells available for emergency hunting of birds and small game, and slugs for large game);

3) A tactical semiautomatic rifle (5.56mm or larger caliber) for self-defense and emergency hunting. (For ranches, farmland and rural living, a scoped 7.62 semiautomatic tactical rifle may be a better choice than 5.56mm); and,

4) A lightweight .22LR rifle with scope for hunting small game.

Further, don't neglect firearm safety, and the safe and secure storage of both guns and ammunition. We need to be intentional about preventing access to firearms by unsupervised children, as well as adults who are not mentally stable or competent. Guns must be inaccessible to anyone who is immature, untrained, unsafe, or untrustworthy. (See the safety rules in the appendix.)

Also, please keep in mind that in most crimes of violence which involve guns, the firearms were stolen from a law abiding citizen's home. Don't inadvertently arm a criminal! Locks which keep a gun from firing may improve safety, but they don't stop thieves. Firearms need to be locked in a gun-storage safe or secure cabinet to prevent them from being taken by a burglar. Hiding a gun is not protection against theft or misuse.

If you don't already own an appropriate firearm, buy one. If you don't have the funds, do what Jesus taught: Sell something so that you can gather the funds needed to buy one. Get going. Purchase the best type of gun for your circumstance (above), buy a quantity of ammunition, get self-defense firearms training, then practice regularly and live as an alert person. If you're financially strapped, get what you can afford, but don't forget that you'll also need self-defense ammunition as well as ammunition for practice.

God tells us that we are not to live in fear.[197] Don't let yourself become paranoid. Rather, be prepared, watchful and ready.

For more on family and personal preparedness, visit:

www.36READY.org

– – – – – – –

If you would like to contact the author of this book, visit: www.SigSwanstrom.com and use the "Contact Me" portion of that website. Corrections and suggestions for improvement are welcomed and valued. If you disagree with something from a biblical viewpoint, be sure to include Bible references which support your viewpoint.

– – – – – – –

About the Author

SIG SWANSTROM is a former police officer and police SWAT team operator who worked in the Los Angeles-area. During his years of service, he personally had many deadly-force encounters with armed criminals, so his writing is real-world practical. And today, as the owner of a highly acclaimed firearms training academy, SIG has also learned how to capture the interest of his audiences and teach them practical real-world skills.

Armed with a university degree in criminology, and his practical experience as a police detective and crime scene investigator (CSI), SIG has had the opportunity to probe many criminal cases in which firearms were used against innocent people. And, he also investigated incidents where law abiding citizens used guns against their attackers.

Since taking an early retirement from law enforcement, these experiences were further enhanced by living with terrorism and guerilla warfare for several years in Guatemala. During that country's bloody civil war, SIG's compound was attacked by guerillas on three occasions, and on one occasion it was overrun. His family was with him at the time. So he also understands these issues from a WTSHTF perspective of widespread mayhem and revolution.

Recognition: During SIG's law enforcement career he was named "Police Officer of the Year," was a "Commendation for Valor" recipient, and he received the Mayor's Commendation, U.S. Attorney General's Commendation, and numerous other awards and citations. He was also the personal bodyguard of president Ronald Reagan during the period after Reagan was governor of California but before he announced his candidacy for president of the United States.

Today, SIG is the owner of Texas Republic Firearms Academy

(www.TXRFA.com), a school based near San Antonio, Texas. It provides firearm self-defense training in handgun, rifle, and tactical shotgun to the general public, as well as training for law enforcement and security-force personnel, both nationally and internationally.

The Most Important Part of This Bio: More important than any life accomplishment, SIG regards a decision he made as a young man to be the most important milestone of his life. Through a series of events he was forced to acknowledge the reality of good and evil in this world, and that we live on one side of this fence or the other. More to the point, that fence-sitting isn't possible.

Though raised in a church-going family, it was as a teenager that SIG made the decision to get serious about his faith in Jesus as his Savior and to serve Jesus wholeheartedly. Far from perfect, since that point SIG has nevertheless been guided by this commitment, and has reveled in a personal relationship with Jesus as his Lord.

The Bible verses which command, *"Seek first the Kingdom of God and His righteousness, and the things needed for life will be added unto you"* (Matthew 6:33), and *"Love the Lord your God with all your heart [passion], and with all your soul [individual uniqueness], and with all your mind [intellect], and with all your strength [energy]."* And, *"Love your neighbor as yourself"* (Mark 12:30-31), guide his daily life.

If you have not made this commitment to ask God to forgive you for your failings, and to accept His free gift of becoming a member of God's family, made possible not by our own goodness but through Jesus sacrifice of His life on the cross, and to become a follower of the living Jesus, consider it now. This decision isn't to believe in a philosophy of biblical living; it's a whole new life. Literally. Without Jesus' free gift of forgiveness, and a personal relationship with the Creator of the universe which He freely offers us, we are incomplete.

Life on earth is only the beginning.

To learn more about the real Jesus, based solely on what the Bible teaches, visit:

www.WhoIsJesus-Really.com

Biblical living is helpful, but to learn about what it means to have a personal relationship with Jesus, visit:

www.GotQuestions.org

For more about the author, visit:

www.SIGSWANSTROM.com

Follow SIG SWANSTROM on Twitter:
www.Twitter.com/SigSwanstrom

To visit the author's blog on disaster and preparedness topics, visit:
www.36ReadyBlog.com

***"A prudent person foresees danger
and takes precautions.
The simpleton goes blindly on
and suffers the consequences."***

- Proverbs 22:3

Appendix:

Jesus' Final Instructions to His Followers, Just Prior to His Arrest

Jesus' teaching at the Last Supper, commonly referred to as Jesus' *Farewell Discourse*, is particularly poignant since He knew that He would be arrested later that evening. He knew that this would be His last opportunity to teach and give instructions to His followers when times were 'normal,' before the dramatic events of His arrest, crucifixion and resurrection.

As you would expect, Jesus used this opportunity to provide an overview of the Gospel, and to provide crucial parting instructions to His followers. It is these *parting instructions* and events that have formed the cornerstone for this book.

Since it is always important to study Bible passages in the context of where they are found, in the following pages you will find Luke 22:35-36 in the context of Jesus' teaching that fateful night. This is essential if we are to properly understand the "big picture" of what the Bible is teaching us with this, or any topic.

With this consideration in mind, I have brought together the various Bible passages which contain Jesus teaching at the Last Supper. Since this was Jesus' last opportunity to teach His followers before his arrest, crucifixion and resurrection, it is particularly poignant.

Below you will find a unified series of verses which together are the entire record of Jesus teaching that night. These passages are sometimes repetitive, as the same teaching is echoed by different disciples in their written record of what happened that night. So though the story flows, it must be understood that the below discourse is as told by several speakers, each chiming in on the same event.

The purpose of this exercise is simple. It is to help us better understand the entirety of Jesus teaching at the Last Supper. In the following collection of Bible passages nothing has been changed. Nothing has been intentionally left out and nothing has been added. I have simply brought together, in approximate chronological order, all of Jesus' teaching that night. This is to help us more fully grasp entirety of Jesus' final teaching that night. And specifically, to better understand the context of Luke 22:35-36, in which Jesus tells us that we should be prepared for adversity, and armed with a weapon.

It's important to acknowledge that we can't know the precise chronological order of these passages. What we do know is that these verses relate the full and complete story of Jesus' teaching that night.

What I have attempted to do here is to group these Bible passages in proximate order, based on the order it appears in the text of the Bible as well as by theme. If you disagree with my ordering of these verses, I invite you to undertake this exercise yourself. To help you accomplish this, at the end of the first section you will find a link to both a Microsoft Word document and a PDF to help you undertake this task. If you would like to accomplish this exercise using a different translation of the Bible (three translations are included here), I have included the Bible references in the left margin of the initial discourse.

Why is this section included in this book? It is to document that the meaning which I have derived for Luke 22:35-36 is consistent in context, and also that it is consistent with all the authoritative translations of the Bible. Here you will find the same Last Supper "Farewell Discourse" repeated three times, each time using a different translation of the Bible. If you take the time to read each, you will note that the details of Jesus' teaching are the same in each, yet understanding is deepened as we compare and consider them together.

Importantly, the words of Jesus as recorded in Luke 22:36 (Jesus injunction that we are to be armed), does not change one iota when considered in the context of the entire discourse. His instructions are clear, and when we consider them in the context of the rest of His teaching that night, we see that these instructions need to be taken literally and seriously.

Reference [198]	Text in Proximate Chronologic Order[199]
	New American Standard Bible (NASB) Translation
Luke 22:14-16	When the hour had come, He reclined at the table, and the apostles with Him. 15 And He said to them, "I have earnestly desired to eat this Passover with you before I suffer; 16 for I say to you, I shall never again eat it until it is fulfilled in the kingdom of God."
Luke 22:24-30	And there arose also a dispute among them as to which one of them was regarded to be greatest. 25 And He said to them, "The kings of the Gentiles lord it over them; and those who have authority over them are called 'Benefactors.' 26 "But it is not this way with you, but the one who is the greatest among you must become like the youngest, and the leader like the servant. 27 "For who is greater, the one who reclines at the table or the one who serves? Is it not the one who reclines at the table? But I am among you as the one who serves. 28 "You are those who have stood by Me in My trials; 29 and just as My Father has granted Me a kingdom, I grant you 30 that you may eat and drink at My table in My kingdom, and you will sit on thrones judging the twelve tribes of Israel.

John 13:5-20

5 Then He poured water into the basin, and began to wash the disciples' feet and to wipe them with the towel with which He was girded. 6 So He came to Simon Peter. He said to Him, "Lord, do You wash my feet?" 7 Jesus answered and said to him, "What I do you do not realize now, but you will understand hereafter." 8 Peter said to Him, "Never shall You wash my feet!" Jesus answered him, "If I do not wash you, you have no part with Me." 9 Simon Peter said to Him, "Lord, then wash not only my feet, but also my hands and my head." 10 Jesus said to him, "He who has bathed needs only to wash his feet, but is completely clean; and you are clean, but not all of you." 11 For He knew the one who was betraying Him; for this reason He said, "Not all of you are clean."

12 So when He had washed their feet, and taken His garments and reclined at the table again, He said to them, "Do you know what I have done to you? 13 "You call Me Teacher and Lord; and you are right, for so I am. 14 "If I then, the Lord and the Teacher, washed your feet, you also ought to wash one another's feet. 15 "For I gave you an example that you also should do as I did to you. 16 "Truly, truly, I say to you, a slave is not greater than his master, nor is one who is sent greater than the one who sent him. 17 "If you know these things, you are blessed if you do them. 18 "I do not speak of all of you. I know the ones I have chosen; but it is that the Scripture may be fulfilled, 'HE WHO EATS MY BREAD HAS LIFTED UP HIS HEEL AGAINST ME.' 19 "From now on I am telling you before it comes to pass, so that when it does occur, you may believe that I am He. 20 "Truly, truly, I say to you, he who receives whomever I send receives Me; and he who receives Me receives Him who sent Me."

Matthew 26:20-25	20 Now when evening came, Jesus was reclining at the table with the twelve disciples. 21 As they were eating, He said, "Truly I say to you that one of you will betray Me." 22 Being deeply grieved, they each one began to say to Him, "Surely not I, Lord?" 23 And He answered, "He who dipped his hand with Me in the bowl is the one who will betray Me. 24 "The Son of Man is to go, just as it is written of Him; but woe to that man by whom the Son of Man is betrayed! It would have been good for that man if he had not been born." 25 And Judas, who was betraying Him, said, "Surely it is not I, Rabbi?" Jesus said to him, "You have said it yourself."
Mark 14:18-21	18 As they were reclining at the table and eating, Jesus said, "Truly I say to you that one of you will betray Me — one who is eating with Me." 19 They began to be grieved and to say to Him one by one, "Surely not I?" 20 And He said to them, "It is one of the twelve, one who dips with Me in the bowl. 21 "For the Son of Man is to go just as it is written of Him; but woe to that man by whom the Son of Man is betrayed! It would have been good for that man if he had not been born."
Luke 22:21-23	21 "But behold, the hand of the one betraying Me is with Mine on the table. 22 "For indeed, the Son of Man is going as it has been determined; but woe to that man by whom He is betrayed!" 23 And they began to discuss among themselves which one of them it might be who was going to do this thing.

John 13:21-30

21 When Jesus had said this, He became troubled in spirit, and testified and said, "Truly, truly, I say to you, that one of you will betray Me." 22 The disciples began looking at one another, at a loss to know of which one He was speaking. 23 There was reclining on Jesus' bosom one of His disciples, whom Jesus loved. 24 So Simon Peter gestured to him, and said to him, "Tell us who it is of whom He is speaking." 25 He, leaning back thus on Jesus' bosom, said to Him, "Lord, who is it?" 26 Jesus then answered, "That is the one for whom I shall dip the morsel and give it to him." So when He had dipped the morsel, He took and gave it to Judas, the son of Simon Iscariot. 27 After the morsel, Satan then entered into him. Therefore Jesus said to him, "What you do, do quickly." 28 Now no one of those reclining at the table knew for what purpose He had said this to him. 29 For some were supposing, because Judas had the money box, that Jesus was saying to him, "Buy the things we have need of for the feast"; or else, that he should give something to the poor. 30 So after receiving the morsel he went out immediately; and it was night.

Matthew 26:31-35

31 Then Jesus said to them, "You will all fall away because of Me this night, for it is written, 'I WILL STRIKE DOWN THE SHEPHERD, AND THE SHEEP OF THE FLOCK SHALL BE SCATTERED.' 32 "But after I have been raised, I will go ahead of you to Galilee." 33 But Peter said to Him, "Even though all may fall away because of You, I will never fall away." 34 Jesus said to him, "Truly I say to you that this very night, before a rooster crows, you will deny Me three times." 35 Peter said to Him, "Even if I have to die with You, I will not deny You." All the disciples said the same thing too.

Mark 14:27-31	27 And Jesus said to them, "You will all fall away, because it is written, 'I WILL STRIKE DOWN THE SHEPHERD, AND THE SHEEP SHALL BE SCATTERED.' 28 "But after I have been raised, I will go ahead of you to Galilee." 29 But Peter said to Him, "Even though all may fall away, yet I will not." 30 And Jesus said to him, "Truly I say to you, that this very night, before a rooster crows twice, you yourself will deny Me three times." 31 But Peter kept saying insistently, "Even if I have to die with You, I will not deny You!" And they all were saying the same thing also.
Luke 22:31-38	31 "Simon, Simon, behold, Satan has demanded permission to sift you like wheat; 32 but I have prayed for you, that your faith may not fail; and you, when once you have turned again, strengthen your brothers." 33 But he said to Him, "Lord, with You I am ready to go both to prison and to death!" 34 And He said, "I say to you, Peter, the rooster will not crow today until you have denied three times that you know Me."
Matthew 26:26-29	26 While they were eating, Jesus took some bread, and after a blessing, He broke it and gave it to the disciples, and said, "Take, eat; this is My body." 27 And when He had taken a cup and given thanks, He gave it to them, saying, "Drink from it, all of you; 28 for this is My blood of the covenant, which is poured out for many for forgiveness of sins. 29 "But I say to you, I will not drink of this fruit of the vine from now on until that day when I drink it new with you in My Father's kingdom."

Mark 14:22-25	22 While they were eating, He took some bread, and after a blessing He broke it, and gave it to them, and said, "Take it; this is My body." 23 And when He had taken a cup and given thanks, He gave it to them, and they all drank from it. 24 And He said to them, "This is My blood of the covenant, which is poured out for many. 25 "Truly I say to you, I will never again drink of the fruit of the vine until that day when I drink it new in the kingdom of God."
Luke 22:17-20	17 And when He had taken a cup and given thanks, He said, "Take this and share it among yourselves; 18 for I say to you, I will not drink of the fruit of the vine from now on until the kingdom of God comes." 19 And when He had taken some bread and given thanks, He broke it and gave it to them, saying, "This is My body which is given for you; do this in remembrance of Me." 20 And in the same way He took the cup after they had eaten, saying, "This cup which is poured out for you is the new covenant in My blood.
1 Corinthians 11:23-26	[23 For I received from the Lord that which I also delivered to you, that the Lord Jesus in the night in which He was betrayed took bread; 24 and when He had given thanks, He broke it and said, "This is My body, which is for you; do this in remembrance of Me." 25 In the same way He took the cup also after supper, saying, "This cup is the new covenant in My blood; do this, as often as you drink it, in remembrance of Me." 26 For as often as you eat this bread and drink the cup, you proclaim the Lord's death until He comes.]

John 14 Do not let your heart be troubled; believe in God,
believe also in Me. 2 In My Father's house are
many dwelling places; if it were not so, I would have
told you; for I go to prepare a place for you. 3 "If I
go and prepare a place for you, I will come again
and receive you to Myself, that where I am, there
you may be also. 4 "And you know the way where I
am going." 5 Thomas said to Him, "Lord, we do
not know where You are going, how do we know
the way?" 6 Jesus said to him, "I am the way, and
the truth, and the life; no one comes to the Father
but through Me.

7 "If you had known Me, you would have known
My Father also; from now on you know Him, and
have seen Him."

8 Philip said to Him, "Lord, show us the Father,
and it is enough for us." 9 Jesus said to him, "Have
I been so long with you, and yet you have not come
to know Me, Philip? He who has seen Me has seen
the Father; how can you say, 'Show us the Father'?
10 "Do you not believe that I am in the Father, and
the Father is in Me? The words that I say to you I
do not speak on My own initiative, but the Father
abiding in Me does His works. 11 "Believe Me that
I am in the Father and the Father is in Me; otherwise believe because of the works themselves. 12
"Truly, truly, I say to you, he who believes in Me,
the works that I do, he will do also; and greater
works than these he will do; because I go to the
Father. 13 "Whatever you ask in My name, that will
I do, so that the Father may be glorified in the Son.
14 "If you ask Me anything in My name, I will do it.

15 "If you love Me, you will keep My commandments.

16 "I will ask the Father, and He will give you another Helper, that He may be with you forever; 17 that is the Spirit of truth, whom the world cannot receive, because it does not see Him or know Him, but you know Him because He abides with you and will be in you.

18 "I will not leave you as orphans; I will come to you. 19 "After a little while the world will no longer see Me, but you will see Me; because I live, you will live also. 20 "In that day you will know that I am in My Father, and you in Me, and I in you. 21 "He who has My commandments and keeps them is the one who loves Me; and he who loves Me will be loved by My Father, and I will love him and will disclose Myself to him." 22 Judas (not Iscariot) said to Him, "Lord, what then has happened that You are going to disclose Yourself to us and not to the world?" 23 Jesus answered and said to him, "If anyone loves Me, he will keep My word; and My Father will love him, and We will come to him and make Our abode with him. 24 "He who does not love Me does not keep My words; and the word which you hear is not Mine, but the Father's who sent Me.

25 "These things I have spoken to you while abiding
with you. 26 "But the Helper, the Holy Spirit,
whom the Father will send in My name, He will
teach you all things, and bring to your remembrance
all that I said to you. 27 "Peace I leave with you;
My peace I give to you; not as the world gives do I
give to you. Do not let your heart be troubled, nor
let it be fearful. 28 "You heard that I said to you, 'I
go away, and I will come to you.' If you loved Me,
you would have rejoiced because I go to the Father,
for the Father is greater than I. 29 "Now I have
told you before it happens, so that when it happens,
you may believe. 30 "I will not speak much more
with you, for the ruler of the world is coming, and
he has nothing in Me; 31 but so that the world may
know that I love the Father, I do exactly as the
Father commanded Me. Get up, let us go from here.

John 15 I am the true vine, and My Father is the vinedresser.
2 Every branch in Me that does not bear fruit, He
takes away; and every branch that bears fruit, He
prunes it so that it may bear more fruit. 3 "You are
already clean because of the word which I have
spoken to you. 4 "Abide in Me, and I in you. As the
branch cannot bear fruit of itself unless it abides in
the vine, so neither can you unless you abide in Me.
5 "I am the vine, you are the branches; he who
abides in Me and I in him, he bears much fruit, for
apart from Me you can do nothing. 6 "If anyone
does not abide in Me, he is thrown away as a branch
and dries up; and they gather them, and cast them
into the fire and they are burned. 7 "If you abide in
Me, and My words abide in you, ask whatever you
wish, and it will be done for you. 8 "My Father is
glorified by this, that you bear much fruit, and so
prove to be My disciples. 9 "Just as the Father has
loved Me, I have also loved you; abide in My love.
10 "If you keep My commandments, you will abide
in My love; just as I have kept My Father's commandments and abide in His love. 11 "These things
I have spoken to you so that My joy may be in you,
and that your joy may be made full.

12 "This is My commandment, that you love one another, just as I have loved you. 13 "Greater love has no one than this, that one lay down his life for his friends. 14 "You are My friends if you do what I command you. 15 "No longer do I call you slaves, for the slave does not know what his master is doing; but I have called you friends, for all things that I have heard from My Father I have made known to you. 16 "You did not choose Me but I chose you, and appointed you that you would go and bear fruit, and that your fruit would remain, so that whatever you ask of the Father in My name He may give to you. 17 "This I command you, that you love one another.

18 "If the world hates you, you know that it has hated Me before it hated you. 19 "If you were of the world, the world would love its own; but because you are not of the world, but I chose you out of the world, because of this the world hates you. 20 "Remember the word that I said to you, 'A slave is not greater than his master.' If they persecuted Me, they will also persecute you; if they kept My word, they will keep yours also. 21 "But all these things they will do to you for My name's sake, because they do not know the One who sent Me. 22 "If I had not come and spoken to them, they would not have sin, but now they have no excuse for their sin. 23 "He who hates Me hates My Father also. 24 "If I had not done among them the works which no one else did, they would not have sin; but now they have both seen and hated Me and My Father as well. 25 "But they have done this to fulfill the word that is written in their Law, 'THEY HATED ME WITHOUT A CAUSE.'

26 "When the Helper comes, whom I will send to you from the Father, that is the Spirit of truth who proceeds from the Father, He will testify about Me, 27 and you will testify also, because you have been with Me from the beginning.

John 16 These things I have spoken to you so that you may be kept from stumbling. 2 They will make you outcasts from the synagogue, but an hour is coming for everyone who kills you to think that he is offering service to God. 3 "These things they will do because they have not known the Father or Me. 4 "But these things I have spoken to you, so that when their hour comes, you may remember that I told you of them. These things I did not say to you at the beginning, because I was with you.

5 "But now I am going to Him who sent Me; and none of you asks Me, 'Where are You going?' 6 "But because I have said these things to you, sorrow has filled your heart. 7 "But I tell you the truth, it is to your advantage that I go away; for if I do not go away, the Helper will not come to you; but if I go, I will send Him to you. 8 "And He, when He comes, will convict the world concerning sin and righteousness and judgment; 9 concerning sin, because they do not believe in Me; 10 and concerning righteousness, because I go to the Father and you no longer see Me; 11 and concerning judgment, because the ruler of this world has been judged.

12 "I have many more things to say to you, but you cannot bear them now. 13 "But when He, the Spirit of truth, comes, He will guide you into all the truth; for He will not speak on His own initiative, but whatever He hears, He will speak; and He will disclose to you what is to come. 14 "He will glorify Me, for He will take of Mine and will disclose it to you. 15 "All things that the Father has are Mine; therefore I said that He takes of Mine and will disclose it to you.

16 "A little while, and you will no longer see Me; and again a little while, and you will see Me." 17 Some of His disciples then said to one another, "What is this thing He is telling us, 'A little while, and you will not see Me; and again a little while, and you will see Me'; and, 'because I go to the Father'?" 18 So they were saying, "What is this that He says, 'A little while'? We do not know what He is talking about." 19 Jesus knew that they wished to question Him, and He said to them, "Are you deliberating together about this, that I said, 'A little while, and you will not see Me, and again a little while, and you will see Me'? 20 "Truly, truly, I say to you, that you will weep and lament, but the world will rejoice; you will grieve, but your grief will be turned into joy.

21 "Whenever a woman is in labor she has pain, because her hour has come; but when she gives birth to the child, she no longer remembers the anguish because of the joy that a child has been born into the world. 22 "Therefore you too have grief now; but I will see you again, and your heart will rejoice, and no one will take your joy away from you.

23 "In that day you will not question Me about anything. Truly, truly, I say to you, if you ask the Father for anything in My name, He will give it to you. 24 "Until now you have asked for nothing in My name; ask and you will receive, so that your joy may be made full.

25 "These things I have spoken to you in figurative language; an hour is coming when I will no longer speak to you in figurative language, but will tell you plainly of the Father. 26 "In that day you will ask in My name, and I do not say to you that I will request of the Father on your behalf; 27 for the Father Himself loves you, because you have loved Me and have believed that I came forth from the Father. 28 "I came forth from the Father and have come into the world; I am leaving the world again and going to the Father."

29 His disciples said, "Lo, now You are speaking plainly and are not using a figure of speech. 30 "Now we know that You know all things, and have no need for anyone to question You; by this we believe that You came from God." 31 Jesus answered them, "Do you now believe? 32 "Behold, an hour is coming, and has already come, for you to be scattered, each to his own home, and to leave Me alone; and yet I am not alone, because the Father is with Me. 33 "These things I have spoken to you, so that in Me you may have peace. In the world you have tribulation, but take courage; I have overcome the world."

Luke 22:35-37

35 And He said to them, "When I sent you out without money belt and bag and sandals, you did not lack anything, did you?" They said, "No, nothing."

36 And He said to them, "But now, whoever has a money belt is to take it along, likewise also a bag, and whoever has no sword is to sell his coat and buy one.

37 "For I tell you that this which is written must be fulfilled in Me, 'AND HE WAS NUMBERED WITH TRANSGRESSORS'; for that which refers to Me has its fulfillment."

38 They said, "Lord, look, here are two swords."

And He said to them, "It is enough."

King James Version

Jesus' Final Instructions to His Followers at the Last Supper (Passover), Just Prior to His Arrest

Text in Proximate Chronologic Order

Luke 22:14-16

14 And when the hour was come, he sat down, and the twelve apostles with him.

15 And he said unto them, With desire I have desired to eat this Passover with you before I suffer:

16 For I say unto you, I will not any more eat thereof, until it be fulfilled in the kingdom of God.

Luke 22:24-30

24 And there was also a strife among them, which of them should be accounted the greatest.

25 And he said unto them, the kings of the Gentiles exercise lordship over them; and they that exercise authority upon them are called benefactors.

26 But ye shall not be so: but he that is greatest among you, let him be as the younger; and he that is chief, as he that doth serve.

27 For whether is greater, he that sitteth at meat, or he that serveth? Is it not he that sitteth at meat? But I am among you as he that serveth.

28 Ye are they which have continued with me in my temptations.

29 And I appoint unto you a kingdom, as my Father hath appointed unto me;

30 That ye may eat and drink at my table in my kingdom, and sit on thrones judging the twelve tribes of Israel.

John 13:5-20

5 After that he poureth water into a basin, and began to wash the disciples' feet, and to wipe them with the towel wherewith he was girded.

6 Then cometh he to Simon Peter: and Peter saith unto him, Lord, dost thou wash my feet?

7 Jesus answered and said unto him, What I do thou knowest not now; but thou shalt know hereafter.

8 Peter saith unto him, Thou shalt never wash my feet. Jesus answered him, If I wash thee not, thou hast no part with me.

9 Simon Peter saith unto him, Lord, not my feet only, but also my hands and my head.

10 Jesus saith to him, He that is washed needeth not save to wash his feet, but is clean every whit: and ye are clean, but not all.

11 For he knew who should betray him; therefore said he, Ye are not all clean.

12 So after he had washed their feet, and had taken his garments, and was set down again, he said unto them, Know ye what I have done to you?

13 Ye call me Master and Lord: and ye say well; for so I am.

14 If I then, your Lord and Master, have washed your feet; ye also ought to wash one another's feet.

15 For I have given you an example, that ye should do as I have done to you.

16 Verily, verily, I say unto you, the servant is not greater than his lord; neither he that is sent greater than he that sent him.

17 If ye know these things, happy are ye if ye do them.

18 I speak not of you all: I know whom I have chosen: but that the scripture may be fulfilled, He that eateth bread with me hath lifted up his heel against me.

19 Now I tell you before it come, that, when it is come to pass, ye may believe that I am he.

20 Verily, verily, I say unto you, He that receiveth whomsoever I send receiveth me; and he that receiveth me receiveth him that sent me.

Matthew 26:20-25

20 Now when the even was come, he sat down with the twelve.

21 And as they did eat, he said, Verily I say unto you, that one of you shall betray me.

22 And they were exceeding sorrowful, and began every one of them to say unto him, Lord, is it I?

23 And he answered and said, He that dippeth his hand with me in the dish, the same shall betray me.

24 The Son of man goeth as it is written of him: but woe unto that man by whom the Son of man is betrayed! it had been good for that man if he had not been born.

25 Then Judas, which betrayed him, answered and said, Master, is it I? He said unto him, Thou hast said.

Mark 14:18-21

18 And as they sat and did eat, Jesus said, Verily I say unto you, one of you which eateth with me shall betray me.

19 And they began to be sorrowful, and to say unto him one by one, Is it I? And another said, is it I?

20 And he answered and said unto them, it is one of the twelve, that dippeth with me in the dish.

21 The Son of man indeed goeth, as it is written of him: but woe to that man by whom the Son of man is betrayed! Good were it for that man if he had never been born.

Luke 22:21-23

21 But, behold, the hand of him that betrayeth me is with me on the table.

22 And truly the Son of man goeth, as it was determined: but woe unto that man by whom he is betrayed!

23 And they began to inquire among themselves, which of them it was that should do this thing.

John 13:21-30

21 When Jesus had thus said, he was troubled in spirit, and testified, and said, Verily, verily, I say unto you, that one of you shall betray me.

22 Then the disciples looked one on another, doubting of whom he

spake.

23 Now there was leaning on Jesus' bosom one of his disciples, whom Jesus loved.

24 Simon Peter therefore beckoned to him, that he should ask who it should be of whom he spake.

25 He then lying on Jesus' breast saith unto him, Lord, who is it?

26 Jesus answered, He it is, to whom I shall give a sop, when I have dipped it. And when he had dipped the sop, he gave it to Judas Iscariot, the son of Simon.

27 And after the sop Satan entered into him. Then said Jesus unto him, that thou doest, do quickly.

28 Now no man at the table knew for what intent he spake this unto him.

29 For some of them thought, because Judas had the bag, that Jesus had said unto him, Buy those things that we have need of against the feast; or, that he should give something to the poor.

30 He then having received the sop went immediately out: and it was night.

Matthew 26:31-35

31 Then saith Jesus unto them, all ye shall be offended because of me this night: for it is written, I will smite the shepherd, and the sheep of the flock shall be scattered abroad.

32 But after I am risen again, I will go before you into Galilee.

33 Peter answered and said unto him, Though all men shall be offended because of thee, yet will I never be offended.

34 Jesus said unto him, Verily I say unto thee, That this night, before the cock crow, thou shalt deny me thrice.

35 Peter said unto him, Though I should die with thee, yet will I not deny thee. Likewise also said all the disciples.

Mark 14:27-31

27 And Jesus saith unto them, All ye shall be offended because of me this night: for it is written, I will smite the shepherd, and the sheep shall

be scattered.

28 But after that I am risen, I will go before you into Galilee.

29 But Peter said unto him, Although all shall be offended, yet will not I.

30 And Jesus saith unto him, Verily I say unto thee, That this day, even in this night, before the cock crow twice, thou shalt deny me thrice.

31 But he spake the more vehemently, If I should die with thee, I will not deny thee in any wise. Likewise also said they all.

Luke 22:31-38

31 And the Lord said, Simon, Simon, behold, Satan hath desired to have you, that he may sift you as wheat:

32 But I have prayed for thee, that thy faith fail not: and when thou art converted, strengthen thy brethren.

33 And he said unto him, Lord, I am ready to go with thee, both into prison, and to death.

34 And he said, I tell thee, Peter, the cock shall not crow this day, before that thou shalt thrice deny that thou knowest me.

35 And he said unto them, When I sent you without purse, and scrip, and shoes, lacked ye any thing? And they said, Nothing.

36 Then said he unto them, But now, he that hath a purse, let him take it, and likewise his scrip: and he that hath no sword, let him sell his garment, and buy one.

37 For I say unto you, that this that is written must yet be accomplished in me, And he was reckoned among the transgressors: for the things concerning me have an end.

38 And they said, Lord, behold, here are two swords. And he said unto them, It is enough.

Matthew 26:26-29

26 And as they were eating, Jesus took bread, and blessed it, and brake it, and gave it to the disciples, and said, Take, eat; this is my body.

27 And he took the cup, and gave thanks, and gave it to them, saying, Drink ye all of it;

28 For this is my blood of the new testament, which is shed for many for the remission of sins.

29 But I say unto you, I will not drink henceforth of this fruit of the vine, until that day when I drink it new with you in my Father's kingdom.

Mark 14:22-25

22 And as they did eat, Jesus took bread, and blessed, and brake it, and gave to them, and said, Take, eat: this is my body.

23 And he took the cup, and when he had given thanks, he gave it to them: and they all drank of it.

24 And he said unto them, This is my blood of the new testament, which is shed for many.

25 Verily I say unto you, I will drink no more of the fruit of the vine, until that day that I drink it new in the kingdom of God.

Luke 22:17-20

17 And he took the cup, and gave thanks, and said, Take this, and divide it among yourselves:

18 For I say unto you, I will not drink of the fruit of the vine, until the kingdom of God shall come.

19 And he took bread, and gave thanks, and brake it, and gave unto them, saying, This is my body which is given for you: this do in remembrance of me.

20 Likewise also the cup after supper, saying, This cup is the new testament in my blood, which is shed for you.

1 Corinthians 11:23-26

23 For I have received of the Lord that which also I delivered unto you, That the Lord Jesus the same night in which he was betrayed took bread:

24 And when he had given thanks, he brake it, and said, Take, eat: this is my body, which is broken for you: this do in remembrance of me.

25 After the same manner also he took the cup, when he had supped, saying, This cup is the new testament in my blood: this do ye, as oft as

ye drink it, in remembrance of me.

26 For as often as ye eat this bread, and drink this cup, ye do shew the Lord's death till he come.

John 14

1 Let not your heart be troubled: ye believe in God, believe also in me.

2 In my Father's house are many mansions: if it were not so, I would have told you. I go to prepare a place for you.

3 And if I go and prepare a place for you, I will come again, and receive you unto myself; that where I am, there ye may be also.

4 And whither I go ye know, and the way ye know.

5 Thomas saith unto him, Lord, we know not whither thou goest; and how can we know the way?

6 Jesus saith unto him, I am the way, the truth, and the life: no man cometh unto the Father, but by me.

7 If ye had known me, ye should have known my Father also: and from henceforth ye know him, and have seen him.

8 Philip saith unto him, Lord, shew us the Father, and it sufficeth us.

9 Jesus saith unto him, Have I been so long time with you, and yet hast thou not known me, Philip? he that hath seen me hath seen the Father; and how sayest thou then, Shew us the Father?

10 Believest thou not that I am in the Father, and the Father in me? the words that I speak unto you I speak not of myself: but the Father that dwelleth in me, he doeth the works.

11 Believe me that I am in the Father, and the Father in me: or else believe me for the very works' sake.

12 Verily, verily, I say unto you, He that believeth on me, the works that I do shall he do also; and greater works than these shall he do; because I go unto my Father.

13 And whatsoever ye shall ask in my name, that will I do, that the Father may be glorified in the Son.

14 If ye shall ask any thing in my name, I will do it.

15 If ye love me, keep my commandments.

16 And I will pray the Father, and he shall give you another Comforter, that he may abide with you for ever;

17 Even the Spirit of truth; whom the world cannot receive, because it seeth him not, neither knoweth him: but ye know him; for he dwelleth with you, and shall be in you.

18 I will not leave you comfortless: I will come to you.

19 Yet a little while, and the world seeth me no more; but ye see me: because I live, ye shall live also.

20 At that day ye shall know that I am in my Father, and ye in me, and I in you.

21 He that hath my commandments, and keepeth them, he it is that loveth me: and he that loveth me shall be loved of my Father, and I will love him, and will manifest myself to him.

22 Judas saith unto him, not Iscariot, Lord, how is it that thou wilt manifest thyself unto us, and not unto the world?

23 Jesus answered and said unto him, If a man love me, he will keep my words: and my Father will love him, and we will come unto him, and make our abode with him.

24 He that loveth me not keepeth not my sayings: and the word which ye hear is not mine, but the Father's which sent me.

25 These things have I spoken unto you, being yet present with you.

26 But the Comforter, which is the Holy Ghost, whom the Father will send in my name, he shall teach you all things, and bring all things to your remembrance, whatsoever I have said unto you.

27 Peace I leave with you, my peace I give unto you: not as the world giveth, give I unto you. Let not your heart be troubled, neither let it be afraid.

28 Ye have heard how I said unto you, I go away, and come again unto you. If ye loved me, ye would rejoice, because I said, I go unto the Father: for my Father is greater than I.

29 And now I have told you before it come to pass, that, when it is come to pass, ye might believe.

30 Hereafter I will not talk much with you: for the prince of this world
cometh, and hath nothing in me.

31 But that the world may know that I love the Father; and as the
Father gave me commandment, even so I do. Arise, let us go hence.

New Living Translation

Jesus' Final Instructions to His Followers at the Last Supper (Passover), Just Prior to His Arrest

Text in Proximate Chronologic Order

Luke 22:14-16

14 When the time came, Jesus and the apostles sat down together at the
table. 15 Jesus said, "I have been very eager to eat this Passover meal
with you before my suffering begins. 16 For I tell you now that I won't
eat this meal again until its meaning is fulfilled in the Kingdom of God."

Luke 22:24-30

24 Then they began to argue among themselves about who would be the
greatest among them. 25 Jesus told them, "In this world the kings and
great men lord it over their people, yet they are called 'friends of the
people.' 26 But among you it will be different. Those who are the greatest among you should take the lowest rank, and the leader should be like
a servant. 27 Who is more important, the one who sits at the table or the
one who serves? The one who sits at the table, of course. But not here!
For I am among you as one who serves.

28 "You have stayed with me in my time of trial. 29 And just as my
Father has granted me a Kingdom, I now grant you the right 30 to eat
and drink at my table in my Kingdom. And you will sit on thrones,
judging the twelve tribes of Israel.

John 13:5-20

5 and poured water into a basin. Then he began to wash the disciples'
feet, drying them with the towel he had around him.

6 When Jesus came to Simon Peter, Peter said to him, "Lord, are you
going to wash my feet?"

7 Jesus replied, "You don't understand now what I am doing, but someday you will."

8 "No," Peter protested, "you will never ever wash my feet!"

Jesus replied, "Unless I wash you, you won't belong to me."

9 Simon Peter exclaimed, "Then wash my hands and head as well, Lord, not just my feet!"

10 Jesus replied, "A person who has bathed all over does not need to wash, except for the feet, to be entirely clean. And you disciples are clean, but not all of you." 11 For Jesus knew who would betray him. That is what he meant when he said, "Not all of you are clean."

12 After washing their feet, he put on his robe again and sat down and asked, "Do you understand what I was doing? 13 You call me 'Teacher' and 'Lord,' and you are right, because that's what I am. 14 And since I, your Lord and Teacher, have washed your feet, you ought to wash each other's feet. 15 I have given you an example to follow. Do as I have done to you. 16 I tell you the truth, slaves are not greater than their master. Nor is the messenger more important than the one who sends the message. 17 Now that you know these things, God will bless you for doing them.

18 "I am not saying these things to all of you; I know the ones I have chosen. But this fulfills the Scripture that says, 'The one who eats my food has turned against me.' 19 I tell you this beforehand, so that when it happens you will believe that I AM the Messiah. 20 I tell you the truth, anyone who welcomes my messenger is welcoming me, and anyone who welcomes me is welcoming the Father who sent me."

Matthew 26:20-25

20 When it was evening, Jesus sat down at the table with the twelve disciples. 21 While they were eating, he said, "I tell you the truth, one of you will betray me."

22 Greatly distressed, each one asked in turn, "Am I the one, Lord?"

23 He replied, "One of you who has just eaten from this bowl with me
will betray me. 24 For the Son of Man must die, as the Scriptures declared long ago. But how terrible it will be for the one who betrays him.
It would be far better for that man if he had never been born!"

25 Judas, the one who would betray him, also asked, "Rabbi, am I the one?"

And Jesus told him, "You have said it."

Mark 14:18-21

18 As they were at the table eating, Jesus said, "I tell you the truth, one of you eating with me here will betray me."

19 Greatly distressed, each one asked in turn, "Am I the one?"

20 He replied, "It is one of you twelve who is eating from this bowl with
me. 21 For the Son of Man must die, as the Scriptures declared long
ago. But how terrible it will be for the one who betrays him. It would be
far better for that man if he had never been born!"

Luke 22:21-23

21 "But here at this table, sitting among us as a friend, is the man who
will betray me. 22 For it has been determined that the Son of Man must
die. But what sorrow awaits the one who betrays him." 23 The disciples
began to ask each other which of them would ever do such a thing.

John 13:21-30

21 Now Jesus was deeply troubled, and he exclaimed, "I tell you the truth, one of you will betray me!"

22 The disciples looked at each other, wondering whom he could mean.
23 The disciple Jesus loved was sitting next to Jesus at the table. 24
Simon Peter motioned to him to ask, "Who's he talking about?" 25 So
that disciple leaned over to Jesus and asked, "Lord, who is it?"

26 Jesus responded, "It is the one to whom I give the bread I dip in the

bowl." And when he had dipped it, he gave it to Judas, son of Simon
Iscariot. 27 When Judas had eaten the bread, Satan entered into him.
Then Jesus told him, "Hurry and do what you're going to do." 28 None
of the others at the table knew what Jesus meant. 29 Since Judas was
their treasurer, some thought Jesus was telling him to go and pay for the
food or to give some money to the poor. 30 So Judas left at once, going
out into the night.

Matthew 26:31-35

31 On the way, Jesus told them, "Tonight all of you will desert me. For the Scriptures say, 'God will strike the Shepherd, and the sheep of the flock will be scattered.'

32 But after I have been raised from the dead, I will go ahead of you to Galilee and meet you there."

33 Peter declared, "Even if everyone else deserts you, I will never desert you."

34 Jesus replied, "I tell you the truth, Peter—this very night, before the rooster crows, you will deny three times that you even know me."

35 "No!" Peter insisted. "Even if I have to die with you, I will never deny you!" And all the other disciples vowed the same.

Mark 14:27-30

27 On the way, Jesus told them, "All of you will desert me. For the Scriptures say,

'God will strike the Shepherd, and the sheep will be scattered.'

28 But after I am raised from the dead, I will go ahead of you to Galilee and meet you there."

29 Peter said to him, "Even if everyone else deserts you, I never will."

30 Jesus replied, "I tell you the truth, Peter—this very night, before the rooster crows twice, you will deny three times that you even know me."

Luke 22:31-38

31 "Simon, Simon, Satan has asked to sift each of you like wheat. 32 But I have pleaded in prayer for you, Simon, that your faith should not fail. So when you have repented and turned to me again, strengthen your brothers."

33 Peter said, "Lord, I am ready to go to prison with you, and even to die with you."

34 But Jesus said, "Peter, let me tell you something. Before the rooster crows tomorrow morning, you will deny three times that you even know me."

35 Then Jesus asked them, "When I sent you out to preach the Good News and you did not have money, a traveler's bag, or extra clothing, did you need anything?"

"No," they replied.

36 "But now," he said, "take your money and a traveler's bag. And if you don't have a sword, sell your cloak and buy one! 37 For the time has come for this prophecy about me to be fulfilled: 'He was counted among the rebels.' Yes, everything written about me by the prophets will come true."

38 "Look, Lord," they replied, "we have two swords among us."

"That's enough," he said.

Matthew 26:26-29

26 As they were eating, Jesus took some bread and blessed it. Then he broke it in pieces and gave it to the disciples, saying, "Take this and eat it, for this is my body."

27 And he took a cup of wine and gave thanks to God for it. He gave it to them and said, "Each of you drink from it, 28 for this is my blood, which confirms the covenant between God and his people. It is poured out as a sacrifice to forgive the sins of many. 29 Mark my words—I will

not drink wine again until the day I drink it new with you in my Father's Kingdom."

Mark 14:22-25

22 As they were eating, Jesus took some bread and blessed it. Then he broke it in pieces and gave it to the disciples, saying, "Take it, for this is my body."

23 And he took a cup of wine and gave thanks to God for it. He gave it
to them, and they all drank from it. 24 And he said to them, "This is my
blood, which confirms the covenant between God and his people. It is
poured out as a sacrifice for many. 25 I tell you the truth, I will not drink
wine again until the day I drink it new in the Kingdom of God."

Luke 22:17-20

17 Then he took a cup of wine and gave thanks to God for it. Then he
said, "Take this and share it among yourselves. 18 For I will not drink
wine again until the Kingdom of God has come."

19 He took some bread and gave thanks to God for it. Then he broke it in pieces and gave it to the disciples, saying, "This is my body, which is given for you. Do this to remember me."

20 After supper he took another cup of wine and said, "This cup is the new covenant between God and his people—an agreement confirmed with my blood, which is poured out as a sacrifice for you.

1 Corinthians 11:23-26

23 For I pass on to you what I received from the Lord himself. On the
night when he was betrayed, the Lord Jesus took some bread 24 and
gave thanks to God for it. Then he broke it in pieces and said, "This is
my body, which is given for you. Do this to remember me." 25 In the
same way, he took the cup of wine after supper, saying, "This cup is the
new covenant between God and his people—an agreement confirmed
with my blood. Do this to remember me as often as you drink it." 26
For every time you eat this bread and drink this cup, you are announcing
the Lord's death until he comes again.

John 14

1 "Don't let your hearts be troubled. Trust in God, and trust also in me. 2 There is more than enough room in my Father's home. If this were not so, would I have told you that I am going to prepare a place for you? 3 When everything is ready, I will come and get you, so that you will always be with me where I am. 4 And you know the way to where I am going."

5 "No, we don't know, Lord," Thomas said. "We have no idea where you are going, so how can we know the way?"

6 Jesus told him, "I am the way, the truth, and the life. No one can come to the Father except through me. 7 If you had really known me, you would know who my Father is. From now on, you do know him and have seen him!"

8 Philip said, "Lord, show us the Father, and we will be satisfied."

9 Jesus replied, "Have I been with you all this time, Philip, and yet you still don't know who I am? Anyone who has seen me has seen the Father! So why are you asking me to show him to you? 10 Don't you believe that I am in the Father and the Father is in me? The words I speak are not my own, but my Father who lives in me does his work through me. 11 Just believe that I am in the Father and the Father is in me. Or at least believe because of the work you have seen me do.

12 "I tell you the truth, anyone who believes in me will do the same works I have done, and even greater works, because I am going to be with the Father. 13 You can ask for anything in my name, and I will do it, so that the Son can bring glory to the Father. 14 Yes, ask me for anything in my name, and I will do it!

Jesus Promises the Holy Spirit

15 "If you love me, obey my commandments. 16 And I will ask the Father, and he will give you another Advocate, who will never leave you. 17 He is the Holy Spirit, who leads into all truth. The world cannot receive him, because it isn't looking for him and doesn't recognize him. But you know him, because he lives with you now and later will be in

you. 18 No, I will not abandon you as orphans—I will come to you.

19 Soon the world will no longer see me, but you will see me. Since I live, you also will live. 20 When I am raised to life again, you will know that I am in my Father, and you are in me, and I am in you. 21 Those who accept my commandments and obey them are the ones who love me. And because they love me, my Father will love them. And I will love them and reveal myself to each of them."

22 Judas (not Judas Iscariot, but the other disciple with that name) said to him, "Lord, why are you going to reveal yourself only to us and not to the world at large?"

23 Jesus replied, "All who love me will do what I say. My Father will love them, and we will come and make our home with each of them. 24 Anyone who doesn't love me will not obey me. And remember, my words are not my own. What I am telling you is from the Father who sent me. 25 I am telling you these things now while I am still with you. 26 But when the Father sends the Advocate as my representative—that is, the Holy Spirit—he will teach you everything and will remind you of everything I have told you.

27 "I am leaving you with a gift—peace of mind and heart. And the peace I give is a gift the world cannot give. So don't be troubled or afraid. 28 Remember what I told you: I am going away, but I will come back to you again. If you really loved me, you would be happy that I am going to the Father, who is greater than I am. 29 I have told you these things before they happen so that when they do happen, you will believe.

30 "I don't have much more time to talk to you, because the ruler of this world approaches. He has no power over me, 31 but I will do what the Father requires of me, so that the world will know that I love the Father. Come, let's be going.

Appendix:

Mayflower Compact

History: This is the first document of governance for what would become the United States. It was signed aboard their ship, the Mayflower, prior to the Pilgrims landing at Provincetown Harbor, Cape Cod, Massachusetts. Its purpose was to have all the settlers agree on the basic tenants of government, prior to forming the Plymouth Colony.

In this short agreement, most of the men (41) aboard ship committed to form a society based on biblical principles. Signers were not just the religious Puritans, but also others who were looking for freedom. In this contract they pledged to institute "just and equal Laws, Ordinances, Acts, Constitutions and Offices," and their obedience to these laws.

The Compact stressed the core civic values of justice, equality, and personal responsibility. It also expressed their mutual commitment to only establish laws and regulations with the consent of the governed. This short document became the foundation on which State government constitutions, and the U.S. Constitution, were later built.

Text of Mayflower Compact (Modern-English)

In the name of God, Amen. We, whose names are underwritten, the Loyal Subjects of our dread [revered] Sovereign Lord King James, by the Grace of God, of Great Britain, France, and Ireland, King, defender of the Faith, etc.:

Having undertaken, for the Glory of God, and advancements of the Christian faith, and the honor of our King and Country, a voyage to plant the first colony in the Northern parts of Virginia; do by these presents, solemnly and mutually, in the presence of God, and one another; covenant and combine ourselves together into a civil body politic; for our better ordering, and preservation and furtherance of the ends aforesaid; and by virtue hereof to enact, constitute, and frame, such just and equal laws, ordinances, acts, constitutions, and offices, from time to time, as shall be thought most meet and convenient for the general good of the colony; unto which we promise all due submission and obedience.

In witness whereof we have hereunto subscribed our names at Cape Cod the 11th of November, in the year of the reign of our Sovereign Lord King James, of England, France, and Ireland, the eighteenth, and of Scotland the fifty-fourth, 1620 [Julian Calendar; November 11, 1620 using our Gregorian calendar].

Text of Mayflower Compact (Original Text)

Note: The original Mayflower Compact document has been lost. The below text comes from the book "Mourt's Relation" by Edward Winslow and William Brandford. Since Bradford was the original author of the Mayflower Compact, and his book was written within two years of the original document, the below text is considered to be reliable. Spelling and grammar is as used in the original source.

\- - - - - - -

In ye name of God Amen. We, whose names are underwritten, the Loyal Subjects of our dread Sovereign Lord King James, by ye Grace of God, of great Britaine, Franc, & Yreland, King, defender of ye Faith, &c.

Haveing undertaken, for ye Glorie of God, and advancements of ye Christian faith, and the honour of our King & countrie, a voyage to plant ye first colonie in ye Northern parts of Virginia; Doe by these presents, solemnly & mutualy, in ye presence of God, and one of another; covenant & combine ourselves together into a Civill body politick; for our better ordering, & preservation & furtherance of ye ends aforesaid; and by vertue hereof to enact, constitute, and frame, such just & equal Lawes, ordinances, Acts, constitutions, & offices, from time to time, as shall be thought most meete and convenient for ye generall good of ye Colonie; unto which we promise all due submission and obedience.

In witnes wherof we have hereunto subscribed our names at Cap-Codd ye 11 of November, in ye year of ye raigne of our soveraigne Lord King James, of England, France, & Yreland, ye eighteenth, and of Scotland ye fiftie fourth, Ano: Dom. 1620.

Appendix:

Declaration of Independence

Official Transcript obtained from the U.S. National Archives

Spelling and grammar is as used in the original document.

\- - - - - - -

In Congress, July 4, 1776

The unanimous Declaration of the thirteen united States of America

When in the Course of human events, it becomes necessary for one people to dissolve the political bands which have connected them with another, and to assume among the powers of the earth, the separate and equal station to which the Laws of Nature and of Nature's God entitle them, a decent respect to the opinions of mankind requires that they should declare the causes which impel them to the separation.

We hold these truths to be self-evident, that all men are created equal, that they are endowed by their Creator with certain unalienable Rights, that among these are Life, Liberty and the pursuit of Happiness. That to secure these rights, Governments are instituted among Men, deriving their just Powers from the consent of the governed, — That whenever any Form of Government becomes destructive of these ends, it is the Right of the People to alter or to abolish it, and to institute new Government, laying its foundation on such principles and organizing its powers in such form, as to them shall seem most likely to effect their Safety and Happiness. Prudence, indeed, will dictate that Governments long established should not be changed for light and transient causes; and accordingly all experience hath shewn, that mankind are more disposed to suffer, while evils are sufferable, than to right themselves by abolishing the forms to which they are accustomed. But when a long train of abuses and usurpations, pursuing invariably the same Object evinces a design to reduce them under absolute Despotism, it is their right, it is their duty, to throw off such Government, and to provide new guards for their future security — Such has been the patient sufferance of these Colonies; and such is now the necessity which constrains them to alter their former Systems of Government. — The history of the present King of Great Britain is a history of repeated injuries and usurpations, all having in direct object the establishment of an absolute Tyranny over these States. To prove this, let facts be submitted to a candid world.

He has refused his Assent to Laws, the most wholesome and necessary for the public good. He has forbidden his Governors to pass Laws of immediate and pressing importance, unless suspended in their operation till his Assent should be obtained; and when so suspended, he has utterly neglected to attend to them.

He has refused to pass other Laws for the accommodation of large districts of people, unless those people would relinquish the right of Representation in the Legislature, a right inestimable to them and formidable to tyrants only.

He has called together legislative bodies at places unusual, uncomfortable, and distant from the depository of their Public Records, for the sole purpose of fatiguing them into compliance with his measures.

He has dissolved Representative Houses repeatedly, for opposing with manly firmness his invasions on the rights of the people.

He has refused for a long time, after such dissolutions, to cause others to be elected; whereby the Legislative Powers, incapable of Annihilation, have returned to the People at large for their exercise; the State remaining in the mean time exposed to all the dangers of invasion from without, and convulsions within.

He has endeavoured to prevent the population of these States; for that purpose obstructing the Laws for Naturalization of Foreigners; refusing to pass others to encourage their migrations hither, and raising the conditions of new Appropriations of Lands.

He has obstructed the Administration of Justice, by refusing his Assent to Laws for establishing Judiciary Powers.

He has made Judges dependent on his Will alone, for the tenure of their offices, and the amount and payment of their salaries.

He has erected a multitude of New Offices, and sent hither swarms of Officers to harrass our People, and eat out their substance.

He has kept among us, in times of peace, Standing Armies without the Consent of our legislatures.

He has affected to render the Military independent of and superior to the Civil Power.

He has combined with others to subject us to a jurisdiction foreign to our constitution, and unacknowledged by our laws; giving his Assent to their Acts of pretended Legislation:

For Quartering large bodies of armed troops among us:

For protecting them, by a mock Trial, from Punishment for any Murders which they should commit on the Inhabitants of these States:

For cutting off our Trade with all parts of the world:

For imposing Taxes on us without our Consent:

For depriving us in many cases, of the benefits of Trial by Jury:

For transporting us beyond seas to be tried for pretended offences:

For abolishing the free system of English Laws in a neighbouring Province, establishing therein an Arbitrary government, and enlarging its Boundaries so as to render it at once an example and fit instrument for introducing the same absolute rule into these Colonies:

For taking away our Charters, abolishing our most valuable Laws, and altering fundamentally the forms of our Governments:

For suspending our own Legislature, and declaring themselves invested with power to legislate for us in all cases whatsoever.

He has abdicated Government here, by declaring us out of his Protection and waging War against us.

He has plundered our seas, ravaged our Coasts, burnt our towns, and destroyed the lives of our people.

He is at this time transporting large Armies of foreign Mercenaries to compleat the works of death, desolation and tyranny, already begun with circumstances of Cruelty and perfidy scarcely paralleled in the most

barbarous ages, and totally unworthy the Head of a civilized nation.
He has constrained our fellow Citizens taken Captive on the high Seas to bear Arms against their Country, to become the executioners of their friends and Brethren, or to fall themselves by their Hands.
He has excited domestic insurrections amongst us, and has endeavoured to bring on the inhabitants of our frontiers, the merciless Indian Savages, whose known rule of warfare, is an undistinguished destruction of all ages, sexes and conditions.

In every stage of these Oppressions we have Petitioned for Redress in the most humble terms: Our repeated Petitions have been answered only by repeated injury. A Prince, whose character is thus marked by every act which may define a Tyrant, is unfit to be the ruler of a free people.
Nor have we been wanting in attention to our Brittish brethren. We have warned them from time to time of attempts by their legislature to extend an unwarrantable jurisdiction over us. We have reminded them of the circumstances of our emigration and settlement here. We have appealed to their native justice and magnanimity, and we have conjured them by the ties of our common kindred to disavow these usurpations, which, would inevitably interrupt our connections and correspondence. They too have been deaf to the voice of justice and of consanguinity. We must, therefore, acquiesce in the necessity, which denounces our Separation, and hold them, as we hold the rest of mankind, Enemies in War, in Peace Friends.
We, therefore, the Representatives of the united States of America, in General Congress, Assembled, appealing to the Supreme Judge of the world for the rectitude of our intentions, do, in the Name, and by Authority of the good People of these Colonies, solemnly publish and declare, That these United Colonies are, and of Right ought to be Free and Independent States; that they are absolved from all Allegiance to the British Crown, and that all political connection between them and the State of Great Britain, is and ought to be totally dissolved; and that as Free and Independent States, they have full Power to levy War, conclude Peace, contract Alliances, establish Commerce, and to do all other Acts and Things which Independent States may of right do.

And for the support of this Declaration, with a firm reliance on the protection of Divine Providence, we mutually pledge to each other our Lives, our Fortunes and our sacred Honor.

The 56 signatures on the Declaration appear in positions indicated:

Column 1

Georgia:

Button Gwinnett
Lyman Hall
George Walton

Column 2

North Carolina:

William Hooper
Joseph Hewes
John Penn

South Carolina:

Edward Rutledge
Thomas Heyward, Jr.
Thomas Lynch, Jr.
Arthur Middleton

Column 3

Massachusetts:

John Hancock

Maryland:

Samuel Chase
William Paca
Thomas Stone
Charles Carroll of Carrollton

Virginia:

George Wythe
Richard Henry Lee
Thomas Jefferson
Benjamin Harrison
Thomas Nelson, Jr.
Francis Lightfoot Lee
Carter Braxton

Column 4

Pennsylvania:

Robert Morris
Benjamin Rush
Benjamin Franklin
John Morton
George Clymer
James Smith
George Taylor
James Wilson
George Ross

Delaware:

Caesar Rodney
George Read
Thomas McKean

Column 5

New York:

William Floyd
Philip Livingston
Francis Lewis
Lewis Morris

New Jersey:

Richard Stockton
John Witherspoon
Francis Hopkinson
John Hart
Abraham Clark

Column 6

New Hampshire:

Josiah Bartlett
William Whipple

Massachusetts:
Samuel Adams
John Adams
Robert Treat Paine
Elbridge Gerry

Rhode Island:
Stephen Hopkins
William Ellery

Connecticut:
Roger Sherman
Samuel Huntington
William Williams
Oliver Wolcott

New Hampshire:
Matthew Thornton

Appendix:

U.S. Constitution

Official Transcript obtained from the U.S. National Archives

Spelling and grammar is as used in the original document.

Underlined text has been amended or superseded.

– – – – – – –

WE THE PEOPLE of the United States, in Order to form a more perfect Union, establish Justice, insure domestic Tranquility, provide for the common defence, promote the general Welfare, and secure the Blessings of Liberty to ourselves and our Posterity, do ordain and establish this Constitution for the United States of America.

Article. I.

Section. 1.

All legislative Powers herein granted shall be vested in a Congress of the United States, which shall consist of a Senate and House of Representatives.

Section. 2.

The House of Representatives shall be composed of Members chosen every second Year by the People of the several States, and the Electors in each State shall have the Qualifications requisite for Electors of the most numerous Branch of the State Legislature.

No Person shall be a Representative who shall not have attained to the Age of twenty five Years, and been seven Years a Citizen of the United States, and who shall not, when elected, be an Inhabitant of that State in which he shall be chosen.

Representatives and direct Taxes shall be apportioned among the several States which may be included within this Union, according to their respective Numbers, which shall be determined by adding to the whole Number of free Persons, including those bound to Service for a Term of Years, and excluding Indians not taxed, three fifths of all other Persons. The actual Enumeration shall be made within three Years after the first Meeting of the Congress of the United States, and within every subsequent Term of ten Years, in such Manner as they shall by Law direct. The Number of Representatives shall not exceed one for every thirty Thousand, but each State shall have at Least one Representative; and until such enumeration shall be made, the State of New Hampshire shall be entitled to chuse three, Massachusetts eight, Rhode-Island and Providence Plantations one, Connecticut five, New-York six, New Jersey four, Pennsylvania eight, Delaware one, Maryland six, Virginia ten, North Carolina five, South Carolina five, and Georgia three.

When vacancies happen in the Representation from any State, the Executive Authority thereof shall issue Writs of Election to fill such Vacancies.

The House of Representatives shall chuse their Speaker and other Officers; and shall have the sole Power of Impeachment.

Section. 3.

The Senate of the United States shall be composed of two Senators from each State, chosen by the Legislature thereof for six Years; and each Senator shall have one Vote.

Immediately after they shall be assembled in Consequence of the first Election, they shall be divided as equally as may be into three Classes. The Seats of the Senators of the first Class shall be vacated at the Expiration of the second Year, of the second Class at the Expiration of the fourth Year, and of the third Class at the Expiration of the sixth Year, so that one third may be chosen every second Year; and if Vacancies happen by Resignation, or otherwise, during the Recess of the Legislature of any State, the Executive thereof may make temporary Appointments until the next Meeting of the Legislature, which shall then fill such Vacancies.

No Person shall be a Senator who shall not have attained to the Age of thirty Years, and been nine Years a Citizen of the United States, and who shall not, when elected, be an Inhabitant of that State for which he shall be chosen.

The Vice President of the United States shall be President of the Senate, but shall have no Vote, unless they be equally divided.

The Senate shall chuse their other Officers, and also a President pro tempore, in the Absence of the Vice President, or when he shall exercise the Office of President of the United States.

The Senate shall have the sole Power to try all Impeachments. When sitting for that Purpose, they shall be on Oath or Affirmation. When the President of the United States is tried, the Chief Justice shall preside: And no Person shall be convicted without the Concurrence of two thirds of the Members present.

Judgment in Cases of Impeachment shall not extend further than to removal from Office, and disqualification to hold and enjoy any Office of honor, Trust or Profit under the United States: but the Party convicted shall nevertheless be liable and subject to Indictment, Trial, Judgment and Punishment, according to Law.

Section. 4.

The Times, Places and Manner of holding Elections for Senators and Representatives, shall be prescribed in each State by the Legislature thereof; but the Congress may at any time by Law make or alter such Regulations, except as to the Places of chusing Senators.

The Congress shall assemble at least once in every Year, and such Meeting shall be on the first Monday in December, unless they shall by Law appoint a different Day.

Section. 5.

Each House shall be the Judge of the Elections, Returns and Qualifications of its own Members, and a Majority of each shall constitute a Quorum to do Business; but a smaller Number may adjourn from day to day, and may be authorized to compel the Attendance of absent Members, in such Manner, and under such Penalties as each House may provide.

Each House may determine the Rules of its Proceedings, punish its Members for disorderly Behaviour, and, with the Concurrence of two thirds, expel a Member.

Each House shall keep a Journal of its Proceedings, and from time to time publish the same, excepting such Parts as may in their Judgment require Secrecy; and the Yeas and Nays of the Members of either House on any question shall, at the Desire of one fifth of those Present, be entered on the Journal.

Neither House, during the Session of Congress, shall, without the Consent of the other, adjourn for more than three days, nor to any other Place than that in which the two Houses shall be sitting.

Section. 6.

The Senators and Representatives shall receive a Compensation for their Services, to be ascertained by Law, and paid out of the Treasury of the United States. They shall in all Cases, except Treason, Felony and Breach of the Peace, be privileged from Arrest during their Attendance at the Session of their respective Houses, and in going to and returning from the same; and for any Speech or Debate in either House, they shall not be questioned in any other Place.

No Senator or Representative shall, during the Time for which he was elected, be appointed to any civil Office under the Authority of the United States, which shall have been created, or the Emoluments whereof shall have been encreased during such time; and no Person holding any Office under the United States, shall be a Member of either House during his Continuance in Office.

Section. 7.

All Bills for raising Revenue shall originate in the House of Representatives; but the Senate may propose or concur with Amendments as on other Bills.

Every Bill which shall have passed the House of Representatives and the Senate, shall, before it become a Law, be presented to the President of the United States: If he approve he shall sign it, but if not he shall return it, with his Objections to that House in which it shall have originated, who shall enter the Objections at large on their Journal, and proceed to reconsider it. If after such Reconsideration two thirds of that House shall agree to pass the Bill, it shall be sent, together with the Objections, to the other House, by which it shall likewise be reconsidered, and if approved by two thirds of that House, it shall become a Law. But in all such Cases the Votes of both Houses shall be determined by yeas and Nays, and the Names of the Persons voting for and against the Bill shall be entered on the Journal of each House respectively. If any Bill shall not be returned by the President within ten Days (Sundays excepted) after it shall have been presented to him, the Same shall be a Law, in like Manner as if he had signed it, unless the Congress by their Adjournment prevent its Return, in which Case it shall not be a Law.

Every Order, Resolution, or Vote to which the Concurrence of the Senate and House of Representatives may be necessary (except on a question of Adjournment) shall be presented to the President of the United States; and before the Same shall take Effect, shall be approved by him, or being disapproved by him, shall be repassed by two thirds of the Senate and House of Representatives, according to the Rules and Limitations prescribed in the Case of a Bill.

Section. 8.

The Congress shall have Power To lay and collect Taxes, Duties, Imposts and Excises, to pay the Debts and provide for the common Defence and general Welfare of the United States; but all Duties, Imposts and Excises shall be uniform throughout the United States;

To borrow Money on the credit of the United States;

To regulate Commerce with foreign Nations, and among the several States, and with the Indian Tribes;

To establish an uniform Rule of Naturalization, and uniform Laws on the subject of Bankruptcies throughout the United States;

To coin Money, regulate the Value thereof, and of foreign Coin, and fix the Standard of Weights and Measures;

To provide for the Punishment of counterfeiting the Securities and current Coin of the United States;

To establish Post Offices and post Roads;

To promote the Progress of Science and useful Arts, by securing for limited Times to Authors and Inventors the exclusive Right to their respective Writings and Discoveries;

To constitute Tribunals inferior to the supreme Court;

To define and punish Piracies and Felonies committed on the high Seas, and Offences against the Law of Nations;

To declare War, grant Letters of Marque and Reprisal, and make Rules concerning Captures on Land and Water;

To raise and support Armies, but no Appropriation of Money to that Use shall be for a longer Term than two Years;

To provide and maintain a Navy;

To make Rules for the Government and Regulation of the land and naval Forces;

To provide for calling forth the Militia to execute the Laws of the Union, suppress Insurrections and repel Invasions;

To provide for organizing, arming, and disciplining, the Militia, and for governing such Part of them as may be employed in the Service of the United States, reserving to the States respectively, the Appointment of the Officers, and the Authority of training the Militia according to the discipline prescribed by Congress;

To exercise exclusive Legislation in all Cases whatsoever, over such District (not exceeding ten Miles square) as may, by Cession of particular States, and the Acceptance of Congress, become the Seat of the Government of the United States, and to exercise like Authority over all Places purchased by the Consent of the Legislature of the State in which the Same shall be, for the Erection of Forts, Magazines, Arsenals, dock-Yards, and other needful Buildings;--And

To make all Laws which shall be necessary and proper for carrying into Execution the foregoing Powers, and all other Powers vested by this Constitution in the Government of the United States, or in any Department or Officer thereof.

Section. 9.

The Migration or Importation of such Persons as any of the States now existing shall think proper to admit, shall not be prohibited by the Congress prior to the Year one thousand eight hundred and eight, but a Tax or duty may be imposed on such Importation, not exceeding ten dollars for each Person.

The Privilege of the Writ of Habeas Corpus shall not be suspended, unless when in Cases of Rebellion or Invasion the public Safety may require it.

No Bill of Attainder or ex post facto Law shall be passed.

No Capitation, or other direct, Tax shall be laid, unless in Proportion to the Census or enumeration herein before directed to be taken.

No Tax or Duty shall be laid on Articles exported from any State.

No Preference shall be given by any Regulation of Commerce or Revenue to the Ports of one State over those of another; nor shall Vessels bound to, or from, one State, be obliged to enter, clear, or pay Duties in another.

No Money shall be drawn from the Treasury, but in Consequence of

Appropriations made by Law; and a regular Statement and Account of the Receipts and Expenditures of all public Money shall be published from time to time.

No Title of Nobility shall be granted by the United States: And no Person holding any Office of Profit or Trust under them, shall, without the Consent of the Congress, accept of any present, Emolument, Office, or Title, of any kind whatever, from any King, Prince, or foreign State.

Section. 10.

No State shall enter into any Treaty, Alliance, or Confederation; grant Letters of Marque and Reprisal; coin Money; emit Bills of Credit; make any Thing but gold and silver Coin a Tender in Payment of Debts; pass any Bill of Attainder, ex post facto Law, or Law impairing the Obligation of Contracts, or grant any Title of Nobility.

No State shall, without the Consent of the Congress, lay any Imposts or Duties on Imports or Exports, except what may be absolutely necessary for executing it's inspection Laws: and the net Produce of all Duties and Imposts, laid by any State on Imports or Exports, shall be for the Use of the Treasury of the United States; and all such Laws shall be subject to the Revision and Controul of the Congress.

No State shall, without the Consent of Congress, lay any Duty of Tonnage, keep Troops, or Ships of War in time of Peace, enter into any Agreement or Compact with another State, or with a foreign Power, or engage in War, unless actually invaded, or in such imminent Danger as will not admit of delay.

Article. II.

Section. 1.

The executive Power shall be vested in a President of the United States of America. He shall hold his Office during the Term of four Years, and, together with the Vice President, chosen for the same Term, be elected, as follows:

Each State shall appoint, in such Manner as the Legislature thereof may direct, a Number of Electors, equal to the whole Number of Senators and Representatives to which the State may be entitled in the Congress: but no Senator or Representative, or Person holding an Office of Trust or Profit under the United States, shall be appointed an Elector.

The Electors shall meet in their respective States, and vote by Ballot for two Persons, of whom one at least shall not be an Inhabitant of the same State with themselves. And they shall make a List of all the Persons voted for, and of the Number of Votes for each; which List they shall sign and certify, and transmit sealed to the Seat of the Government of the United States, directed to the President of the Senate. The President of the Senate shall, in the Presence of the Senate and House of Representatives, open all the Certificates, and the Votes shall then be counted. The Person having the greatest Number of Votes shall be the President, if such Number be a Majority of the whole Number of Electors appointed; and if there be more than one who have such Majority, and have an equal Number of Votes, then the House of Representatives shall immediately chuse by Ballot one of them for President; and if no Person have a Majority, then from the five highest on the List the said House shall in like Manner chuse the President. But in chusing the President, the Votes shall be taken by States, the Representation from each State having one Vote; A quorum for this purpose shall consist of a Member or Members from two thirds of the States, and a Majority of all the States shall be necessary to a Choice. In every Case, after the Choice of the President, the Person having the greatest Number of Votes of the Electors shall be the Vice President. But if there should remain two or more who have equal Votes, the Senate shall chuse from them by Ballot the Vice President.

The Congress may determine the Time of chusing the Electors, and the Day on which they shall give their Votes; which Day shall be the same throughout the United States.

No Person except a natural born Citizen, or a Citizen of the United States, at the time of the Adoption of this Constitution, shall be eligible to the Office of President; neither shall any Person be eligible to that Office who shall not have attained to the Age of thirty five Years, and been fourteen Years a Resident within the United States.

In Case of the Removal of the President from Office, or of his Death, Resignation, or Inability to discharge the Powers and Duties of the said Office, the Same shall devolve on the Vice President, and the Congress may by Law provide for the Case of Removal, Death, Resignation or Inability, both of the President and Vice President, declaring what Officer shall then act as President, and such Officer shall act accordingly, until the Disability be removed, or a President shall be elected.

The President shall, at stated Times, receive for his Services, a Compensation, which shall neither be increased nor diminished during the Period for which he shall have been elected, and he shall not receive within that Period any other Emolument from the United States, or any of them.

Before he enter on the Execution of his Office, he shall take the following Oath or Affirmation:--"I do solemnly swear (or affirm) that I will faithfully execute the Office of President of the United States, and will to the best of my Ability, preserve, protect and defend the Constitution of the United States."

Section. 2.

The President shall be Commander in Chief of the Army and Navy of the United States, and of the Militia of the several States, when called into the actual Service of the United States; he may require the Opinion, in writing, of the principal Officer in each of the executive Departments, upon any Subject relating to the Duties of their respective Offices, and he shall have Power to grant Reprieves and Pardons for Offences against the United States, except in Cases of Impeachment.

He shall have Power, by and with the Advice and Consent of the Senate, to make Treaties, provided two thirds of the Senators present concur; and he shall nominate, and by and with the Advice and Consent of the Senate, shall appoint Ambassadors, other public Ministers and Consuls, Judges of the supreme Court, and all other Officers of the United States, whose Appointments are not herein otherwise provided for, and which shall be established by Law: but the Congress may by Law vest the Appointment of such inferior Officers, as they think proper, in the President alone, in the Courts of Law, or in the Heads of Departments.

The President shall have Power to fill up all Vacancies that may happen during the Recess of the Senate, by granting Commissions which shall expire at the End of their next Session.

Section. 3.

He shall from time to time give to the Congress Information of the State of the Union, and recommend to their Consideration such Measures as he shall judge necessary and expedient; he may, on extraordinary Occasions, convene both Houses, or either of them, and in Case of Disagreement between them, with Respect to the Time of Adjournment, he may adjourn them to such Time as he shall think proper; he shall receive Ambassadors and other public Ministers; he shall take Care that the Laws be faithfully executed, and shall Commission all the Officers of the United States.

Section. 4.

The President, Vice President and all civil Officers of the United States, shall be removed from Office on Impeachment for, and Conviction of, Treason, Bribery, or other high Crimes and Misdemeanors.

Article III.

Section. 1.

The judicial Power of the United States shall be vested in one supreme Court, and in such inferior Courts as the Congress may from time to time ordain and establish. The Judges, both of the supreme and inferior Courts, shall hold their Offices during good Behaviour, and shall, at stated Times, receive for their Services a Compensation, which shall not be diminished during their Continuance in Office.

Section. 2.

The judicial Power shall extend to all Cases, in Law and Equity, arising under this Constitution, the Laws of the United States, and Treaties made, or which shall be made, under their Authority;--to all Cases affecting Ambassadors, other public Ministers and Consuls;--to all Cases of admiralty and maritime Jurisdiction;--to Controversies to which the United States shall be a Party;--to Controversies between two or more States;--between a State and Citizens of another State,--between Citizens of different States,--between Citizens of the same State claiming Lands under Grants of different States, and between a State, or the Citizens thereof, and foreign States, Citizens or Subjects.

In all Cases affecting Ambassadors, other public Ministers and Consuls, and those in which a State shall be Party, the supreme Court shall have original Jurisdiction. In all the other Cases before mentioned, the supreme Court shall have appellate Jurisdiction, both as to Law and Fact, with such Exceptions, and under such Regulations as the Congress shall make.

The Trial of all Crimes, except in Cases of Impeachment, shall be by Jury; and such Trial shall be held in the State where the said Crimes shall have been committed; but when not committed within any State, the Trial shall be at such Place or Places as the Congress may by Law have directed.

Section. 3.

Treason against the United States, shall consist only in levying War against them, or in adhering to their Enemies, giving them Aid and Comfort. No Person shall be convicted of Treason unless on the Testimony of two Witnesses to the same overt Act, or on Confession in open Court.

The Congress shall have Power to declare the Punishment of Treason, but no Attainder of Treason shall work Corruption of Blood, or Forfeiture except during the Life of the Person attainted.

Article. IV.

Section. 1.

Full Faith and Credit shall be given in each State to the public Acts,

Records, and judicial Proceedings of every other State. And the Congress may by general Laws prescribe the Manner in which such Acts, Records and Proceedings shall be proved, and the Effect thereof.

Section. 2.

The Citizens of each State shall be entitled to all Privileges and Immunities of Citizens in the several States.

A Person charged in any State with Treason, Felony, or other Crime, who shall flee from Justice, and be found in another State, shall on Demand of the executive Authority of the State from which he fled, be delivered up, to be removed to the State having Jurisdiction of the Crime.

No Person held to Service or Labour in one State, under the Laws thereof, escaping into another, shall, in Consequence of any Law or Regulation therein, be discharged from such Service or Labour, but shall be delivered up on Claim of the Party to whom such Service or Labour may be due.

Section. 3.

New States may be admitted by the Congress into this Union; but no new State shall be formed or erected within the Jurisdiction of any other State; nor any State be formed by the Junction of two or more States, or Parts of States, without the Consent of the Legislatures of the States concerned as well as of the Congress.

The Congress shall have Power to dispose of and make all needful Rules and Regulations respecting the Territory or other Property belonging to the United States; and nothing in this Constitution shall be so construed as to Prejudice any Claims of the United States, or of any particular State.

Section. 4.

The United States shall guarantee to every State in this Union a Republican Form of Government, and shall protect each of them against Invasion; and on Application of the Legislature, or of the Executive (when the Legislature cannot be convened), against domestic Violence.

Article. V.

The Congress, whenever two thirds of both Houses shall deem it necessary, shall propose Amendments to this Constitution, or, on the Application of the Legislatures of two thirds of the several States, shall call a Convention for proposing Amendments, which, in either Case, shall be valid to all Intents and Purposes, as Part of this Constitution, when ratified by the Legislatures of three fourths of the several States, or by Conventions in three fourths thereof, as the one or the other Mode of Ratification may be proposed by the Congress; Provided that no Amendment which may be made prior to the Year One thousand eight hundred and eight shall in any Manner affect the first and fourth Clauses in the Ninth Section of the first Article; and that no State, without its Consent, shall be deprived of its equal Suffrage in the Senate.

Article. VI.

All Debts contracted and Engagements entered into, before the Adoption of this Constitution, shall be as valid against the United States under this Constitution, as under the Confederation.

This Constitution, and the Laws of the United States which shall be made in Pursuance thereof; and all Treaties made, or which shall be made, under the Authority of the United States, shall be the supreme Law of the Land; and the Judges in every State shall be bound thereby, any Thing in the Constitution or Laws of any State to the Contrary notwithstanding.

The Senators and Representatives before mentioned, and the Members of the several State Legislatures, and all executive and judicial Officers, both of the United States and of the several States, shall be bound by Oath or Affirmation, to support this Constitution; but no religious Test shall ever be required as a Qualification to any Office or public Trust under the United States.

Article. VII.

The Ratification of the Conventions of nine States, shall be sufficient for the Establishment of this Constitution between the States so ratifying the Same.

The Word, "the," being interlined between the seventh and eighth Lines of the first Page, the Word "Thirty" being partly written on an Erazure in the fifteenth Line of the first Page, The Words "is tried" being interlined between the thirty second and thirty third Lines of the first Page and the Word "the" being interlined between the forty third and forty fourth Lines of the second Page.

Attest William Jackson Secretary

done in Convention by the Unanimous Consent of the States present the Seventeenth Day of September in the Year of our Lord one thousand seven hundred and Eighty seven and of the Independance of the United States of America the Twelfth In witness whereof We have hereunto subscribed our Names,

Go. Washington
Presidt and deputy from Virginia

Delaware
Geo: Read
Gunning Bedford jun
John Dickinson
Richard Bassett
Jaco: Broom

Maryland
James McHenry
Dan of St Thos. Jenifer
Danl. Carroll

Virginia
John Blair
James Madison Jr.

North Carolina
Wm. Blount
Richd. Dobbs Spaight
Hu Williamson

South Carolina
J. Rutledge
Charles Cotesworth Pinckney
Charles Pinckney
Pierce Butler

Georgia
William Few
Abr Baldwin

New Hampshire
John Langdon
Nicholas Gilman

Massachusetts
Nathaniel Gorham
Rufus King

Connecticut
Wm. Saml. Johnson
Roger Sherman

New York
Alexander Hamilton

New Jersey
Wil: Livingston
David Brearley
Wm. Paterson
Jona: Dayton

Pennsylvania
B Franklin
Thomas Mifflin
Robt. Morris
Geo. Clymer
Thos. FitzSimons
Jared Ingersoll
James Wilson
Gouv Morris

Appendix:

U.S. Bill of Rights

Official Transcript obtained from the U.S. National Archives
Spelling and grammar is as used in the original document.

The *Bill of Rights was added by the nation's Founding Fathers to provide additional clarity to the U.S. Constitution.*

\- - - - - - -

Congress of the United States
begun and held at the City of New-York, on Wednesday the fourth of March, one thousand seven hundred and eighty nine.

THE Conventions of a number of the States, having at the time of their adopting the Constitution, expressed a desire, in order to prevent misconstruction or abuse of its powers, that further declaratory and restrictive clauses should be added: And as extending the ground of public confidence in the Government, will best ensure the beneficent ends of its institution.

RESOLVED by the Senate and House of Representatives of the United States of America, in Congress assembled, two thirds of both Houses concurring, that the following Articles be proposed to the Legislatures of the several States, as amendments to the Constitution of the United States, all, or any of which Articles, when ratified by three fourths of the said Legislatures, to be valid to all intents and purposes, as part of the said Constitution; viz.

ARTICLES in addition to, and Amendment of the Constitution of the United States of America, proposed by Congress, and ratified by the Legislatures of the several States, pursuant to the fifth Article of the original Constitution.

Amendment I

Congress shall make no law respecting an establishment of religion, or prohibiting the free exercise thereof; or abridging the freedom of speech, or of the press; or the right of the people peaceably to assemble, and to petition the Government for a redress of grievances.

Amendment II

A well regulated Militia, being necessary to the security of a free State, the right of the people to keep and bear Arms, shall not be infringed.

Amendment III

No Soldier shall, in time of peace be quartered in any house, without the consent of the Owner, nor in time of war, but in a manner to be prescribed by law.

Amendment IV

The right of the people to be secure in their persons, houses, papers, and effects, against unreasonable searches and seizures, shall not be violated, and no Warrants shall issue, but upon probable cause, supported by Oath or affirmation, and particularly describing the place to be searched, and the persons or things to be seized.

Amendment V

No person shall be held to answer for a capital, or otherwise infamous crime, unless on a presentment or indictment of a Grand Jury, except in cases arising in the land or naval forces, or in the Militia, when in actual service in time of War or public danger; nor shall any person be subject for the same offence to be twice put in jeopardy of life or limb; nor shall be compelled in any criminal case to be a witness against himself, nor be deprived of life, liberty, or property, without due process of law; nor shall private property be taken for public use, without just compensation.

Amendment VI

In all criminal prosecutions, the accused shall enjoy the right to a speedy and public trial, by an impartial jury of the State and district wherein the crime shall have been committed, which district shall have been previously ascertained by law, and to be informed of the nature and cause of the accusation; to be confronted with the witnesses against him; to have compulsory process for obtaining witnesses in his favor, and to have the Assistance of Counsel for his defence.

Amendment VII

In Suits at common law, where the value in controversy shall exceed twenty dollars, the right of trial by jury shall be preserved, and no fact tried by a jury, shall be otherwise re-examined in any Court of the United States, than according to the rules of the common law.

Amendment VIII

Excessive bail shall not be required, nor excessive fines imposed, nor cruel and unusual punishments inflicted.

Amendment IX

The enumeration in the Constitution, of certain rights, shall not be construed to deny or disparage others retained by the people.

Amendment X

The powers not delegated to the United States by the Constitution, nor prohibited by it to the States, are reserved to the States respectively, or to the people.

\- - - - - - -

To read the amendments to the Constitution which were enacted after the Bill of Rights was ratified, follow this link to Amendments 11-27: http://www.archives.gov/exhibits/charters/constitution_amendments_11-27.html

Appendix:

Christian Lyrics of U.S Patriotic Music

Songs like the official U.S. national anthem, "The Star Spangled Banner," as well as the "Battle Hymn of the Republic" (both included below) are just two of the many examples of the strong Christian heritage of the United States expressed in music.

The spirit of sacrifice which these lyrics demonstrate is a reminder of the cost of freedom. These words also remind us that Bible-believing people have always been at the forefront of America's battles, paying the price for justice and liberty. This isn't a new concept; it's a return to our founding principles.

The Star Spangled Banner was originally titled, "In Defense of Fort McHenry." Composed by Francis Scott Key who wrote it during the war with the British, the U.S. Congress proclaimed it the National Anthem in 1931. You will find more about the history of this patriotic song after the lyrics.

Lyrics for *"The Star Spangled Banner"*

Oh, say, can you see, by the dawn's early light,
What so proudly we hailed at the twilight's last gleaming?
Whose broad stripes and bright stars, thru the perilous fight,
O'er the ramparts we watched, were so gallantly streaming?
And the rockets' red glare, the bombs bursting in air,
Gave proof through the night that our flag was still there.
O say, does that star-spangled banner yet wave
O'er the land of the free and the home of the brave?

On the shore dimly seen through the mists of the deep,
Where the foe's haughty host in dread silence reposes,
What is that which the breeze, o'er the towering steep,

As it fitfully blows, half conceals, half discloses?
Now it catches the gleam of the morning's first beam,
In full glory reflected, now shines on the stream:
'Tis the star-spangled banner: O, long may it wave
O'er the land of the free and the home of the brave!

And where is that band who so vauntingly swore
That the havoc of war and the battle's confusion
A home and a country should leave us no more?
Their blood has washed out their foul footsteps' pollution.
No refuge could save the hireling and slave
From the terror of flight or the gloom of the grave:
And the star-spangled banner in triumph doth wave
O'er the land of the free and the home of the brave.

O, thus be it ever when freemen shall stand,
Between their loved home and the war's desolation!
Blest with victory and peace, may the heav'n-rescued land
Praise the Power that hath made and preserved us a nation!
Then conquer we must, when our cause it is just,
And this be our motto: "In God is our trust"
And the star-spangled banner in triumph shall wave
O'er the land of the free and the home of the brave!

History of *The Star Spangled Banner:* In 1814, about a week after the city of Washington, DC and the White House had been burned, British troops moved up Baltimore Harbor in Maryland. Francis Scott Key risked his life by visiting the British fleet on September 13th, in an attempt to negotiate the release of Dr. William Beanes, a medical doctor who had been captured by the British during their raid. The British agreed to release the noncombatant doctor, but the two were detained on the ship so as not to warn the Americans that the British Navy was going to bombard Fort McHenry that night.

At dawn on the 14th, Key noted that the huge American flag (which now hangs in the Smithsonian National Museum of American History) was still waving, indicating that the soldiers at the fort had not surrendered despite the withering bombing. The sight of that battle-torn flag inspired him to write a poem titled Defense of Fort McHenry, which was later put to music. In 1931 this song officially became the U.S. national anthem.

Lyrics for the *Battle Hymn of the Republic*

By Julia Ward Howe

Mine eyes have seen the glory of the coming of the Lord;
He is trampling out the vintage where the grapes of wrath are stored;
He hath loosed the fateful lightning of his terrible swift sword:
His truth is marching on.

I have seen him in the watch-fires of a hundred circling camps;
They have builded him an altar in the evening dews and damps;
I can read his righteous sentence by the dim and flaring lamps;
His day is marching on.

I have read a fiery gospel, writ in burnished rows of steel:
"As ye deal with my contemners, so with you my grace shall deal;
Let the Hero, born of woman, crush the serpent with his heel,
Since God is marching on."

He has sounded forth the trumpet that shall never call retreat;
He is sifting out the hearts of men before his judgment-seat;
Oh, be swift, my soul, to answer him! Be jubilant, my feet!
Our God is marching on.

In the beauty of the lilies Christ was born across the sea,
With a glory in his bosom that transfigures you and me:
As he died to make men holy, let us die to make men free,
While God is marching on.

History of the *Battle Hymn of the Republic*: Considered to be one of the nation's finest patriotic songs, the *Battle Hymn of the Republic* was written during the U.S. Civil War, by Julia Ward Howe. As she watched the men march away from their homes and loved ones, she penned the words of this hymn as an acknowledgement that we have a responsibility to fight against injustice, and that this sometimes requires the use of the sword in battle. Her words remind us that just as Jesus *died to make men holy,* we must be prepared to *die to make men free.*

As we consider the history behind this song we can appreciate why it has such a solemn tone. God's physical protection is never guaranteed even to the faithful, but it also reminds us that eventually He will triumph over evil. Victory is costly, but certain.

A soloist sung this hymn at a large public gathering attended by Abraham Lincoln during the war. The audience responded with loud applause, but the weeping president cried out, *"Sing it again!"* And as it was belted out again, the entire audience succumbed to tears as they reflected more deeply on the meaning of the words.

Patriotic music has now become unfashionable, partly because many of our contemporaries don't want to acknowledge the spiritual underpinnings which have supported this nation since its founding. Yet, despite the best efforts of those who write revisionist history, the biblical principles on which this nation was founded remain crystal clear when we read these historic documents. More to the point, this spirit of sacrifice must be revived if our nation is to survive. We need a revival, and this needs to start with us.

– – – – – – –

For more about the spiritual heritage of the United States, contact "WallBuilders" at www.WallBuilders.org. For young people, the "Early American" section of the video series, "Drive Through History" by ColdWater Media is an excellent and fun teaching tool:
http://www.drivethruhistory.com/series/american-history/

Appendix: TXRFA Firearm Safety Rules

(Adapted and expanded from the NRA Gun Safety Rules)

1. Treat all guns as if they are always loaded and ready to fire.

Using good common sense is the first rule of firearms safety. If you observe unsafe behavior immediately take appropriate action, and bring the violation to the attention of the Range Master or your instructor.

2. Always keep a gun pointed in a safe direction.

Always point the muzzle in a safe direction; never point a firearm at anyone or anything you are not willing to destroy.

A safe direction means that the gun is pointed so that even if it were to go off accidently, it would not cause injury or damage. The key to this rule is to control where the barrel is pointed at all times. Keeping a gun pointed downrange or in a safe direction when not on the gun range, and at a downward angle (approximately a 45-degree downward angle), is generally the safest. However, common sense dictates the safest direction, and this can change as circumstances change.

Even when putting a gun into a holster or storage container, make sure that the muzzle is pointed in a safe direction until the gun is safely secured.

3. Never touch the trigger unless you are ready to shoot.

Keep your finger off the trigger until your sights are on the target and you have made the decision to shoot.

When holding a gun, rest your finger on the trigger-guard (not the trigger) or along the side of the gun. Do not touch the trigger until you are actually ready to fire. When putting a gun in a holster, storage container or anywhere else, watch to make sure that nothing snags the trigger.

4. Be sure of your target—*and what is behind it.*

Confirm your target before pointing your gun at it. Be aware of what is behind your target.

Even if the area between you and your target is clear, the area behind your target may make it unsafe for you to shoot. Bullets penetrating the target, or missing the target, go somewhere. Also, a ricochet can still be deadly, so consider this possibility before shooting.

Since a bullet can travel more than a mile, it is essential that you are sure of your backstop. It is essential to use due care and caution to avoid unintended consequences of death, injury or property damage. Never shoot unless you are sure that the area is safe, and that you have a legal right to shoot.

5. Always keep the gun securely locked or unloaded until ready to use.

The act of legally carrying a concealed weapon is "use" of the gun, so carrying a loaded gun in a safe concealed-carry holster is reasonable as long as proper safety precautions are observed. However, other guns should be kept securely locked or unloaded until they are ready to be used.

Guns should be transported to and from the gun range unloaded. When possible, semi-automatic firearms should be transported to the range with the action open and magazine removed. No unlocked firearms should be handled in the parking lot of the gun range.

For TXRFA range instruction and gun range activities, guns should be transported to the range in either a locked container, or with a highly-visible gun lock installed. Guns must be inspected by a TXRFA instructor or the Range Master prior to being unlocked. Guns cannot be handled until the TXRFA instructor or Range Master directs the student(s) to ready their firearm for inspection or use. Even locked and unloaded guns must always be pointed in a safe direction.

6. The first activity of handling a firearm is to render it safe and verify that it is unloaded.

While keeping the muzzle of the gun pointed in a safe direction, remove the magazine (clip) if it has one, open the action of the firearm, and verify that it is unloaded. Be sure to look, and also to manually check the chamber with your finger, to verify that a cartridge is not inserted.

Whenever a firearm is handed to another person, repeat this exercise, and show the open action and unloaded condition to that person, *before* handing it to them.

When receiving a firearm from another person, repeat this same process even if you have already observed that the gun is unloaded.

7. Never rely on a gun's safety mechanism, or a mechanical device, to render it safe.

Any mechanical safety device can fail. Always treat a gun as if it is loaded and ready to fire.

8. When at the gun range, do not handle a firearm except as directed by your instructor or Range Master.

Wait for instructions before handling a firearm at the gun range. Fire-arms should only be handled when on the firing line, and only after verifying that no one is downrange or forward of your location.

When it is your turn to approach the firing line, when directed by the Range Master or your instructor, remove your gun from its place of storage and only when no one is forward of the firing line.

Know the rules for the gun range you are using, and the commands which will be used on the range, and what they mean.

Do not handle a firearm at the range, or in the parking lot of the range, except as directed by the Range Master or your instructor. Do not handle a firearm except on the firing line.

Do not handle a gun when anyone has moved forward of the firing line, when the firing area has become unsafe, or when targets are being replaced or adjusted.

When at the range, never shoot at anything other than your assigned target. Make sure that the target area is free from rocks, metal and other objects which might cause a bullet to ricochet.

9. Be sure that the gun you are about to use is safe to operate; and that you know how to operate it safely, before loading it.

It is the responsibility of the user of a gun to make sure that it is safe and in good working condition; and that the user knows how to render the gun safe, how to load and unload it, how the mechanism operates, how to clean and maintain it, and (if a semiautomatic) how to disassemble and reassemble it after cleaning and lubrication.

Even if you are familiar with the weapon, it should be inspected before you load it, to make sure that it is safe and that the action and barrel is clear and free of obstructions. Ammunition should be similarly inspected to make sure that it is undamaged and clean. Do not use damaged, corroded or dirty ammunition.

If you are not familiar with the gun you are about to use, learn how to use it before you load it. And, know what to do in the event of a misfire. If the gun is old or may be damaged, have it inspected by a licensed gunsmith before attempting to use it.

10. Use only ammunition that is appropriate for the gun you are about to use.

Use only clean, non-corroded, undamaged ammunition in your gun. And, only use ammunition of the type and caliber recommended by the manufacturer. If the gun is new to you, confirm a match between the gun and ammunition. Note: the caliber and ammunition type is stamped into the barrel or action of the gun. Compare this to the ammunition box and the base of the handgun cartridge. If in doubt, do not proceed until you have verified that the ammunition is appropriate for the gun.

Further, even ammunition which is suitable for use in a particular firearm may not be suitable for in every situation. Or, it may not be approved or appropriate for the gun range or place where you plan to shoot. Some calibers, loads and bullet types are not allowed on a particular range due to their power, environmental considerations, tendency to ricochet, or because they are of a type that is likely to damage the range. Similar factors must be considered when you plan to use the ammunition anywhere else. Tracers, armor piercing and various other specialty-ammunition types are also illegal to use.

Ammunition used for any Texas Republic Firearms Academy class or activity must be SAAMI approved. SAAMI ammunition includes most major brands such as: Black Hills, Cor-Bon, Federal, Fiocchi, Hornady, Remington, Sellier and Bellot, Speer, Ultra Max, and Winchester. Brands specifically prohibited are: Magtech, Monarch, Wolf, and any ammunition manufactured in Russia, China or one of the former Easter Bloc countries. Further, no re-loads or hand-loads are permitted at any Texas Republic firearms Academy sponsored activity.

For self-defense use, use only quality ammunition of a type designed for self-defense, and made by one of the SAAMI approved manufacturers.

11. When in the proximity of someone who is shooting, utilize appropriate safety equipment.

Whether on the grounds of a gun range or shooting anywhere else, wear suitable safety equipment.

When on the range for TXRFA activity, even when not on the firing line, appropriate safety equipment must be worn. This includes:

a) Eye-protection in the form of safety glasses, shooting glasses, or prescription glasses made from polycarbonate and of a design and material that is suitable for protecting the wearer's eyes. Note: It is the responsibility of the individual to make sure that eye protection is adequate.

b) Hearing protection which is muff-style, that has a Noise Reduction Rating (NRR) of 27 or higher, but still allows the wearer to hear range commands. (Ear plugs may be worn in addition to ear-muffs for added hearing protection). However, ear-muff style protection is required so that the instructor and Range Master can see that everyone has ear protection in place. Also, recent studies indicate that the area behind the ear (protected by muff-style hearing protection) is also vulnerable and may be susceptible to hearing damage if not protected.

12. No guns are allowed in a classroom being used by Texas Republic Firearms Academy.

Except for those guns carried or used by TXRFA instructors or certified law enforcement officers, weapons are not allowed in the classroom. This also applies to those who have a State issued license authorizing them to carry a concealed handgun.

13. Alcohol and/or drugs do not mix with firearms use.

Do not carry or use a firearm if you have been drinking any alcoholic beverage or using any drug that might impair your judgment, or your ability to safely operate a gun. It is not sufficient that you are not intoxicated. Even the smallest impairment due to alcohol consumption or drug use is unacceptable. This includes the use of legal drugs which are prescribed by a doctor. If the medication has a cautionary label warning about possible adverse effect to your driving ability or the use of equipment, do not carry or use a firearm until the effects of that drug are completely out of your bloodstream.

14. No horseplay or "joking around" when handling a firearm; or when on the firing-line.

Gun use is serious business. Firearm safety and range safety must always be in the forefront of thought and actions when dealing with firearms. Joking and horseplay can be a distraction to you or other shooters, so save it for later when guns are not involved.

15. Keep your firearms secure and safe.

Even a firearm that is being legally carried should be transported in a secure holster or container, and never allowed to be out of your immediate control.

An unattended firearm is a danger to children, and to adults who do not know how to safely handle a firearm. Stored firearms should be unloaded, locked, and securely stored so that a burglar or thief cannot easily use or steal the gun. Criminals rarely purchase guns from a store; they either steal their guns or purchase a stolen gun. Don't inadvertently arm a criminal as a result of your negligent storage.

It is unlawful to store, transport, or abandon an unsecured firearm in a place where children are likely to be and can obtain access to a firearm. (46.13a-g). Even if you are confident that your child is mature enough to handle a firearm, their friends may not be. Except when used under your supervision and a few other specific exceptions, it is a crime to let a person under 18-years of age to gain access to a firearm.

For extended storage and in situations where a gun safe is not available, consider storing the slide, bolt, and other components of the gun separately. Still utilize a gun lock to keep the gun inoperable even if the pieces are found and reassembled.

Many factors must be considered when deciding where and how to store guns. A person's particular situation will be a major part of the consideration. Dozens of gun storage devices, as well as locking devices that attach directly to the gun are available. However, mechanical locking devices, like the mechanical safeties built into guns, can fail and should not be used as a substitute for safe gun handling and the observance of all gun safety rules.

16. Clean and lubricate your firearm after each use.

Regular cleaning is important in order for your gun to operate correctly and safely. Taking proper care of it will also maintain its value and extend its life. Your gun should be cleaned every time that it is used. For extended storage, use gun oil or a metal preservative made specifically for gun storage. Most lubricants do not adequately protect gunmetal from rust. Additionally, handguns used for concealed carry should be wiped-down with a gunmetal preservative or silicon-impregnated cloth daily, especially if carried in a warm or humid climate.

A gun brought out of prolonged storage should also be cleaned before shooting. Accumulated moisture and dirt, or solidified grease and oil, can prevent the gun from operating properly. Heavily oiled barrels can cause a bullet to be unstable in flight and inaccurate.

Before cleaning your gun, check and double-check to ***make absolutely sure that it is unloaded.***

Use your eyes to visually inspect the firearm, and then insert your little finger into the chamber to make a tactile (by feel) check to confirm that the weapon is unloaded. The gun's action should be open during the cleaning process. Confirm that no ammunition is present in the cleaning area. Do not clean your gun when you are tired, or if you have consumed alcohol, drugs, or any medicines that might cloud or impair your judgment. Remember that even during the activities of cleaning a firearm; it must always be pointed in a safe direction.

17. Do not dry fire or quick-draw your gun in an unsafe place or manner.

A gun should not be dry fired (the trigger pulled on an empty gun) and quick-draw should not be practiced, except when an accidental discharge would not bring the risk of death, injury or unintended property damage. Treat all guns as if they were loaded and ready to fire.

Quick-draw practice, or quickly removing a gun from a holster or storage device, can be extremely dangerous. If you elect to engage in such practice, you need to begin with slow-draw, and over time gradually build to a more rapid presentation of the handgun. The trigger-finger should never touch the trigger until the gun is on target. Quick-draw practice also brings a much greater risk of self-injury. Whether engaged in quick-draw or slow draw of a firearm, holsters and clothing can snag or impede the draw (presentation) of a handgun or accidently pull the trigger, so extreme care must be used to avoid an accidental discharge.

Remember, it is rarely the speed of your draw that will save the day; it is the accuracy of your shots. The benefit of a quick-draw is overrated. We do not allow quick-draw on the range.

To download a PDF of these safety rules formatted for printing, visit: www.TXRFA.com

- To contact the author, visit: www.SigSwanstrom.com
- Follow the author at: www.twitter.com/SigSwanstrom

Footnotes / Endnotes:

---

1 During our four years living in Guatemala, our installation was attacked by Marxist guerillas three times. Additionally, during our travels around the region we encountered bombings and guerilla operations on numerous other occasions.

2 Proverbs 6:12-19

3 In Joel 3:10 the people of Israel are told by God to turn their plows into swords and their pruning hooks into spears, so that they can fight against their oppressors. In Micah 4:3, the Isaiah 2:4 concept is repeated again, but it specifically states that it will occur after God's judgment on the nations of the world.

4 *'Worldview'* is the overall perspective from which a person sees and interprets what is happening in the world, as well as human nature and beliefs about life and the origin of the universe. To learn more about the contrast between secular and biblical worldviews,

check out:

Focus on the Family's *The Truth Project,*

http://www.thetruthproject.org/; also:
the Chuck Colson Center for Christian Worldview,

http://www.colsoncenter.org; and
the *Centurions Program* (founded by Chuck Colson),

http://www.breakpoint.org/resources/centurions.
For high school age students, visit: Probe Ministries,

http://www.probe.org; and
Summit Ministries: http://www.summit.org.

[5] At the end of my time in college I lived in Haiti with three close friends. During these months we were exposed to the cruelty and murders of Haiti's secret police, the Tonton Macoute. For me this was the first time that I had faced the cold reality of institutionalized evil, and our need to stand up for justice. It was also a wake-up call as I realized that I could donate everything I own, and give everything I would ever own to the poor—and it would not move Haiti's problem even an inch in the right direction. Living in the midst of this oppression, a key detail became obvious. The main problem was not a lack of resources; it was the crushing presence of evil. The good people of Haiti were unable to resist the perpetrators of evil, primarily because they were unarmed.

[6] Photo: This stained glass church window depicts Moses with the Ten Commandments. Contrary to the claim of some, Commandment #6 (Exodus 20:13) does not say "Thou shalt not kill." Properly translated from the original Hebrew language, it says that we are prohibited from engaging in murder. The 'Ten Commandments' are found in Exodus 20:1-17, and these Commandments are further elaborated in other parts of the Bible.

[7] *Law Enforcement Code of Ethics*, based on the recommended model published by the International Association of Chiefs of Police. (theIACP.org)

[8] Matthew 5:17; 2 Timothy 3:12-17.

[9] Photo at Top of Page: Statue of the Apostle Peter holding a sword and the Bible. Located within Vatican City, this historic work of art is prominently displayed in front of Saint Peter's Basilica. The concept of being a godly person, who is equipped with Bible knowledge and also prepared to use deadly force, is not a new idea. Note: This statue does not depict the Bible as our Sword, but rather being prepared with the Bible *and* a sword.

[10] Matthew 16:18

[11] The root word of máchairan (pronounced makh'-ahee-rah) is the Greek word *mákhaira,* which means "a battle" or "to fight." Historically, scholars made a clear distinction between the máchairan sword and the *kopis,* which was a large knife used for cutting meat and other peaceful purposes. Both have a single-edged curved blade, but the máchairan is larger and was made exclusively for fighting. Since máchairan swords (and all bladed implements) were handmade in this era, for the civilian market they were produced in various sizes, dimensions and shapes, ac-

cording to regional preferences and the specifications of the buyer. Xenophon, a Greek historian who is highly regarded for his descriptions of life in ancient Greece, was also a soldier and mercenary. He commended the máchairan for use by cavalry, and we know from the art of that period that these had wider blades than the modern *saber,* and were more akin to a *falchion* which had the weight and power of a battle axe, but the versatility of a sword. Notwithstanding, many modern scholars contend that in the Koine Greek language of the New Testament, the word 'máchairan' refers to a sword generically, not making any particular distinction between indigenous blades, nor the *gladius* which was used by Roman soldiers.

12 Similar to Jesus situation, we may encounter a situation where God wants us to accept persecution. Therefore, we must keep in mind that if we encounter a situation in which self-defense and the use of deadly force is permitted by man's law and God's law, it may nevertheless not be the right choice to fight back. For example, in some situations involving persecution due to our Faith, it may be appropriate to accept the persecution because that is the more powerful witness. For examples of this, read: Luke 21-12-15; Acts 14:5-7; Acts 14:19-22; and Hebrews 11:32-38. Notwithstanding, throughout history there have been many occasions where a person has accepted abuse when they should have fought back for the good of themselves and others. For example, if Jews in Hitler's Germany had fought back they might have still died, but their resistance would have hobbled Hitler's war machine. To learn more about Christians martyred for their Faith and the subversion of a biblical legal process which seeks justice, read the Christian classic, "Foxe's Book of Martyrs" by John Foxe. In this historical account you will find many examples of people who might have served God better by fighting back, and others who surrendered their lives willingly, to accomplish a higher purpose.

13 Exodus 20:7; Leviticus 19:12; Deuteronomy 6:13-17; 10:20.

14 Letter to the Clergy of Philadelphia, March 3, 1797

15 Source: John Quincy Adams, "*The Works of John Adams, Second President of the United States*," Charles Francis Adams, editor (Boston: Little, Brown, and Co. 1854), Vol. IX, p. 229, October 11, 1798.

16 Source: *Connecticut Courant*, June 7, 1802, p. 3, Oliver Ellsworth, to the General Assembly of the State of Connecticut.

---

[17] Source: James Madison, *The Records of the Federal Convention of 1787*, Max Farrand, editor (New Haven: Yale University Press, 1911), Vol. I, pp. 450-452, June 28, 1787.

[18] Matthew 7:24-27; Luke 6:47-49.

[19] Source: Noah Webster, *History of the United States*, "Advice to the Young" (New Haven: Durrie & Peck, 1832), pp. 338-340, par. 51, 53, 56.

[20] Source: Daniel Webster, *The Writings and Speeches of Daniel Webster* (Boston: Little, Brown, & Company, 1903), Vol. XIII, p. 492. From "The Dignity and Importance of History," February 23, 1852. Voted by the U.S. Senate as one of the top-5 senators of all time: "United States Senate website at www.Senate.gov". Retrieved 2011-01-03. Source: http://www.senate.gov/artandhistory/history/common/briefing/Famous_Five_Seven.htm

[21] Mark 2:16-17; Luke 7:34; 15:1-2.

[22] Matthew 19:13-14

[23] Luke 7:33-34. Also, John 2:3-10, Jesus' first miracle. He was at a party where the host couple ran out of wine. Jesus turned water into wine, so the host couple would not be embarrassed by running out.

[24] Matthew 5:5, "Meek" as translated in KJV and NIV; "Gentle" in NASB; "Humble" in NLT.

[25] Matthew 6:33

[26] Matthew 21:12-13; Mark 11:15-17; and John 2:13-22.

[27] Mark 10:16; Luke 16:8.

[28] John 2:18-22; 1 Corinthians 3:16; 2 Corinthians 6:16-18.

[29] Matthew 6:33; Mark 12: 28-33.

[30] Counsel: Proverbs 11:14; 24:6; Wisdom: Proverbs 1:2-5; 8:5, 10; 13:10; 19:20.

[31] John 2:17; 2 Corinthians 7:9-11.

[32] Issues regarding firearms and national and local laws, are primarily addressed in the chapters, "The Law: What is legal in regard to firearms?" and "The Law: The U.S. Constitution trumps other laws."

[33] Jesus' four discourses are: The *'Sermon on the Mount,'* recorded in Matthew 5-7; the *'Mystery Parable Discourse,'* Matthew 13; the *'Olivet Discourse,'* Matthew 24-24; and the *'Farewell (Last Supper) Discourse,'* John 13-17, Matthew 26, Mark 14, and Luke 22. See Appendix for the full narrative of Jesus' teaching during the Last Supper, just before His arrest.

[34] Photo at Top of Page: In the original Greek, the word used for "sword" in Luke's Gospel (Luke 22:35) is "Machairan." Historic works of art from this period often depict a Machairan as a short sword, as illustrated above, with a blade of at least 18-20" (Judges 3:16). It was not just a large knife as some claim. It was a sword designed specifically for fighting. It was a tool to deliver deadly force.

There were also cavalry versions of the Machaira sword with a blade considerably longer. So we don't know the exact size or shape of Peter's sword, but the swords of this era which were commonly carried by civilians, typically had a blade length of about 23" with an overall length of 29."

The modern-day sword is a handgun. Jesus didn't just say it was "okay" to own a sword, He told his followers that it was important for them to have one (see Luke 22:36).

[35] For more about GO-Bags, visit www:36Ready.org.

[36] If you elect to carry Pepper Spray, be sure to pick a brand that contains at least 10% Oleoresin Capsicum (OC). The "Pepperblaster II" made by Kimber is a good example.

[37] Romans 12:18; 14:19; Hebrews 12:14.

[38] James 3:17-18; Hebrews 12:14-16.

[39] Proverbs 19:11; Matthew 5:7; Luke 6:35-37; Ephesians 4:32.

[40] Romans 3:23

[41] Romans 12:21

[42] Genesis 22:2

[43] Ephesians 6:14

[44] Jesus injunction in Luke 22:36 tells us that we are to be ready financially, ready with provisions, and ready for defense. It's not an optional assignment.

[45] Image at Top of Page: This painting depicts Nehemiah and citizens of Jerusalem who carried their swords as they worked to construct the wall around their city (Nehemiah 4:14).

[46] Nehemiah 4:1-8

[47] Nehemiah 4:9

[48] Photo: General Efraín Rios Montt with President Ronald Reagan. Often unfairly berated by American politicians and journalists, Montt was a brilliant military strategist. Recognizing that the military and police couldn't respond fast enough, his strategy was to arm civilians so they could protect themselves from the guerrillas who were attacking their villages. According to the official U.S. State Department report, this arming of civilians turned the tide of the war and helped bring an end to the protracted conflict in Guatemala.

[49] Note: Though the 2nd Amendment of the U.S. Constitution provides for civilian-created armed militias, local and state laws though perhaps unconstitutional, may nevertheless require security guard-type licenses if participants are carrying guns. If your jurisdiction issues Concealed Handgun Licenses, participants can generally carry guns as long as this isn't a requirement for participation. If you are involved with such a group, be sure to check with your local law enforcement agency to make sure you understand the law.

[50] Judges 20; Matthew 10:34, Romans 8:35-39, Hebrews 11:36-38.

[51] Today, over 100-million Christians worldwide suffer interrogation, arrest, torture, and even death for their faith. Millions more face serious discrimination and alienation. http://www.opendoorsusa.org/about-us/faq See also: http://www.opendoorsusa.org/about-us/quick-faqs.

[52] Timothy 1:18; 6:12; 2 Timothy 4:7.

[53] Lyrics from the National Anthem of the United States: "*... through the perilous fight, O'er the ramparts we watched, were so gallantly streaming? And the rockets' red glare, the bombs bursting in air, Gave proof*

through the night that our flag was still there; O say does that star-spangled banner yet wave, O'er the ***land of the free and the home of the brave?"***

[54] St. Cyril of Alexandria (c. 376-444 AD); Commentary on Luke, Homily 145, GGSL 579.

[55] St. Ambrose; Exposition of the Gospel of Luke; 10.53-55, EHG 405-6.

[56] Thayer's Lexicon, NT:2425, 'It is enough;' *"Jesus, saddened at the paltry ideas of the disciples, breaks off in this way the conversation; the Jews, when a companion uttered anything absurd, were accustomed to use this phrase."*

[57] Jesus exhibited similar aggravation with their thickheaded lack of understanding in Mark 14:41. See also Deuteronomy 3:26b, where the same phrase is used by God to express frustration toward Moses.

[58] Plato, *Republic*, pg. 20 (B. Jowett translation. 1946).

[59] Plato, *Republic* 139-40 (E. Cornford translation. 1945).

[60] Aristotle, *"Athenian Constitution,"* (H. Rackham translation. 1935).

[61] I *Livy* 148 n.2 (B. Foster translation 1919).

[62] Cicero, *"Selected Political Speeches,"* 77-83, 221-222

[63] Id. at 222. This same quote was cited by Founding Fathers of the United States, such as John Adams and Thomas Jefferson.

[64] Caesar, "The Gallic War" 109, 131, 303, 204-5, 309, 575 (H. Edwards translator 1966).

[65] Genesis 34:1-31; 48:5-7; Judges 19.

[66] Examples of retribution: Matthew 7:2; and Psalm 18:25-26.

[67] 1 Samuel 17-30

[68] Romans 3:23

[69] Ibid.

---

[70] Additional reading: Ephesians 4:32; Colossians 3:13; 1 Peter 3:9.

[71] Psalms 14:2-3: *The Lord has looked down from heaven upon the sons of men to see if there are any who understand, who seek after God. They have all turned aside, together they have become corrupt; there is no one who does good, not even one.* (NASB).

[72] Ezekiel 36:26; Psalms 51:10. We must be *born again*, John 3:1-21; 1 Peter 1:3-13.

[73] The Bible makes it clear that there is only one way to get to heaven; accepting that Jesus died in our place, and by accepting His offer of a restored relationship with our Creator. Jesus wouldn't have come to earth and willingly sacrificed Himself to a tortuous, excruciatingly painful death if there had been another way. He did it for us because He loves us and we can't do it ourselves. We can never be good enough to earn it.

It is a free gift that is offered to everyone, but it must be accepted by each individual. All we need to do is express a simple prayer to God, asking Him to forgive us for the wrongs we have done, and telling him that we accept His gift of life. As we thank Him for the sacrifice of His son, Jesus, who died in our place, we are literally born again into a new life with our Creator. It's a free gift, we can't earn it, but to receive it we must accept it. See: John 3:16-19; Romans 3:23; 5:8-11; Acts 4:12; Ephesians 2:8-9.

[74] Genesis 3

[75] For additional examples, read: Hebrews 10:30, 31; and I Samuel 12:15, 16.

[76] Signed by President Obama on March 16, 2012. See the White House website for details: http://www.whitehouse.gov/the-press-office/2012/03/16/executive-order-national-defense-resources-preparedness.

[77] Something similar to this happened after the Boston bombing on April 15, 2013, when the terrorists were fleeing the area.

[78] Known as the Luby's Massacre, this incident occurred October 16, 1991. One of those present, Suzanna Gratia Hupp, was dining with her parents. Both her mother and father were killed by the gunman, who shot

50-people that day. Her testimony to congress can be found by using her name to search www.YouTube.com.

79 2 Timothy 3:16-17 *"All Scripture is inspired by God and profitable for teaching, for reproof, for correction, for training in righteousness; so that the man of God may be adequate, equipped for every good work."*

80 Acts 13:22; 1 Samuel 13:14; Psalms 89:20; Acts 7:46.

81 David's life is chronicled in the Bible books of Samuel, Kings, and Chronicles, but I Samuel, chapters 16-30, is a good place to start this study.

82 I Samuel 17:32-54; 30:1-31; 23:1-5.

83 I Samuel 19:10-23:29; I Samuel 26.

84 I Samuel 24:1-7; 25:14-35; 26:6-12.

85 I Samuel 26:17-25

86 Ibid.

87 1 Samuel 23:1-14

88 1 Samuel 21:8-9

89 Colossians 4:5-6

90 Dietrich Bonhoeffer (1906-1945), author of the Christian classic "The Cost of Discipleship," was arrested by the Gestapo during World War II and killed just 23 days before the German surrender. Prior and during World War II, Bonhoeffer opposed the Nazis, and tried to wake-up the Christian churches to the evil of the National Socialist Party. Most of the churches had capitulated, falling victim to the political correctness which the Nazis used to neuter the Church. Bonhoeffer initially used only words and his pen to oppose the Nazi programs of euthanasia and the genocide of the Jews, but he eventually came to grips with the need to use violence to counter the violence of Hitler and the Nazi regime. He became a member of the underground resistance movement.

91 Deuteronomy 4:9, 14; 11:18-19; Proverbs 22:6 et al.; Book of Esther; Matthew 4:23; 28:19-20; Luke 4:14; Romans 12:5-9; Galatians 6:7-10.

92 For an overview of the details, see the chapter, "Summary of Relevant Crime Statistics."

93 Ibid.

94 Photo: Red laser mounted on a pistol, aimed at a B-27 law-enforcement type paper target. Scoring on this target is based on center-mass shooting. This is because it's not about shooting to wound vs. shooting to kill. It's only about shooting to *stop*. That's it. The goal is to stop an act of serious violence. Nothing more.

95 This is a bit off topic, but it is worth noting that survival, after being shot or stabbed, is often a matter of attitude. As odd as this sounds, people who think they are going to die, often do. Those who fight to survive have a good chance of winning against their assailant, even after they are seriously wounded. And they also have a much better chance of surviving their injuries. Fight to win. Fight to survive.

96 Federal *HST* is the handgun cartridge which was at the center of the controversy in 2012, when the Department of Homeland Security (DHS) issued a purchase order to ATK for the purchase of 450,000,000 rounds of .40 ACP ammunition for use within the United States. *HST* ammunition is unusually destructive against soft (human) targets, so this advanced-design cartridge, plus the staggering quantity of ammunition and the fact that this is just one of the handgun calibers in use by DHS, is what sparked this controversy. Verification: The author confirmed the accuracy of this information with the manufacturer.

97 For more on gun selection, read "Family and Personal Protection: Selecting the Best Gun for Self-Defense at Home." Available on Amazon.com: http://www.amazon.com/Family-Personal-Protection-Self-Defense-ebook/dp/B00ADT1NTA/ref=sr_1_2?ie=UTF8&qid=1377800886&sr=8-2&keywords=sig+swanstrom

98 Research Compendium: "Gun Control Facts." To download this PDF document, visit:
http://www.texasrepublicfirearmsacademy.com/uploads/Gun_Ownership-Gun_Control-Statistics-101222.pdf

99 The U.S. Bureau of Alcohol, Tobacco, Firearms, and Explosives. www.ATF.gov. To download the *National Firearms Act Handbook*: http://www.atf.gov/publications/firearms/nfa-handbook/.

---

[100] We don't have a viable option to use a non-lethal tool for self-defense. Products like pepper spray and stun guns might be worth owning, but they cannot take the place of a firearm in regard to reliability for stopping a violent attacker.

[101] For more about the constitutional amendment process, read Article V in the U.S. Constitution, which is included in the appendix of this book.

[102] Report of the Congressional Research Service, "Representatives and Senators: Trends in Member Characteristics Since 1945," (February 17, 2012). http://www.fas.org/sgp/crs/misc/R42365.pdf

[103] U.S. Law Shield: http://www.uslawshield.com/. Additional information about this legal service is contained in the chapter, "The Law: What is legal in regard to firearms?"

[104] U.S. Concealed Carry Association's "Self-Defense Shield":

http://www.usconcealedcarry.net/join-now/;

National Rifle Association's "Self-Defense Insurance":

http://www.locktonrisk.com/nrains/defense.htm.

Additional information about these legal service is contained in the chapter, "The Law: What is legal in regard to firearms?"

[105] Thomas Jefferson was the principal author of the Declaration of Independence and third president of the United States. This motto was probably proposed by Benjamin Franklin, but was later appropriated by Thomas Jefferson after it was not used for the Great Seal. Source: Thomas Jefferson Encyclopedia, Jefferson's home at Monticello. http://www.monticello.org/site/jefferson/personal-seal

[106] The first words of preamble of the U.S. Constitution, which talks about the prerogative of citizens to take action to establish justice, insure domestic tranquility, provide for the common defense, etc.

[107] Since the Founding Fathers of the United States were such prolific writers, it is a relatively simple matter to determine their original intent in regard to the 2nd Amendment and the rest of the Bill of Rights, and why they appended these Amendments (clarifications) to the U.S. Constitution.

[108] The preamble of the U.S. Constitution establishes the citizen prerogative and responsibility to take whatever action is necessary to act together to establish justice, insure domestic tranquility, provide for the common defense, promote the general welfare, and secure the blessing of liberty for ourselves and our children.

[109] Patrick Henry was one of the Founding Fathers of the United States, and was the first governor of Virginia. His powerful words, "Give Me Liberty, or Give Me Death" became the cry of all Americans who had a passion for a free America and a small federal government. Henry was also a major advocate for the Bill of Rights.

[110] Statement made by Patrick Henry. Source: United States Government, Department of Justice, "Liberty Watch,"

http://www.dojgov.net/Liberty_Watch.htm

[111] This assumes that the prescribed Constitutional Amendment process has not been invoked, and passed by a two-thirds majority of the States.

[112] Luke 14:28-35

[113] United States Constitution, Article V.

[114] According to a recent poll, 81% of Americans do not trust their government to do the right thing. Source: Gallup

http://www.gallup.com/poll/5392/trust-government.aspx

[115] Segment of Charlton Heston's May 20, 2000 speech, presented to the attendees of the 129th NRA Convention, held in Charlotte, North Carolina.

[116] To get started, visit the website of the American history organization, WallBuilders, www.WallBuilders.com, or write or phone: WallBuilders, PO Box 397, Aledo, TX 76008 – (800) 873-2845.

[117] For more on the character, beliefs and motivations of the Founding Fathers of the United States, or the spiritual heritage of the nation, visit: WallBuilders: http://www.wallbuilders.com/ WallBuilders has a great selection of books, articles, pamphlets and DVDs for adults, teens and children. The book, audio or DVD set, "A Spiritual Heritage Tour of the United States Capitol" is a great place to start. Another great resource

is, "The Founder's Bible" which is a Bible that includes study notes and citations made by the Founders themselves.

Once we get away from the revisionist history espoused in most modern history textbooks, and into the writings of our nation's Founders themselves, there is no doubt: The United States was founded on biblical principles, and the nation was designed to include God in our public life. The Founders intended justice and freedom for all, but they recognized that the security and blessing of the nation would only come as a result of honoring and invoking the help of the God of the Bible.

[118] Matthew 11:16-24; Luke 7:31-35.

[119] Poll taken by David Barton of WallBuilders (www.WallBuilders.com) in 2012.

[120] Deconstruction is a term that has different meanings, particularly when used in science and literary criticism. In philosophy and sociology the terms are more closely aligned but with somewhat different meaning. The popular use of the term is derived from the literal definition. For example, to "construct" or develop a historical account of an event, is to pull together the important parts of the story, and put them together in a cohesive narrative. To "deconstruct" history is to disassemble the elements of the story and change the emphasis on what is important, or to introduce new elements which change the meaning. History is not just the recording of past events; it is the summation of noteworthy events so that meaning can be derived from them.

The traditional of view of history in the United States has been to: 1) Record ("construct") the progress of human affairs as directed by the Providence of God; His-story. 2) To connect a series of events, to better understand cause and effect. 3) To display the character of man and/or man's Creator. (Jedidiah Morse, early American textbook writer and Father of Geography). Conversely, "deconstruction" involves the disassembly of a historical account for the purpose of changing its meaning, with the goal of fabricating a different significance. Deconstructionists often cloud or overwhelm with details, causing confusion, and they sometimes invent details which they assume were present at the time but for which there is no documentary evidence.

[121] Tyranny has arrived when the national government is vested with absolute power over the people, especially when it is wielded unjustly. Indicators of tyranny include developments which include several of these factors: the loss of freedoms, limitations placed on the exercise of rights, disarmament, the loss of privacy, impediments to free speech, a

media which consistently advances the agenda of government leaders, voter fraud, excessive taxation, the seizure of private land or resources and giving it to others, the use of police to protect government interests rather than the people, masked law enforcement or military, domestic shows of force or superiority by the government, the use of public agencies to intimidate, constant wars and insufficient public safety, economic policies which force people to work harder so they can't afford to dissent, control over education, government intrusion into the private life of its citizens, etc.

[122] The Constitution's *Bill of Rights* (including the 2nd Amendment) was adopted by the House of Representatives on August 21, 1789, formally proposed by a joint resolution of the U.S. Congress on September 25, 1789, and after successfully passing the constitutionally-mandated amendment process which requires ratification by three-fourths of the States, it became the supreme law of the land on December 15, 1791.

This same process could be used today by the anti-gun crowd to eliminate the 2nd Amendment. However, they would need to utilize the same Congressional and State ratification process, including securing endorsement of three-fourths of the States. Since they realize that this is unlikely to succeed, they use various slight-of-hand maneuvers and illegal tricks to circumvent the Constitution. So it isn't that the 2nd Amendment can't be changed, it's just that the anti-gun crowd is not willing to follow the will of the people, and they are unwilling to follow the established legal process for changing the Constitution.

[123] If you don't have time to study the American Revolution in depth, the booklet "The Patriot's Essential Liberty Pocket Guide" produced by Patriot Post www.PatriotPost.us is a great place to start. If you have an Internet connection and would like to read it online, visit: www.EssentialLiberty.us. If you would like to purchase this Pocket Guide in inexpensive booklet form to read or distribute, visit their online store at www.PatriotPostShop.com. If you want to study the American Revolution in more depth, the Patriot Post has an online store which offers a number of good books and DVDs. If you are looking for books and DVDs on the Founding Fathers and the Christian and Bible-based roots of the U.S., visit the online Wall Builders store at:

www.WallBuilders.com.

[124] This was before the U.S. Constitution and the 2nd Amendment, but the colonists did have rights of citizenship as actuated in British law and the *Magna Carta* (1215). Even more important was the Rights provided by

"The Laws of Nature and Nature's God," which were well known and widely accepted biblical concepts. This was the basis of British Common Law; the laws we all have in common because they are provided to us by our Creator and common sense. British thought on these subjects was heavily influenced by the writings of legal minds such as Charles Montesquieu and John Locke, but the principles are as old as mankind.

[125] Benjamin Franklin, U.S. Founding Father; author, diplomat, inventor, physicist, politician, and printer (1706 - 1790).

[126] Text from the U.S. National Anthem, "The Star Spangled Banner" (in appendix).

[127] Mark 12:28-31

[128] John 19:11; Mark 12:13-17; Romans 13; as opposed to degenerate government, Revelation 13. God-given function of government, 1 Peter 2:11-12. Once government exalts itself over all of life it has overstepped its God-authorized bounds and become evil, and obedience to it is no longer required. In Acts 4-5 the Apostles made it clear that obedience to God and His work supersedes manmade rules, laws, and court decisions. Romans 11 contains the Bible passage known as the "Faith Hall of Fame" and it cites many people who were faithful to God and in the process, disobeyed their wayward government.

[129] Letter from Thomas Jefferson to James Madison. *PTJ* 11:92-93.

Letterpress copy at the Library of Congress: Also available online at: http://www.monticello.org/site/jefferson/little-rebellionquotation.

[130] Photo at Top of Page: Photograph of the Declaration of Independence. The preamble of the Declaration of Independence, the founding document for the United States, includes this statement: *"We hold these truths to be self-evident, that all men are created equal, that they are endowed by their Creator with certain unalienable Rights, that among these are Life, Liberty and the pursuit of Happiness."*

The point is clear. These "Rights" are not bestowed by a president or government legislature, nor by a court of law. Furthermore, these Rights cannot be taken away or suspended by any person or government because they were given to us by our Creator. The Founders of the United States clearly understood that the citizens of the United States cannot allow their government, nor any person or even international entity, to revise, limit, usurp or subordinate these Rights of humanity.

---

131 Photo of Toolbox, Saw and Handgun: A gun is simply a tool to be carried in case it is needed. Like any other tool in our toolbox of options, it can be used properly or improperly. In the right hands, it is an instrument to protect life and restore peace.

132 Press Release by Nancy Pelosi, July 19, 2013, "Pelosi Statement on the One-Year Anniversary of the Aurora Tragedy"

http://pelosi.house.gov/news/press-releases/2013/07/pelosi-statement-on-the-one-year-anniversary-of-the-aurora-tragedy.shtml

133 John 15: 18-20; Proverbs 14:4.

134 1 Peter 2:13-17; Romans 13:1-7.

135 National Rifle Association, www.NRA.org; and NRA-ILA, Institute for Legislative Action, http://www.nraila.org/.

136 The *Bill of Rights* was added to the U.S. Constitution by the same Founding Fathers who wrote the Constitution. It was understood to be integral to the Constitution, and an essential elaboration of our Rights. Our Founders were better students of history than most of us are today, and many of them had experienced government excesses and abuses first-hand in Europe or England, before coming to America. They understood that the expansion of government power, and the diminishment of the rights of the people, has been a standard problem of governments throughout history. So they formulated a brilliant strategy to protect the American people, the Constitution and Bill of Rights. For freedom loving people around the world, these documents have become the gold-standard for protecting liberty.

137 WallBuilders (www.WallBuilders.org) is a nonprofit educational organization dedicated to upholding our nation's biblical heritage and honoring the sacrifice and wisdom of our Founders. Their recommended reading list, and online store (http://shop.wallbuilders.com/), are good places to start. Additionally, their DVD collection is entertaining and educational (http://shop.wallbuilders.com/dvds), and useful for stimulating conversations with family and friends.

138 Matthew 6:24-33

139 Ephesians 2:10

---

140 A 'GO-Bag' or Get-Out Bag (aka/ GOOD Bag, Get-Out-of-Dodge Bag, Bug-Out Bag, etc.) is a knapsack which is ready to grab if you need to evacuate, suddenly relocate, or remain in place for several days. This bag contains essential items such as 100^{+}-oz of water and the means to purify water, emergency food rations for 3-5 days, shelter, first-aid kit and medicine, and basic survival tools. Each family member should have their own Go-Bag. For more on this subject, visit: www.36Ready.org.

141 The FBI and the Department of Justice have officially sought to report reliable crime statistics since 1930. Unfortunately, these statistics are often misused and poorly interpreted. Today, due to political machinations and political correctness, relevant statistics are often obscured or buried in volumes of data. Notwithstanding, these reports remain a valuable source of information for those who are willing to distill the data, and have sufficient understanding to accurately interpret it.

http://www.fbi.gov/about-us/cjis/ucr/crime-in-the-u.s/2011/crime-in-the-u.s.-2011/index-page

Reliable research such as that done by Professor John R. Lott, Jr., and documented in his book, "More Guns, Less Crime" (Third Edition), is an easy way for the layman to gain an understanding of the key facts.

http://www.amazon.com/More-Guns-Less-Crime-Understanding/dp/0226493660/ref=sr_1_1?ie=UTF8&qid=1376959517&sr=8-1&keywords=More+Guns%2C+Less+Crime

142 Paper: "Armed Resistance to Crime: The Prevalence and Nature of Self-Defense with a Gun." By Gary Kleck and Marc Gertz. *Journal of Criminal Law and Criminology*, Fall 1995.

http://www.law.northwestern.edu/jclc/backissues/86-1.html

143 Paper: "Estimating intruder-related firearm retrievals in U.S. households, 1994." By Robin M. Ikeda and others. *Violence and Victims*, Winter 1997. Pages 363-372. http://www.ncbi.nlm.nih.gov/pubmed/9591354

144 Report: "Lifetime Likelihood of Victimization." By Herbert Koppel. Bureau of Justice Statistics, U.S. Department of Justice, March 1987.

http://www.ncjrs.gov/pdffiles1/bjs/104274.pdf

145 "More Guns, Less Crime," Third Edition. By Dr. John R. Lott, Jr., University of Chicago Press, 2010.

[146] "The Swiss and the Nazis," by Stephen P. Halbrook, Casemate Press, Phildelphia, 2006.

[147] "Target Switzerland," by Stephen P. Halbrook, Da Capo Press, Cambridge, MA, 1998.

[148] Eurostat (the European Union's Commission which gathers statistics), "Statistics in Focus," 2013. http://epp.eurostat.ec.europa.eu/cache/ITY_OFFPUB/KS-SF-13-018/EN/KS-SF-13-018-EN.PDF

[149] Ibid.

[150] Ibid.

Also, London Telegraph article, "UK is violent crime capital of Europe," By Richard Edwards, Crime Correspondent. 02 Jul 2009 http://www.telegraph.co.uk/news/uknews/law-and-order/5712573/UK-is-violent-crime-capital-of-Europe.html

[151] Ibid.

[152] This data is for 2011, the most recent statistics available from the U.S. Department of Justice at the time this book was written. This 3% figure cite4d in the text represents the maximum possible benefit. However, as the remainder of this article will demonstrate, the actual number is far lower, probably less that 1/10th of 1%.

[153] In 2011, the most recent year of crime statistics available at the time of writing, 728 people were murdered by assailants using hands, feet, elbows, etc. Compare this to 679 people murdered using all types of rifles (323) and shotguns (356). Assault rifles and assault-style tactical shotguns, which are the subject of many gun control efforts, are included in these rifle and shotgun figures. Knives were used more than twice as often (1,694) in homicides compared to all rifles and shotguns (679). Source: FBI, Criminal Justice Information Services Division, Uniform Crime Report for 2011: http://www.fbi.gov/about-us/cjis/ucr/crime-in-the-u.s/2011/crime-in-the-u.s.-2011/tables/expanded-homicide-data-table-8.

[154] Machine guns, submachine guns, and fully-automatic rifles, fall into the "other firearms" category for law enforcement reporting. Source of statistics: FBI, Criminal Justice Information Services Division, Uniform Crime Report for 2011: http://www.fbi.gov/about-us/cjis/ucr/crime-in-the-u.s/2011/crime-in-the-u.s.-2011/tables/expanded-homicide-data-table-8.

[155] "More Guns, Less Crime," Third Edition. By Dr. John R. Lott, Jr. University of Chicago Press, 2010.

[156] The city of New York also has strict gun control laws, but their reduction in crime is the result of other illegal and unconstitutional policies. This includes Third World-like check points, raids and random searches of people without probable cause, and various intimidation tactics; activities of a police state, not a free society. Notwithstanding, despite these illegal and unconstitutional activities of New York's government, these extreme measures are still far less effective than simply allowing good people to be armed and able to defend themselves.

More to the point, the cities of Chicago and Washington, DC, have primarily utilized extreme gun control measures to reduce crime. Rather than admit that their efforts are ineffective, they have progressively become more extreme in their anti-gun legislation and enforcement, and yet their streets are increasingly unsafe.

Since these city governments have repeatedly been embarrassed by having the highest violent crime rates in the country despite their extreme anti-gun efforts, these municipalities are increasingly using other unconstitutional and reprehensible tactics. Chicago and Washington, DC, are now using malicious prosecution and black-shirt intimidation tactics (including those employed in New York), in an attempt to stem the growing tide of violence that has come from their anti-gun and anti-self defense policies.

[157] The most recent government report by the U.S. Bureau of Alcohol, Tobacco, Firearms and Explosives (ATF) indicates that 1,458,782 self-defense style handguns were sold in the U.S. in 2010. This is a 208% increase from a decade earlier (2000).

U.S. Murder Rate: Year 1992 - 23,760, Year 2011 – 14,612 / Rate per 100,00 population: 1992 – 9.3, 2011 – 4.7. Violent Crime (General): Year 1992 – 1,932,274, Year 2011 – 1,203,564 / Rate per 100,000 population: 1992 – 758, 2011 – 386. Source: FBI Unified Crime Report 2011

http://www.fbi.gov/about-us/cjis/ucr/crime-in-the-u.s/2011/crime-in-the-u.s.-2011/tables/table-1

[158] For more about the pre-American history of the Right to keep and bear arms, read: "That Every Man Be Armed: The Evolution of a Constitutional Right" by Stephen P. Halbrook (University of New Mexico Press, Revised and Updated Edition 2013)

[159] In the scholarly community two books stand out as the most authoritative on this subject. These are the same books cited by Supreme Court Justice Clarence Thomas in his opinion on the 2nd Amendment:

Stephen P. Halbrook, *The Founders' Second Amendment: Origins of the Right to Bear Arms* (Independent Study in Political Economy, 2012)

Joyce Lee Malcom, *To Keep and Bear Arms: The Origins of an Anglo-American Right"* (Harvard University Press, 1996)

[160] Virginia`s U.S. Constitution ratification convention, 1788

[161] "Additional Letters From The Federal Farmer," 1788

[162] On the *2nd Amendment* of the U.S. Constitution's Bill of Rights, Federal Gazette, June 18, 1789

[163] An Examination of The Leading Principles of the Federal Constitution, Philadelphia, 1787

[164] Jefferson`s "Commonplace Book," 1774-1776, quoting from On Crimes and Punishment, by criminologist Cesare Beccaria, 1764.

[165] The Federalist, No. 29.

[166] Virginia`s U.S. Constitution ratification convention.

[167] Ex.: Richard Cloward and Frances Fox Piven both highly regarded in the 'Progressive' community, made many public statements about the need to collapse the economy of the United States to achieve their Progressive agenda. These are just two of the many Progressive leaders who have made public statements, or written about their plans to instigate disaster to advance their political and social objectives.

Others, like George Soros, are simply greedy and power hungry. Since 1979, Soros has given more than $8 billion to finance Progressive causes which further his personal power-grabbing agenda. He has become a billionaire by using vicious tactics to control financial markets, and has literally collapsed national economies for his own financial gain, and for his own entertainment. Soros is known as "the man who broke the Bank of England" when he orchestrated Britain's "Black Wednesday" (1992) financial disaster. He has publically expressed his distain for the United States and his desire to destroy the U.S. as an economic and political power. He said, "the main obstacle to a stable and just World Order is the United States." (*"The Age of Fallibility,"* 2006)

[168] "A Government of Wolves: The Emerging American Police State," by John W. Whitehead, Select Books, New York, 2013. The author is the president of the highly regarded Rutherford Institute, and is also an experienced constitutional law attorney. His articles have been published nationally in more than 300 newspapers.

[169] Oath Keepers (www.OathKeepers.org) is a nonprofit organization started by law enforcement officers and military personnel, which is dedicated to helping government employees understand how to discern when an order is unlawful, and to support them when they take a stand.

[170] The "Brights Movement" is a sociocultural crusade which claims to be scientific, but which is really just an anti-God worldview. It actively promotes the naturalistic belief that life is a cosmic accident and without purpose. As a consequence, there is no right and wrong, and morality and virtue are outdated concepts. These people use the term "Brights" to describe themselves because they think they are more enlightened and smarter than the rest of the population. The writings and statements of the leaders of this Internet-based movement make it clear that they should be in charge of the world. This is their quest, followed closely by extreme environmentalism, which includes the objective of dramatically reducing the earth's population by whatever means is necessary. These pseudo-intellectuals have established a beachhead on our university campuses where their beliefs and values are taught with evangelistic fervor by elitist professors. 'Brights' often use various forms of retribution to silence their opponents.

[171] Luke 16:8; Psalms 83:3; Acts 7:18-19.

[172] Article: Michael Snyder, *Dumb As A Rock: You will be absolutely amazed at the things that U.S. high school students do not know*, (End of the American Dream, 10-Jan-2012)

http://endoftheamericandream.com/archives/dumb-as-a-rock-you-will-be-absolutely-amazed-at-the-things-that-u-s-high-school-students-do-not-know

[173] An 8th grade test from the year 1912 was recently donated to the Bullitt County History Museum in Kentucky. Most college graduates, who were educated in the U.S., would not be able to pass this test even though they have spent twice as many years in school.

http://www.bullittcountyhistory.com/bchistory/schoolexam1912.html

[174] The NRA's *Institute for Legislative Action* is one of the best groups to support financially, and one of the best sources of trustworthy information: http://www.nraila.org/

[175] Pennsylvania Assembly: Reply to the Governor, November 11, 1755.—The Papers of Benjamin Franklin, ed. Leonard W. Labaree, vol. 6, p. 242 (1963).

[176] No one knows what the future holds, but there are solid economic and cultural indicators which provide us with evidence that change is underway. We can benefit from observing and analyzing these changes in relationship with other events and changes, as this will help us anticipate and prepare for the future. Investors do this all the time. We need to do it too, not just for financial planning, but for life planning, too. Jesus criticized the church leaders of His time for being able to recognize the signs in the sky which indicate changes in weather, but not the signs of the times which are far more important. Matthew 16:1-3.

[177] Though the composition of each of our classes is different, on average, 55% of our students are women. Yet, the number of students who are taking the class as part of their disaster preparation effort is divided equally between men and women.

[178] Throughout the Bible it is important to take time off from work for rest, rejuvenation and reflection on God and other good things. The Ten Commandments even require us to take one day off from work each week (Exodus 20:8-11). Notwithstanding, the issue here is that preparing for the future is a required task; an additional responsibility to our regular day-to-day work.

[179] Proverbs 27:17

[180] Available on the White House's website, www.WhiteHouse.gov

[181] Huffington Post, "Barack Obama Prepares for War Footing," by Edwin Black. March 19, 2012. http://www.huffingtonpost.com/edwin-black/obama-national-defense-resources-preparedness_b_1359715.html

[182] This information was validated by the author during a telephone interview with the public relations office of ATK, the parent company of Remington Arms Company. It was further validated by a press release given to the author during that interview. A copy of that press release is available by following this link:

---

http://www.texasrepublicfirearmsacademy.com/uploads/ATK-Press_Release-Ammo_Purchased__2_.pdf

This is only one example of an ammunition company that has received purchase orders from the U.S. Dept. of Homeland Security. When these orders are combined, they represent more than a billion rounds of anti-personnel ammunition for handguns, assault rifles and machine guns. These purchase orders were issued by the Department of Homeland Security, not the U.S. military which makes its purchases through the Department of Defense.

[183] To view or download a copy of the U.S. Army training manual, "Internment and Resettlement Operations," visit:

http://36readyblog.files.wordpress.com/2012/11/fm_3-39dot40-usarmy-internmentresettlement.pdf

[184] Some have suggested that these are simply grave liners stored at this location by the manufacturer. However, grave liners used in the U.S. (designed to contain coffins buried in a cemetery), have traditionally been made of concrete. Plastic grave liners used by budget-conscious cemeteries have a domed or curved lid which corresponds to the design of most coffins, as the curved top is more effective for distributing the weight of the soil which will be piled on top of it. Whereas the plastic coffins stored in Georgia are sized to accommodate three body bags, and have flat lids and interlocking notches to make them stackable. Further, the land where these plastic coffins were stored in Madison, Georgia, was leased by the CDC. It's interesting to note that these coffins were moved within days of the public release of this information.

[185] Presidential Executive Order, National Defense Resources Preparedness, Authorization Act, March 16, 2012; White House website:

http://www.whitehouse.gov/the-press-office/2012/03/16/executive-order-national-defense-resources-preparedness

[186] Rapture, or "harpazo" which is the Greek word for "caught-up," references a future occurrence when Jesus will instantly remove His true followers from the earth, both living and dead. 1 Thessalonians 4:13-18; John 14:1-3; Job 19:25-27; I Corinthians 15:1-55.

[187] Matthew 25:1-13

[188] Luke 12:35-37, 22:36; Proverbs 6:6-11, 22:3; Ezekiel 38:7.

[189] Matthew 25:14-30

[190] Matthew 10:16

[191] Proverbs 15:30; Isaiah 61; Acts 8:12; 13:32-39; Romans 10:14-15; Hebrews 4:2-7.

[192] The context of the following verses makes it clear that these lists of gifts are not exhaustive, but rather representative of various special skills and abilities, given by God, for the purpose of advancing His work on earth. These are not given to each follower of Jesus, but rather to certain individuals. These gifts may increase or expand the natural gifting that a person already has, or be wholly new and unprecedented in their life. As the name "gift" implies, these are not necessarily rewards for faithfulness, or as a result of asking, but in each case given for the purpose of serving God, His Church, and for service to people. See: 1 Peter 4:10; Romans 12:6-8; 1 Corinthians 12:4-11; 28-30; Ephesians 4:7-12.

[193] Some may prefer death, rather than live through the dark days ahead, but God birthed us into this time for a purpose (Ephesians 2:10). Just as with Queen Esther (Esther 4:13-14) we have a purpose to fulfill. The Apostle Paul said it best when he declared, "For to me, living means living for Christ, and dying is even better. But if I live, I can do more fruitful work for Christ (Philippians 1:21-22 NLT).

[194] Matthew 6:33

[195] Ephesians 2:10

[196] 1 Corinthians 10:13; 13:13

[197] **Old Testament:** Numbers 14:9-10; Deuteronomy 31:6; 1 Chronicles 28:20; Isaiah 41:10, 13; Psalms 23:4; 27:1; 56:3-4; 118:6; Proverbs 3:5-7, 21b-26; **New Testament:** Matthew 10:28-29; 2 Timothy 1:7; Romans 8:15-17; 1 Corinthians 16:13; 1 Peter 3:13-14.

[198] These passages are from the New American Standard translation of the Holy Bible.

[199] Unlike our modern method of relating a story in chronological order, in Bible times the writers were primarily concerned with topics, not timing. This makes it difficult to reconstruct the exact order of Jesus teachings at the Last Supper in the precise sequence.

Further, since Jesus' teaching from that evening was recorded by four different eye witnesses, each account includes different nuances of Jesus' teaching that night. This explained, the text contained here is accurate in regard to what was said, but may be slightly off in regard to the order of the subject matter.

This compilation of Jesus' Last Supper teaching is included here to help put His teaching of Luke 22:36 in the full context of Jesus teaching that fateful night. Keep in mind that this teaching occurred immediately before Jesus' arrest and His crucifixion the next day.

This expanded narrative is additionally helpful because the modern preaching which focuses on this *Farewell Discourse* is often limited to the account in John 14-17. However, since we have additional eyewitness accounts in other Gospels, we are enriched by bringing all the pieces together.

Because Jesus had so much to say that night, most of our pastors and Bible teachers don't talk about Jesus teaching that night as a complete body of instruction. He covered a lot of ground with His instruction that night, so this compilation is additionally helpful.

Lastly, when we concentrate on an individual element of Jesus' teaching that night to the exclusion of the whole discourse, we fail to fully grasp the big picture. As a result, we miss the power of Jesus' discourse as a package of final instructions.

These instructions were for His followers in that era and also for us. So as you read the following Bible passages, I encourage you to picture yourself sitting in a room with four reliable friends who were all eyewitnesses to the events that unfolded that night. Listen to them as they each tell the story, interrupting each other to add insights from their own individual viewpoint. The same story, but related by four different witnesses. After you are done listening to what your four trusted friends have said, think about how you would react. This isn't just history; this teaching is relevant to our life today, too. How will you respond to Jesus?

Notes

Made in the USA
San Bernardino, CA
26 February 2014